GOD'LL CUT YOU DOWN

GOD'LL CUT YOU DOWN

The Tangled Tale of a White Supremacist,
a Black Hustler, a Murder, and How I Lost
a Year in Mississippi

John Safran

RIVERHEAD BOOKS I A member of Penguin Group (USA) I New York 2014

RIVERHEAD BOOKS
Published by the Penguin Group
Penguin Group (USA) LLC
375 Hudson Street
New York, New York 10014

USA · Canada · UK · Ireland · Australia
New Zealand · India · South Africa · China

penguin.com
A Penguin Random House Company

Originally published under the name *Murder in Mississippi* by Hamish Hamilton,
an imprint of Penguin Books Australia, 2013.

Library of Congress Cataloging-in-Publication Data

Safran, John.
God'll cut you down : the tangled tale of a white supremacist, a black hustler,
a murder, and how I lost a year in Mississippi / John Safran.
p.   cm.
ISBN 978-1-59463-335-5
1. Murders—Mississippi—History—21st century.   2. White supremacy
movements—Mississippi—21st century.   3. Racism—Mississippi—21st century.   I. Title.
HV6533.M7S34   2014   2014017207
364.152'3092—dc23

Printed in the United States of America
1   3   5   7   9   10   8   6   4   2

Book design by Gretchen Achilles

For my family, especially Lachlan Stewart

CONTENTS

You can run on for a long time,

but sooner or later God'll cut you down.

TRADITIONAL
(although in this case, Johnny Cash)

GMAILS WITH A FRIEND

On Thurs, Dec 09, at 2:10 a.m., Lally wrote:

Seriously, J. Safran, I really do want to know what you thought of *The Tell-Tale Heart.* X

On Sun, Dec 12, at 10:27 p.m., John Safran wrote:

Hi Lally,

I forgot to concentrate at the start of the play, so later on when the actor started talking about a murder it was too late and I couldn't follow! It was basically one guy climbing up and down a ladder for 50 minutes. Are you still in USA? When will you be back? Should I go to Mississippi and write a true crime book? I know of a murder there. I've been reading true crime books in the last month—*In Cold Blood, Midnight in the Garden of Good and Evil,* and a couple of less famous ones. I've never read true crime before, so I'm buzzing with how good they can be. X

On Sun, Dec 12, at 11:59 p.m., Lally wrote:

I get back to Melbourne on the 5th of January. I was very happy being in New York, but then I got sick, and now I've turned slightly against it. You know what, I absolutely think you should go to Mississippi and write a true crime book. Without a doubt. What an exciting thing to do. You'd have such a great and sometimes dangerous adventure. Your part in writing it would become part of the story perhaps. Yes—I'm all for you doing that! When would you go? X

On Mon, Dec 13, at 12:23 a.m., John Safran wrote:

Not sure when I'd go to Mississippi. I just sent a Facebook friend request to the accused killer. He's got a photo labeled "first day out." I assume he's just out pending a trial. It's a bit fuzzy where things stand, just going by Google.

On Mon, Dec 13, at 12:36 a.m., Lally wrote:

How great that you requested to be his friend on Facebook! What's the case? What did he do?

On Tues, Dec 14, at 9:54 p.m., John Safran wrote:

Did I tell you anything about meeting this white supremacist? Because it's tied in with that, and I want to know how much background I need to give you.

On Tues, Dec 14, at 10:01 p.m., Lally wrote:

No—you haven't told me any of that. Please tell me the whole thing. From beginning to end.

1.

THE BEGINNING

Melbourne

This story begins when I'm ten years old. I'm at a bar mitzvah with my family. And my dad taps me on the shoulder and points to a guy by the buffet, scooping food onto his plate.

"See that man?" my dad whispers.

"Yes," I say.

"See the tie he's wearing?"

"Yes."

"See that little symbol on his tie?"

"Yes," I reply, squinting my eyes.

"That's the Freemason symbol," he says. "They're a secret society. They don't like it when you ask them about it."

"Wow."

"Go up and ask him about it," he tells me.

So I shuffle over to the guy and ask if he's a Freemason.

"Yes, um," he splutters, his eyes darting about. "But, listen, we don't do anything unusual." He then backs away from the buffet and creeps out of the room.

In that moment I learned there are secret worlds out there. We can glance over a landscape and think we're seeing everything, but there are realms operating just out of our lines of sight.

I became hooked on secret worlds. And the clunky encounter with the Freemason taught me you can ask questions even when you're not supposed to. That's why I became what I became, a documentary film-maker of sorts. I say "of sorts" because mine are not the straightest of documentaries. I often ask dangerous people indelicate questions and try not to get thumped. And I often ask them about race. I'm a bit of a Race Trekkie—like a sci-fi Trekkie, but with race, not space.

So the murder at hand? That part of the story begins—although I didn't know it at the time—about ten years ago. I was filming a segment for a television series called *John Safran vs God*, in which I tried to join the secret world of the Ku Klux Klan even though I'm a Jew.

My First Meeting with the Klan

I'm boxed in at the Ku Klux Klan compound in Orange County, California. Swastika flags run along the wall. I sit across the desk from the Grand Dragon, a man called Chris. Jesus Christ eyeballs me from the painting hanging behind the Grand Dragon. Four Klansmen stand at attention along the edge of the room.

"I'm a little confused about who can and can't join the Klan," I tell the Grand Dragon. "Are you allowed to join the Klan if you're not American?"

"Yes, absolutely!" he assures me.

"And what about if you're Catholic?"

"You know, Catholics are every bit as Christian as anyone else," he says. "Sure."

"And what happens," I ask, trying hard not to squirm in my seat, "if you were brought up Jewish but you don't do anything Jewish anymore? Because that's where I'm at."

The Grand Dragon shoots his eyes to his fellow Klansmen.

"Was your mother Jewish?" he asks.

"Yes," I say.

His face sours.

"Jewish life flows through Jewish women," he says, pointing to a Biblical Racial Identity chart pinned up next to his desk. "Jews are from their father, the devil. They're from the Synagogue of Satan."

"So I can't join the Klan?" I ask.

"The answer is no."

I lean forward.

"I understand if someone came in here wearing a skullcap and said, 'Hey, can I join the Klan?' that would be ridiculous. But I don't do anything Jewish anymore. I haven't stepped in a synagogue since my bar mitzvah."

The Grand Dragon looks like he's about to breathe fire.

"I drive on the Sabbath," I say. "I eat pork."

"Yes," he says, "but we believe that Judaism is both a race and religion."

I point to my face.

"I'm whiter than Hitler. I've got blond hair and blue eyes. He had brown hair and brown eyes. If I went to school with Hitler, I'd be the one beating him up for being a wog."

The Grand Dragon asks me to leave.

God and/or Fate blows a ripple into the ocean.

Several Years Later

Several years later, the Australian Broadcasting Corporation airs another series I pull together called *John Safran's Race Relations*. This series pokes its nose into cross-cultural, interracial, and interfaith love.

The ABC forbids one story I film from airing. This is the story in which the ripple from years before drifted me into the arms of a man named Richard Barrett.

I have to give away a magician's trick to explain this, but so be it.

The Unaired Story

Rabbis would wag their fingers in front of the class at my all-boys school. They would tell us that if we married a non-Jew, our children would not be Jewish. "If you marry a non-Jew, you're finishing Hitler's work for him!" is how one of them put it.

To be a Jew, according to the rabbis (like the Klan), your mother must be Jewish. And for her to be Jewish, *her* mother had to be Jewish. And for *her* to be Jewish, *her* mother had to be, too, rolling all the way back to the Hebrews plodding through the desert with Abraham.

DNA testing has made things awkward for the Jewish community. Now it's quite simple to check whether your mother's mother's mother's mother's mother was Jewish. Some folk who have lived their lives as Jews have popped off to take a DNA test and found out they are not.

The *Race Relations* story opens with me stomping out of my bedroom.

"Jews make up 0.25 percent of the world's population," I lisp aggressively to the camera. "If I'm going to rule out 99.75 percent of women on the pretext that Jews should only marry Jews, I'm going to make damn sure I'm actually one."

Cut to my bathroom.

I'm staring in the mirror, poking a little plastic rod in and out of my mouth. The rod is for scraping saliva from one's cheek.

"I'm going to the USA," I say, "to Family Tree DNA, the world's largest genetic testing firm. They send you out this kit."

I snap the head of the rod into a vial and twist on the lid.

Cut to my living room. My laptop is throwing blue light on my face.

"Now," I say to the camera, "here's an interesting little sidebar . . ."

I swivel my laptop around to the camera. The web page reads WHITE PRIDE WORLDWIDE.

"Someone sent me a link to the American white pride website Stormfront," I say, "where they have an alert."

I read it out: "Alert: John Safran Coming to the USA. I have it on very good authority that the Australian Jewish documentary maker/comedian John Safran will be coming to the United States sometime between now and the middle of the year to film his new show for the ABC, *Race Relations*.

"John Safran was the blond, blue-eyed Jew from Australia who tried to enlist in the Ku Klux Klan in his series *John Safran vs God*.

"I personally felt this episode was in particular poor taste, and would warn white nationalists across the States to keep a watchful, close eye out for John Safran attempting to set up other white separatist groups in a similar way."

I stare down the camera, addressing the white supremacists.

"Hey, guys," I say. "I wasn't even thinking about you. But now that you've brought it up . . . Seeing as I'm going to America for a DNA test, why don't I go get a DNA test done on one of you?"

I whip out of my pocket another Family Tree DNA kit.

"Oh, I don't know," I say, "how about the founder of the Nationalist Movement, Richard Barrett?"

I make out I know who this guy is, but I don't. I'm familiar with the lowercase "white nationalist movement," which just includes any group that's proud to be white. As to this specific uppercase "Nationalist Movement"—no idea. The reason I'm off to see Richard Barrett specifically? My researcher shot off e-mails to a dozen Klan types, and he's the one who got back to us. On his web page, Richard says he's also the founder of the American skinhead movement. He's sixty-seven years old.

A plane flies on a map from my flat to Mississippi.

The Mississippi State Legislature is bright white and gorgeous, a bit Greek temple, a bit *Gone with the Wind* mansion. I trot up the steps and between the white pillars. A black member of the House of Representatives, Robert Johnson, meets me on one of the marble walkways.

"Can you tell us who Richard Barrett is?" I ask.

"Richard Barrett is an avowed racist, white supremacist, who believes the only true Americans are white Americans," he says, his mustache bouncing up and down. "And he's one of the most outspoken white supremacists here in the state."

Coincidentally, my visit collides with a ceremony run by Richard Barrett.

"And what is the Spirit of America Day banquet?" I ask.

"It is an award ceremony," he answers, "that Richard Barrett alleges recognizes athletes, male athletes, football players, who represent the best of what is America. But he's never recognized an African American or a black student at all. And in the past he's acknowledged that it's only for white students."

Fade down. Fade up.

It's night. A black pickup truck speeds down a road in rural Mississippi. The moon must be somewhere, but I can't find it and there are no streetlights, either. An old man with liver spots controls the wheel: Richard Barrett. I sit beside him. The damaged road rattles my teeth. For the "founder of the American skinheads," he's sure trying hard to hide that he's going bald. He has thin gray hair he's styled into a comb-over. Perhaps to make up for that, Richard is driving so fast, the wind gusting in the windows is drying out my eyeballs.

Richard wears glasses, but refuses to be filmed wearing glasses. He slides them off whenever the camera points his way. I also wear glasses but decide not to wear them, convinced they make me look Jewish.

Two blind phonies drive into the night.

Tomorrow I plan to secure a saliva sample from Richard for the DNA test. Tonight I want to find out more about the man.

"There was a colored woman on television not long ago," Richard Barrett tells me, "and they asked her what she thought of me." Richard had been running for office. "And she said, 'When we had segregation, I didn't have the bullet holes you see in my house.' She said, 'I didn't have the syringes from the drug users on my front lawn.' And the reporter said, 'Do you think we would be better off with segregation?' And she said,

'I do.' Now, that colored woman may be the sort of person that voted for me."

Richard lost his election.

"So, you are for segregation?" I ask.

"Yes," he says, not even making it to the *s* in *yes* before sounding like he regretted committing that to camera.

Richard steers off the road and heads deep into a field. A redbrick wall rolls into the glow of the headlights. This is the Nationalist Movement headquarters.

Inside, bookshelves tighten up an already tight hallway. We head down into a tiny study. The black night hides the fact that the Nationalist Movement headquarters is in fact just a small house in rural Mississippi.

In the study, green-spined law books color up one whole wall. Red-spined law books color up another. A large red flag flops on a brass pole in the corner. I pull it up, hoping, for the sake of my show, that it's a swastika.

It isn't. Rather, it recalls a swastika with the elements moved around a bit, as if to avoid infringing Hitler's copyright.

"What does it mean?" I ask.

"That's the Nationalist Movement flag," Richard replies. "It's called the Cross Star. It means victory, North, South, East, and West, victory over communism. It was used in Vietnam."

Richard points to a photo on the wall behind the photocopier.

"This is where an anarchist attacked me, shouting, 'Kill, kill!'" The photo in fact seems to show Richard grabbing a protester's T-shirt. "He was nineteen years old, and I'm quite a bit older. But I got him in a headlock. I used my skills from Vietnam. I stomped him on the ground and held him for the police."

In another photo he grins next to Miss America.

A WHITES ONLY sign is taped to the back of the study door.

"So what's this 'Whites Only' thing?" I ask.

"Oh that," Richard says, a little coy. "Someone put that up there and I'm not sure why, but it's just kind of interesting."

"Okay, so I understand nationalism," I say. "So, it's not racism?"

Richard looks offended by the vulgar term.

"Well, it's not so much a matter of what it's not. Let's talk about what it is. Nationalism is blood-based. Where you have a feeling for your own self, your own people, your own children, your own family, your own countrymen. It's really what makes the world tick."

"But so many young people today are a mixture of things," I say. "Like, they'll have one Lebanese grandparent. So if you're an American with one Lebanese grandparent—"

"You don't have that," Richard interrupts.

"Yes, you do."

"Not really."

I find it odd I have to argue the point that mixed-race people exist.

"Go to New York," I say.

"Sure, New York." Richard chuckles. "You know what Senator Goldwater from Arizona said? He'd like to cut it off and let it float into the Atlantic." Richard chuckles again. "I was born in New York."

Next to the WHITES ONLY sign is a flag that looks incredibly like a swastika. "That's from South Africa," Richard says. "Eugène Terre'Blanche's party." And next to the flag is a plaque: FAG-FREE ZONE.

"So you're not allowed to be gay in the Nationalist Movement?"

"Well, of course not," Richard replies.

Leaving the study, I ask, "Why all the law books?"

Richard tells me he's a lawyer. (Of course. Some of the hairsplitting begins to make sense.) Richard says the law is his weapon. He says he grinds his enemies to dust with legal action. When a county in Georgia tried to charge Richard for the extra police it put on to cover a protest he planned, he dragged the county through court after court, all the way to the US Supreme Court, until he won. He lawyered a black family out of a home in Jackson, Mississippi. Something about "blockbusting" maybe? I don't really follow.

We're in the Nationalist Movement's lounge area. The first thing I notice is a rifle, propped up in the corner like a mop.

"What kind of gun is that?" I ask.

"A Chinese gun," Richard replies, plucking it up by the barrel, a little clunkily, I reckon.

"A Chinese gun! In a white supre—" I hit the brakes on my mouth. "Shouldn't you have an American one?"

"Someone gave this to us." He's not quite pointing the muzzle to his face, but he's not many degrees off, either. "I do have American ones," he mutters. "In fact, they're all around here. And in fact, did you notice the ax handle?" He perks up, pointing to an ax handle mounted on the wall. "The ax handle was given to me by Lester Maddox, who in Georgia was the one who took up the ax handle to keep the Negroes out of his restaurant. And he was elected governor of the state because of it."

I'm pretty excited that not only is he saying *Negroes*, he's pronouncing it *Nigroes*, like an old Southern plantation owner.

Next to that is a black-and-white photo, where (Christ, this is an embarrassing example of my postmodern education) he's dressed like the Illinois Nazis in *The Blues Brothers*.

"The Nazis in *The Blues Brothers*, they dress like that," I say.

"I don't know." He chuckles. "I'm trying to dress like that because it's reminiscent of the skinheads that we know from England. We have many here, and it has, you know, a certain appeal."

Richard passes me the latest issue of his newsletter.

The front-page headline: INTEGRATED LICENSE PLATE DITCHED. Below that is a picture of the special-edition license plate. The design is a brown boy's face and a white girl's face drawn in crayon by a child.

"Yes," Richard tells me, "we had actually a license plate that had a Negro and a white. And we lobbied against it and we had it taken out. And thank goodness we did."

"But it's just a license plate, isn't it?"

"Well, that's something contrary to what the American people stand for. People can *do it*, but don't put an official seal of the state on it."

People can "do it"? People can "do" what? I scrutinize the crayon drawing.

"But . . . what . . . Is that meant to be a boyfriend and a girlfriend, do you think?"

"Yes, it's just not done, it's not proper, it's not part of our heritage. People find it offensive. If you had two homosexuals there, kissing each other, we'd find that offensive. People can *do it*, but you don't flaunt it, you don't give the stamp of approval."

Two crayon children smile up at me from the license plate.

It's one thirty a.m. Richard starts his rounds of the headquarters, flicking off each room light and desk lamp.

"Okay, we're done here, yes?" Richard asks me.

"Yes, I'll see you tomorrow," I say.

He flicks the final switch.

Fade to black.

Fade up. It's morning.

I'm walking through the parking lot of a motel. The sun is trying hard to perk things up, but it can only do so much for the Budget Inn parking lot. My voiceover announces, "This is the place where Richard will be hosting his whites-only sports awards, the Spirit of America Day banquet."

I push open the glass door and cross the lobby. I lean into the camera and mumble a very quiet aside. "I have to get a saliva sample from Richard Barrett for the DNA test. He's in the Diplomat Ballroom apparently."

I push open the door to the Diplomat Ballroom. Red, white, and blue stings my eyes, the colors crisp, bright, and everywhere. It's like walking off a gray street into a candy shop. Balloons and bunting run from wall to wall. A Confederate flag hangs behind a raised stage.

Six helpers, including two black children, mope about. Should the black kids be here? The black kids are with a white man and a helium tank, inflating balloons. A white kid runs about, placing a small Confederate flag in the center of each round dinner table.

Up a ladder, a body is lost in a bundle of thirty-odd balloons. Two legs poke out.

"Hello, Richard!" I shout up.

"Wuh, herlow!" he shouts down, muffled by the balloons.

Months earlier, the researcher and I had been slumping in a TV production office in Melbourne, trying to figure out a way to thieve saliva from a white supremacist. Coffee cup? Toothbrush? Chewing tobacco? When Richard told the researcher I'd be arriving just as he was preparing his banquet—hanging streamers, blowing up balloons—I thought, *God really wants me to do this.*

I wag two uninflated balloons.

"Can we bother you for your time for ten seconds?" I say. "The camera guy is saying it'll be a good shot if you and me are blowing up balloons together."

Richard and I purse our lips to our floppy balloons, the raised stage behind us. The American football beefcake painted on the big Spirit of America Day crest looks down on us as we huff, huff, huff.

Richard ties a knot in his red balloon.

"How's that?" he asks.

I pluck the red balloon from his hands.

"Thank you very much," I say.

I creep out of the Diplomat Ballroom.

Fade down. Fade up.

The hinges squeak on the door of the motel lobby bathroom as it swats shut behind me. I crouch on the floor, the urinals lined up behind me, and paw through my backpack.

"This is the Family Tree DNA kit," I whisper to the camera, ripping open the vacuum-sealed package. I hold up the plastic scraper in my left hand and the vial in my right.

Three stabs with the scraper bursts the balloon. The boom bounces wall to wall. I scrape Richard's saliva off the shreds of red balloon.

I snap the head of the scraper into the vial and twist on the lid.

I dart out of the motel lobby bathroom.

Fade to black. Fade up.

A small man in a blue suit stands at the end of a silver corridor.

"Mr. Greenspan?" I ask, rolling forward, my arm outstretched, ready for a shaking.

"I am," says Mr. Greenspan, and we shake and shake and shake. Mr. Bennett Greenspan is the CEO of Family Tree DNA.

"Well, here's me and my friend's samples." I hand over a package of two vials.

"Good," he says. "We'll get them processed for you and hope you'll find the results interesting."

Fade to black. *6 Hours Later* snaps up on the screen. Fade up.

In an office, bald little Mr. Greenspan is pecking at his laptop. I'm parked next to his desk in a swivel chair.

"I was brought up," I explain to him, "to marry a Jew, because I'm a Jew, and I just thought, I just want a 100 percent guarantee that I am a Jew so I'm not wasting my time."

Mr. Greenspan ignores my shtick and rotates his laptop so I can see the screen.

"Looking at your results," he says, "it's very clear that you have a . . . what we call an Ashkenazi background. And so what that means is, you descend on your mother's side from Eastern European Jewish stock."

"What about my dad's side?" I ask.

"Your dad's side, well . . ." He spools down the screen. "So you are J1. In that respect, your DNA is commonly found among Jews all over the Middle East. So on your mom's side you're Jewish and your dad's side you're Jewish."

From spit in a jar, he can tell I'm an Ashkenazi Jew.

"Well, can we look at my friend's DNA?" I say.

Mr. Greenspan types in a code and a new page pops up.

"The father's side is European," he says. "There's no question about that."

Mr. Greenspan spools down the page.

"On your friend's mother's mother's mother's side, your friend has African ancestry."

I swivel a little happy swivel.

"And so on your friend's mother's mother's mother's side, he descends from an African."

"My friend is really, really, really white," I say.

"Okay," he says. "That tells us that this event, this black marriage to a Caucasian, happened a long time ago."

"Wow. I cannot tell you how white this person is. And how white this person thinks they are."

"I cannot tell you how African they are, if they'll scratch the surface a little bit."

Fade to black. Fade up. Nighttime.

I'm pulling at the lapels of my best suit, stepping through the parking lot of the Budget Inn. Car headlights blind me, but I march on.

Richard Barrett is held together in a sharp suit, too. His fingers wriggle up and down a Casio keyboard in the corner of the Diplomat Ballroom. The ballroom is even more colored in than this morning. Confederate battle flags are planted across the stage.

Six white athletes march in to Richard's "Onward, Christian Soldiers."

The athletes' families are seated at round tables across the room. A candle has joined the Confederate battle flag in the center of each. The mayor and other special guests look down from a long dining table on the stage.

The Nationalist Movement's second-in-command, a potbellied man called Vince Thornton, bends down until his lips nearly touch the microphone on the podium.

"Please join me in welcoming Richard Barrett," he announces.

A local beauty queen's tiara twinkles as Richard passes behind her on his way to the microphone.

"Thank you, Vince. American youth, because you are special, you deserve a special day," Richard reads from his cards. "Ever since the days when youngsters were pressured toward long hair, loose living, and drugs, the Spirit of America Day has showcased clean-cut, clean-living youth who are patriotic to the core."

Richard tells us what makes Mississippi Mississippi. He gushes over the mayor, the beauty queen, and a local country singer in attendance.

"At this time," he continues, "we'd like to thank Australian television, which is here covering the banquet and the Spirit of America Day. And John, if you'll come up? He wanted to say a few words of appreciation. John, we'd be honored to have you."

I walk from the back of the ballroom, straightening the Windsor knot in my tie. The stage lighting burns my eyes, and the crowd turns to shadows. I lean down to the microphone.

"Um, well, thank you to the people of Mississippi and, um, congratulations to all the, er, participants in the Spirit of America Day awards."

I suck in a little air. I turn my head to Richard and then turn back to the crowd.

"Now, this is a bit awkward. But, er, earlier when I interviewed you, Richard, I procured a saliva sample. And I took it to a DNA testing plant. And the results are in, as they say. And there's no real easy way to put this, but you have African DNA."

Perhaps three confused giggles arise from an otherwise silent ballroom.

"You're part African," I continue. "But don't worry, you're not, you're not, it's not like you're *black* black. It's more you're white and a bit black. Like Barack Obama. But it doesn't really matter because we're, like, all mixed up. All of us. Like, if we went back far enough, I probably wouldn't even be Jewish. Anyway, thank you, everybody, and enjoy the Spirit of America Day banquet."

I turn my head to Richard. He is pulling a smile so wide and so fake, I can see his decaying gums.

"Ha, ha," mumbles Richard with a clap, "very good."

It is a tribute to the politeness of Mississippians that I receive a light applause.

I dart out of the ballroom and loosen my Windsor knot as I head down to the motel lobby. An asthma whistle pushes up my lungs and out my throat. I pull off my jacket as I exit to the parking lot. A gust of wind hits the sweat on my back and I feel good.

Fade to black. End of segment.

The Magician's Trick

Okay. Here's the magician's trick: We're all from Africa.

A thorough DNA test of anyone will reveal African roots. As this is the case—and as DNA testing without permission is a murky legal/ethical area—after I scraped saliva from Richard's balloon, I did a switcheroo with a sample from a consenting person.

So I'm P. T. Barnum. Can we move on?

The Next Morning

My baseball cap is pulled down like Matt Damon trying not to be noticed. The four-man film crew and I slouch low in a booth in a Mississippi diner confusingly called Texas.

Will Richard send his footballers out to get us? We only have to make it to the afternoon, when our plane leaves.

The director, Craig, chews a fried calamari ring the size of a doughnut. Cameraman Germain scratches his face until it's as red as his stubble and eyes. Production assistant Richie is on the phone haggling down the cost of a prosthetic nose. In two days I'll be going undercover as a black man in Chicago.

The producer, Jonathan, plucks the last "pretzel chicken tender" from the basket. It seems to push his Adam's apple to one side as it goes down his throat. After he's recovered, he says that when we were packing up at the Nationalist Movement headquarters two nights ago, Richard Barrett put his hand on his back and left it there too long.

We agree that Mississippi's most prominent white supremacist gave off a bit of a gay vibe.

Richie slides his phone in his pocket and says the prosthetic nose will be waiting with the concierge at the hotel in Chicago. I pull out my phone and e-mail my ABC boss back in Australia.

> *On Tues, Mar 3, at 11:09 a.m., John Safran wrote:*
>
> Hi Debbie! Well, I did the speech. And I wasn't murdered. I don't have too much of a read on how it went because I was at the podium with lights in my eyes and Richard Barrett was standing behind me. But Craig and Germain said it was awkward. We got a great interview with the black House of Rep politician, Robert Johnson, who's opposing Richard Barrett's Spirit of America Day banquet, so that really sells to the Aussie audience that Richard is a "someone," and a dangerous someone, without me having to say much. I also went to Barrett's office and he gave me skinhead pamphlets and showed me his gun. My read is there's close to zero chance Barrett's going to pursue legal action or the like. Time to turn black! X

I press send, smudging catfish grease all over the screen.

One Day Later

Richard Barrett visits a post office somewhere in Mississippi. He sends a registered letter to the Chief Operating Officer of the Australian Broadcasting Corporation.

You and your agents acted in the utmost bad faith . . . they claimed that theirs was a legitimate news operation . . . they used the permission to disrupt the ceremonies, insult the guests, slander the state . . . the releases were obtained by fraud and misrepresentation . . .

Richard demands the ABC drop the footage or face his legal wrath.

Four Months Later

Chris Lilley, in various sexes and ethnicities, pulls faces at me from the walls of the Melbourne television production office.

I am sucking on a mint ball from the goldfish bowl of mint balls in the middle of the table. Through the bowl I see the distended face of producer Jonathan. He presses the red button on the speakerphone. The ABC has instructed us to seek advice from US lawyers. The network is happy to defend us against defamation. That's a civil action and all part of the rough-and-tumble of this type of television. However, Richard is alleging fraud, and possibly therefore trespass, which are criminal offenses.

The US lawyers tell us Richard has a case. One he might well eventually lose, but a case nonetheless. They also tell me what Richard told me back in his Nationalist Movement office, something I'd chosen not to think about. Richard-the-lawyer had hauled a county in Georgia through the US Supreme Court, lawyered a black family out of their home, and snuffed out two crayon kids on a Mississippi license plate. The US lawyers also mention *Richard Barrett v. Oldsmobile Division General Motors Corporation* and *Richard Barrett v. Some Guy Who Came to Repair His Xerox Machine*.

The ABC forbids the story from airing. Not a frame of Richard Barrett or Mississippi makes it to the show.

That was that.

One Year After Filming Richard Barrett, and Three Months After the Airing of *Race Relations*

Johnny Cash is in my living room.

What's done in the dark will be brought to the light, says Johnny.

Johnny Cash isn't the only singer here. Cries float up the staircase and push under my door: "We want Moshiach! We want Moshiach now! We want Moshiach! We want Moshiach now!"

Moshiach is the Messiah. A sect of black-hatted Jews are convinced their dead leader is the Moshiach. They sing for an hour a day, waving King Moshiach flags on the corner just outside my flat. They hope this will hasten his return to earth, at which time my fellow Jews and I will fly to Israel on clouds with wings of eagles.

I'm slumped on the couch, poking around the Internet.

I download conspiracy podcasts, spool through Scientology tweets, and search for exorcisms on YouTube. I punch in *vanguardnewsnetwork .com*, one of my white supremacist faves. *No Jews. Just Right* is their motto.

A redheaded woodpecker swoops over the Vanguard News Network masthead.

Beneath is the headline: MISSISSIPPI: WHITE NATIONALIST LEADER MURDERED; BLACKS CHARGED.

Below that: *Sad news, but* what *was Barrett thinking? White leaders usually* avoid *Blacks*.

Vanguard links to a Mississippi television report. Richard Barrett has been found, stabbed to death, in his burning house. A twenty-two-year-old, Vincent McGee, has confessed to the murder. Members of the McGee family have been arrested as accessories after the fact.

"Yes sir, we interviewed him and he told us basically what happened," Sheriff Pennington tells a reporter.

The reporter asks if he knows the motive. Sheriff Pennington will not answer.

I don't notice I'm biting the inside of my cheek until it starts to sting.

My E-mail to the *Race Relations* Crew

I e-mail the *Race Relations* crew.

> On Sat, April 24, at 10:06 a.m., John Safran wrote:
> Jesus Christ. Richard Barrett murdered.

The replies:

> Director Craig: Holy shit!

> Researcher Roland: Jesus Christ.

> My manager, Kevin: Cool. I'll ring the ΛBC and see what this means about the footage. We can probably use it now.

What Happened?

People are punching in their opinions on message boards all over the Internet.

Vincent McGee is a civil rights hero!

I can only imagine the circumstances behind this, but I shake your hand, man.

The racist guy got what he deserved. All racists should die . . . I'm sure the black guy was not a racist. He just was pissed off at some evil, pompous white guy who hated him without a just reason.

It's not all good reviews for the killer Vincent McGee.

Will the black man be charged with a HATE crime?

What if a white had killed a black activist???

Just another day in a troubled country where the truth is spoken and the victim murdered, thus proving the truth. But there can never be a black supremacist, can there? That would be racist.

It's a hate crime, but who committed it? Richard Barrett, for being a white supremacist, or Vincent McGee, for hating someone with views other than his own?

I hit refresh, refresh, refresh.

Pretty soon more news blows out of Mississippi. Vincent's stepfather has told a local paper Vincent did yard work for Richard. The day of the killing, Richard had paid Vincent twenty-six dollars for a whole day's work. Vincent argued with Richard and the fight blew up.

Now the murder's about money as well as race.

White supremacist hires black youth, pays him as if he were a slave, says who knows what when confronted . . . dispute ends badly.

I hit refresh, refresh, refresh.

Two days later a bulletproof vest is strapped on Vincent McGee. He is led from his cell to a courthouse in Rankin County, Mississippi.

An investigator from the sheriff's department walks to a podium, facing the judge. He tells the judge what Vincent has told investigators: He had been doing yard work at Richard's Nationalist Movement headquarters. (The tiny house! I didn't see the yard in the dark.) But he adds another element. Richard then drove him to Richard's house in another part of Mississippi. Inside this house, Richard made a sexual advance.

Vincent knifed Richard and lit his house on fire.

So now the murder's about race, money, and sex.

The district attorney now speaks to Vincent. He tells Vincent he is being charged with capital murder. Capital murder is when you murder so you can commit another crime, like burglary. Does that mean the district attorney doesn't believe Vincent's story? Capital murder, rather than simple murder, means that Vincent could be put to death by lethal injection.

Jesus. Richard Barrett—so careful, so evasive—managed to get himself killed in a race crime. Hater of, employer of, possible lover of, a black man. Vanguard was indeed just right: What *was* Richard Barrett thinking?

In the Ghetto

Here's what I was thinking.

I live in a flat up a stairwell. The walls of the stairwell are streaked with skid marks. I carried my bicycle up the stairs, often and badly, before it was nicked.

I moved in here when my grandfather died ten years ago and kept most of my grandparents' furnishings. Seventies wallpaper, cream and gold, rolls along the hallway and through most of the rooms. Grandma-needled tapestries stare at me whichever way I turn. An aristocratic woman plucking a harp, a gypsy patting a rabbit, a Dutch boy blushing before a windmill, and thirteen others. A dining room table for six stretches out in the dining room. And there's one of me.

The cupboards are squeezed full of crockery. The type of china you could whip out if the Queen dropped by; enough for the Queen to bring her family. Tucked among the china are shoehorns and wooden contraptions for stretching leather. My grandparents ran the shoe repair shop under the rail bridge on the same street as the flat. My high school rabbi, who taught me Torah, had his heels fixed there. Old Jews stop me in the street to tell me my grandparents did their shoes, too.

If I turn right out the front of my apartment block, the first shop I hit is Glick's Cakes & Bagels. Along the one-minute walk from my flat to Glick's, I pass three Jewish prayer houses catering to slightly different sects of Orthodox Jews. Next to Glick's is Daneli's, a kosher deli. Next to that is Gefen Liquor, which carries kosher wines.

The kosher certificate pasted on the window of Glick's is signed by Rabbi Gutnick. He belongs to an Orthodox sect called Lubavitch. An even more Orthodox sect, Adass Israel, prefers something more stringent to Rabbi Gutnick's kosher certifications. They buy their bagels across the street at Lichtenstein's Bakehouse. Those bagels are certified by Rabbi Beck.

Near Lichtenstein's is Hadar Judaica, for all your bar mitzvah gift needs. Just down from that is Balaclava Jewish & Continental Deli, where the food is Jewish (gefilte fish, cholent, matzo ball soup) but not kosher. Not far is Melbourne Kosher Butchers, where all the recent Israeli arrivals buy their phone cards. Also nearby is La Cafe on Nelson, where the hottest recent Israeli arrivals are hired as waitresses.

When I haul my rubbish bags to the lane at the rear of my block of flats, I see across the way B'nai B'rith, a Jewish organization that fights anti-Semitism. If I traipse thirty seconds up the lane I hit Yeshivah College, my old Jewish high school. Next to that is the synagogue, where the rabbis wear plastic bags on their hats on rainy days. Also within a short schlep is the headquarters of a Zionist youth group and a Kabbalah center.

In summary: I live in the worst place in Australia you could live if you ever piss off the Jews.

I pissed off the Jews.

I began to get greasy looks about two weeks before *Race Relations* aired, when some of the show's content leaked. People began to keep their distance. Any Jew would recognize the signs: Why was I making trouble?

My mother kept my scrapbook in better shape when she was alive. I still need to paste in the *Race Relations* clippings from the *Australian Jewish News*.

SAFRAN CRUCIFIED OVER NEW SHOW

Comedian John Safran's new show has caused a public outcry, even though its debut on ABC TV is still a week away. The Australian Family Association last week hit out at the show, describing it as "filth."

In episode one of the series, in which Safran explores interracial attraction, the former Yeshivah College student donates sperm at a Palestinian sperm bank, while looking at a picture of US President

Barack Obama. In a later episode, Safran is crucified as part of a religious ritual in the Philippines.

But the scene that will likely generate the most controversy in the Jewish community involves Safran going to his mother's grave with a shovel and Kabbalah prayer book to discover what she would think of him if he married a non-Jew.

"Safran's actions are to be deplored," the Executive Council of Australian Jewry president told the *Australian Jewish News*. "They are extremely insensitive and not only bring disrepute on the Jewish people, but adversely affect interfaith relationships."

—ADAM KAMIEN

The ABC has shamed itself with the showing of John Safran's *Race Relations* program. He appears desperate for subject matter, having to resort to underpants stealing and sniffing (stealing is a crime—not a joke) and the degrading deceit of insulting both Jews and Palestinians by substituting each other's sperm in sperm banks (also a crime—not a joke). The entire subject matter and execution is despicable, and no doubt more bad publicity has been showered on us Jews.

—NOAH LEVIN, MALVERN, VIC, LETTERS

Safran's carnival approach to the Holocaust continued in last week's episode when he mock-gassed Holocaust denier David Irving. Safran claimed he was following the lead of Nazi hunter Simon Wiesenthal. Prior to "luring his prey" for the interview, Safran "rigs" the radio studio by inserting a pipe through the ventilation system so as to convert the room into a "gas chamber." Taking pause from their chat, Safran walks out, jams the door with a broom, and opens a gas bottle while screaming at Irving through the glass: "You're locked in a room and it's filling with gas, and if you try and tell anyone, I'm going to deny it." Safran not only distorts Wiesenthal's message of justice, instead of revenge, but given that his own grandmother lost her family in the Holocaust, he should have known better.

—DR. DVIR ABRAMOVICH

And Then One Night

As well as all of that, the theme blaring through *Race Relations* is that the Australian Jewish community bullies their young to marry Jewish and bullies their non-Jewish partners to back off.

Not long ago, my Jewish friend Leah was preparing to marry a non-Jew named Ant. One afternoon Ant visited Leah's family while Leah was out of town. Over an hour, one by one, Leah's mother, father, and brother floated out of the living room. Ant sat alone, disconcerted. Finally a man Ant had never seen before strolled in.

The man sat down and looked at Ant.

"You'll never be accepted here," the man said.

"Why?"

"Because you're not Jewish."

Then the man stood up and left.

As well as locking David Irving in a radio studio, in *Race Relations* I ran a yellow highlighter over little events like this. I learned people in small towns don't like the man with the yellow highlighter pen.

The afternoon before the first episode aired, I bought hundreds of dollars of food from the supermarket so I wouldn't have to leave the flat for a while. Good decision. Even now, I try to avoid it. Months ago I gave up walking down the street. If I need to catch up for coffee, I catch up somewhere else. I do my grocery shopping a few suburbs up.

One night, well out of my Jewish ghetto, as my head sloshed with alcohol, a girl holding a plastic cup of wine drifted over.

"Hello," I said.

Her face twisted to fury.

"If you're going to take my Jewish background," she shrieked, "and put it up on the television, you better do better than sniffing Eurasian underpants!"

All heads on the rooftop turned to us. The Jewess escaped down the stairs.

That was an hour ago. Now I'm hunched over my laptop at my dining room table for six.

I punch in the address I've been punching in for weeks: *tripadvisor .com.au*.

I punch the words into the box I've been punching in for weeks: *Jackson, Mississippi*.

Tonight I go one step further. I slap my wallet onto the dining room table. I slide out my credit card. I bash in the numbers and hit confirm.

How can I *not* get on a plane to Mississippi? I'm a Race Trekkie. I *met* the dead white supremacist. Why would God and/or Fate have arranged that if not for me to now get on that plane? I know that man at the book publisher sneered when I told him my idea. *John, a book is a little more difficult than a comedy TV show.* I know I have no book deal. But the trial's not going to wait for me. There's not going to be a *second* white supremacist who I hung out with murdered. This is my sweet spot, right? As well as race and money and sex and death, this thing with Richard Barrett is about small towns, tribalism, and old ways. I'm going to escape my ghetto, thank God, for a new one across the sea.

2.

MISSISSIPPI

The Airport

It's winter in Mississippi and drizzling. My feet squelch on my untied shoelaces as I jerk my luggage across the parking lot at Jackson–Medgar Wiley Evers International Airport.

Mississippi doesn't waste any time. That *Jackson* is President Andrew Jackson, pro-slavery campaigner and master to three hundred slaves. That *Medgar Wiley Evers* was a black activist who collapsed and died outside his house in 1963 after a Klansman had shot him in the back. You land straight in a race war.

And Mississippi wants to get something else out in the open, too. Tennessee Williams is looking down at me like I'm a piece of dirt. John Grisham wants to stab me. William Faulkner sneers.

YES, WE CAN READ, says the headline on the welcome billboard. A FEW OF US CAN EVEN WRITE.

Way to try to psych me out, Mississippi. Why not just put up a sign: *John, a book is a little more difficult than a comedy TV show*? All up, a dozen Mississippi writers scorn me from the billboard, glowing in the night, as I steer out of the airport.

One Mississippi stereotype collapses as I drive into downtown Jackson. Jackson is the state capital, but from the little I can see, the Mississippi with white plantation mansions is somewhere else. I pull in to the motel, a hunk of concrete in a parking lot of concrete in a city of concrete.

In the entrance, a black man in black is pacing with a thumping stick. I try to remember if motels usually have guards with thumping sticks out front.

The man attending the front desk has a neck that flops over his collar. He looks at me as if an elf has just turned up on his doorstep. Overseas folk, I gather, don't really stop by downtown Jackson. Or is that white folk? A gold Freemason ring, of all things, twinkles on his fat black finger as he signs me in.

I'll be the first person to stay in room twenty-two, he tells me. The motel fresh opened just two weeks ago.

Glue fumes follow me through the lobby, up the elevator, down the hall, into my room, and into the shower. Those twenty hours of planes. Mr. Sandman has not only sprinkled sand in my eyes, but grouted over my nostrils and under my fingernails. I scratch the asthma tickle in my chest.

I'm not going for the sympathy vote, but I can tell you I don't really know what I'm doing. For weeks I've been reading true crime book after book after book for hints. I've got a month before the trial starts. You can't just rock up on the day of the trial and expect to be able to work out what's going on. That's what I learned from *Midnight in the Garden of Good and Evil*: Arrive early and befriend the local yahoos. That's how you paint a picture of the town, understand the context. Start getting an idea of what really happened.

What have I got? I've got the names of the killer's lawyers from the news reports: Chokwe Lumumba and Precious Martin. And what names they are. I don't even know whether Precious is a man or a woman. And Chokwe? I've also got the number of a black journalist, Earnest McBride. And there's this white separatist podcaster, Jim Giles.

Out of the shower, I pace, one towel as a kilt, one towel as a cape. I wiggle my toes. The carpet feels like mini golf Astroturf. Everything here, from the bed headboard to the venetian blinds, is both brand-spanking-new and about to fall apart, like counterfeit Nikes at the market. You know, I saw on an Internet message board that John Berendt fudged the start of *Midnight in the Garden of Good and Evil*.

John Berendt barely knew the killer Jim Williams; he had never met him at the time of the murder, and the entire first chapter of the book in which Williams's violent lover comes in and throws a fit is made up (or at least is told in first person with Berendt as the observer when in fact he wasn't there).

The pedants are even after Truman Capote. *Truman said he went to the house on Tuesday! It was Wednesday!*

And all those true crime books were written before the Internet. These days, you can't get away with anything. Everyone has a Twitter account. Just hours after I was crucified (literally, by the way) in a tiny village in the Philippines for *Race Relations*, an Australian journalist had tracked down a local online to see if my version of events matched what he saw. I unpack my Flip video camera and my Zoom Dictaphone. I'll get everything on tape, so none of my frenemies can trip me up later.

My eyes fall on the bedside table, as yet untouched by a guest's hands.

My God! I skip over and creak open the drawer. Can it be true? Will I be the first to open a brand-new Gideon Bible?

The spine indeed squeaks a most pleasing never-been-opened squeak. I flick the pristine white pages to John 8:44.

You belong to your father, the devil.

Ever since the Grand Dragon quoted that to me, it's been my fave! Because *You* is the Jews and John is my name.

My neck already aches, and I've only been lying here two minutes. My lungs clench up. I huff and huff. A green leech crawls from my mouth into my Delta Air Lines serviette.

I puff my Ventolin puffer five times, rub my neck, and fall asleep.

The White Supreme

The sharp winter sun rises. Outside my window, down the road, four black convicts plod and mope. I know they are convicts because CON-VICT is printed on the back of their green-and-white-striped shirts.

They're stroking a fresh coat of white paint on a fire hydrant. A black bus with tinted windows, marked SHERIFF, trails the men by a hundred meters or so.

I flick on the coffee machine in the kitchenette.

"If it pleases the court, this is Jim Giles, and you're listening to *Radio Free Mississippi*," says my laptop on the kitchenette bench. Jim pulls up his theme song, "Amerika" by Rammstein.

Jim Giles is a white separatist who lives in Pearl, in Rankin County. More specifically, he lives in a trailer on his mother's farm. Each weekday morning he hunches over a microphone in that trailer and broadcasts *Radio Free Mississippi* live over the Internet. This one isn't live, though. I'm working my way through his old podcasts, from the weeks after Richard's death.

"I had a Rankin County deputy sheriff call me from a crime scene," Jim says, "Richard Barrett's crime scene where he had been killed, and he was trying to figure out did I do it! He actually lived fairly close to me, Barrett did, I still don't know where exactly."

Jim Giles takes a sip of something in his trailer; I take a sip of coffee in the kitchenette.

"Who was Richard Barrett?" Jim asks. "Richard Barrett was an asset. Not to white people. He was an asset to the FBI and to the fucking media. He was a sick puppy, and I'm suggesting sexual perversion on his part. He was a little man. He was a lawyer. He was a scrawny man and he had a look in his face that was one of distortion, of perversion. He would call me on the telephone incessantly."

You should know, white separatists are always kvetching about one another. In fact, most white supremacists hate: (1) white liberals, (2) white conservatives, and (3) other white supremacists, making it unclear which whites they have in mind when proclaiming their love of the white race. It's not uncommon for them to accuse one another of working for the FBI, although already I'm hoping it's true in Richard's case.

"Richard Barrett, the most famous European supremacist Mississippi has ever known." That's a big claim. Bigger than the Mississippi Burning Klansmen? Maybe he's being sarcastic. "He is dead now, though, boys, if y'all didn't know that! An African killed him, and I'd say that's an appropriate end to his life. His demise was rooted in his conduct as a man. He was somewhere he did not belong. He was from . . . He wasn't originally from the South. He was a Yankee from up in New Jersey, who came down here like those Freedom Riders."

The Freedom Riders were civil rights activists in the 1960s. Odd comparison, but perhaps it's a white supremacist insult. Barrett was an outsider, coming down to meddle in things that weren't his birthright to meddle in.

"I have read brand-new Freedom Riders will be marching on Mississippi this month. Well, let me tell you, folks, this might be called the hospitality state, but I'm not offering you any hospitality. I hope an African kills you dead. And your demise will be rooted very appropriately where Richard Barrett's demise was rooted. Come on down! I'm praying one of the Africans kills you dead as Abraham Lincoln."

I've made Jim first on my list of people to pursue. He sounds emotional with nothing to lose. They're the people who blurt out the truth. Back in Melbourne, I flicked a Facebook message to Jim. He never responded. But his home address is online. Jim had claimed in an interview he's such a good fighter, he can beat up 95 percent of people in the street. So an anti-racist activist posted a smart-aleck poll on a message board.

POLL: Can you beat up Jim Giles?

---

a. Yes

---

b. No

---

c. Maybe

Jim Giles responded to the poll.

In Reply To: POLL: Can you beat up Jim Giles?

I live at 6 Oakland Lane, Pearl, Mississippi 39208.

If any of you bitches want to fight me, meet there.

---

t's still cement in all directions in downtown Jackson. In the daytime, even the sky is cement. Walking through the motel parking lot, I pull my jacket sleeves over my hands—the air cuts that cold. But when the sun elbows its way through the clouds now and then, it laser-beams my eyes.

The Stepford Wife inside the GPS says it's forty-five minutes to Jim Giles's. I want to know more about why he hated Richard so much. Does he really think that he was a sexually perverted FBI agent who was killed in some horrible misunderstanding? And I want to know what *he's* like, the white supreme in the trailer.

The Stepford Wife directs me past vast abandoned concrete lots in Jackson, where things once were but I don't know what. In one, the mangled metal innards of a building twist to the heavens. I can't tell if the building was never fully built or never fully torn down. I'm then directed through a designated "historic district." It tricks the eye. First glance, you see gorgeous, old-world white cottages, the charming heart of the American South. Second glance, you see they've been gutted, vandalized, stripped for firewood. Several sit there collapsed in on themselves.

By the way, where is everyone? Those extras in your life, lurking the streets, just aren't here.

My flavorless red rental weaves onto I-55. Walmarts, Taco Bells, and Red Roof Inns build and build till logos stumble over one another in the blur out my side window. Half a Hank Williams CD later, that thins out and giant golden-tip oak trees take over. Not just lining the road but running thick and deep. Suddenly America has gone and Mississippi has appeared. I've crossed from Jackson into Rankin County, where Pearl is.

A silver castle sparkles in the distance. It rolls closer. Golden sunshine pings off the tips of the barbed wire of the Central Mississippi Correctional Facility. Is Vincent locked up in there? How many jails are there in Mississippi?

Opposite the prison is a sign saying MORE SWEAT IN TRAINING, LESS BLOOD ON THE STREET, with *Sweat* dripping sweat and *Blood* dripping blood. It's the sign for the police academy.

I need to talk with the police, too, before the trial, get the lowdown.

As I push on, the grass bordering the road collapses into marshland. These could even be "backwoods." I curve off the highway.

The trees reach over the road to touch one another, blocking out the sun, and now I bolt through green for miles and miles, until a parked fire engine throws a whoosh of red at my windshield. The trees become older and the trunks become thicker, the closer I get to Jim's. I don't think it's just my imagination. Moss has climbed all over the drooping branches; the trees look like they're dripping green fur.

I slow from a bolt to a crawl to a stop.

Jim Giles's street is a dirt path off the road. Gently, I poke up the path toward a bend.

I hear before I see.

A wave of wounded howls bursts from beyond the bend and rolls toward my car.

Mississippi's coming to get me.

Giles Farm

Ten huge gray dogs yowl and leap in one tangled bundle behind barbed wire. This one airborne, then that one airborne, then that one, then that one, then that, like they are being juggled. Their teeth make it higher than the barbed wire, but the rest of them remains below. The farm is tucked away behind the bend, hidden from the main road and the world.

I step from the car. The sound of my door slamming behind me is drowned out by the dogs. Their howls shatter through the air and through the ground, through my body and eardrums. My bearings are toppled, leaving me blinking, disoriented.

First thing. Triggering the hound alarm has tipped me past the point of no return. Any fear I have about Jim and his fighting must be folded away in my pocket for later.

Okay, the vehicle gate in front of me is shut. Okay, it's a small farm. Okay, barbed wire holds in the farm on the three sides I can see. Okay, I'll walk the perimeter to see whether there's a walk-in gate.

I affect a confident stride.

"Jim? Jim! Hello? Hello?"

I'm reverse-psychology snooping. *If he's shouting he can't be snooping,* I hope Jim is thinking from wherever he is.

"Jim? Jim!"

The half of the farm closest to my car is green and open. A white trailer squats in the corner. I assume that's the trailer where Jim flicks on a microphone and rants *Radio Free Mississippi.* Is Jim in there? If he is, doesn't look like he's coming out.

The other half of Giles Farm is tightly packed with oak trees, the ground coated with rusty leaves. I squint, and deep behind the black trees, I make out the blur of a two-story wooden house. Is Jim Giles in there, staring at me from the second-story window?

I journey the length and breadth of the barbed wire. There's no walk-in entrance. The vehicle entrance is bolted shut. No one comes out.

Under a Hunchbacked Tree Dripping Green Fur

The shrieks of the hellhounds are faint and far behind. I park under a hunchbacked tree and pull my phone from my pocket. My thumb taps out a reverse-psychology e-mail. (*If he's e-mailing me he can't have been snooping just then.*)

Hi Jim,

I'm an Australian writer, in Mississippi at the moment, trying to contact you regarding Richard Barrett. Would you be able to get back to me, please?

All the best,
John

I drive off, twiddling the dial to American Family Radio. A man explains, point by point, why Mormons aren't Christian, so no one should be fooled by presidential candidate Mitt Romney.

I curve into a Walmart to buy some groceries. A set of bulbous black twins, in matching pink denim, totter to the entrance in matching cherry high heels.

Jackson is roughly 80 percent black, 18 percent white, and 2 percent everyone else. The lack of everyone else really hits you. I noticed it while filming for *Race Relations*. It's like if a tornado in Australia sucked away the Greeks, Italians, Asians, and Arabs and all that was left were the white Anglo-Saxon Protestants and Aboriginal Australians gawking at one another.

I feel a tickle in my pocket.

Hello John,

I will be on the air in the morning and would be happy to speak with you live. I'll try to reach you by Skype in the morning between seven and nine a.m. CST.

Yours Truly,
Jim Giles

The white separatist has done what the Jewish writer would probably have done and made danger into a show. I go home and, riding my luck, make some calls to the answering machines of the lawyers Precious and Chokwe, and the DA.

Then I read about another case Chokwe's working on—the Scott sisters, who sixteen years ago were sentenced to double life for armed robbery. Chokwe saw racism and prized a pardon out of the governor just this month. The governor placed one condition on their release: Gladys had to agree to have her kidney scooped out, to be then sewn up into her sick sister, Jamie. This is being reported as "touching" in the Mississippi media and "erghh" in all non-Mississippi press.

Radio Free Mississippi

It's seven a.m. and I poke my face out the window of my room. Jackson still insists on being sunny enough to burn your eyes while cold enough to wear gloves.

"If it pleases the court, this is Jim Giles, and you're listening to *Radio Free Mississippi*," Jim announces live from my laptop. "I have an inquiry from someone. I've mentioned him to you before."

"What!" I say, turning from the window.

"His name is John Safran. I've some concerns about him. And if he's listening, well, I'll just air them now. 'Well-known for pranks and indelicate handling.' I believe this is from his Wikipedia page."

Uh-oh.

"So, this might be an attempt on his part to make me look bad," Jim continues. "John, that's real hard to do. I do a good job with that myself. I don't really need any help from you. I'm not so much like probably anybody you've dealt with. I'm certainly no Richard Barrett.

"Barrett was not a legitimate voice for the local people here in Mississippi. I've long suspected him of being a police informer. Something that—John, I hope I don't hurt your feelings—but honestly, I think that's probably what you are as well, John—a police informer."

He pauses.

"Let me just break this to you delicately if you are listening now. I do not use the *J* word here because it confers upon those folks two things I don't think they deserve. That is victim status and a religion. Rather, I use the term *Israeli*, stripping them of both their victim status and their religion. It's my argument here, John, that Israelis are first and foremost a foreign and alien race of people.

"And that's who you are.

"John, don't get your feelings hurt. I'll still be nice and respectful to you if you want to talk with me. You can ask me a question and I'll answer. And you can chop it up and put it out there and say, 'This is the redneck from Mississippi I interviewed. Don't you just love the way they talk down there in Mississippi?'

"John, I'm used to people making fun of me. Thinking low of me. Thinking I'm kind of stupid and ignorant."

I lean forward, hunching over my computer on the little coffee table.

"Okay. I am gonna go get some orange juice and then I will try to reach Mr. Safran if he's reachable. Mr. Safran, if you are listening, I am about to try to reach you as soon as I get through getting some orange juice."

There's dead air. Then a slurp.

"All right, let's give Mr. Safran a ring-a-ling," he says.

My laptop starts to bleep and bloop.

"Ha-ha," Jim says. "I think he has got a gun and a baseball bat over his shoulder."

I forgot about my Skype profile picture. I'm Photoshopped as the Bear Jew from *Inglourious Basterds*.

"Good morning, Mr. Safran," Jim says, like a coyote feeling out another coyote who has wandered onto his prairie. And for all I know he may be dressed as a coyote—his video is flicked off.

"Is this one of your spoofs?" he asks.

"No, no. That's why I should tell you my connection to Richard Barrett. Because it'll explain why I'm calling you." I take him through the whole *Race Relations* story, how I announced at the Spirit of America Day that Richard had African DNA.

"That's funny." Jim laughs. "That's actually funny." He takes a sip of juice and laughs some more. "You might have a best seller on your hands with your book, given the market out there. There seems to be a hearty appetite for this sort of thing."

Jim starts one of his trademark pauses, which make you think his equipment has broken, or yours.

"Richard Barrett, even in death, lives on," Jim says finally. "And so my concern about your focus is he continues to haunt and do what he did best. And that is tar and tarnish anyone who is—and I hate, I don't use the *W* word here, I use *European*. *W* is just . . . I have concluded that *W*, to use the *W* word, is just too frightening for most people."

Jim claims he's no Richard Barrett, but he can't come out and say what he means, either.

I tell Jim that there was something that didn't stack up about the Spirit of America Day. Not everyone seemed in on the deal.

"He was forever doing that," Jim says. "That was his MO. All geared around young white males, too. He was forever clinging to young white males. And one of them got charged with . . . some kind of bomb crime."

"Oh really? Who is that?" Immediately I scribble down *Bomb Crime*.

"I've forgotten the boy's name, but . . . And I knew another young boy that was associated with him, very troubled boy, and yeah, he is just, you know, the whole thing with Barrett—nothing smacked of wholesome, he was anything but wholesome. Richard never failed to make Europeans look stupid and goofy. Richard Barrett was tampering with something that was very important to the lives and fortunes of the people who live here in Mississippi in a hurtful way. He has made my tasks harder."

"Is your family from Mississippi?" I ask.

Jim pauses.

"I am a very open and direct person; there is nothing that I shirk from talking about."

Jim tells me how he got to be a white separatist living in a trailer.

The Ballad of Jim Giles

One thing about poor folk, you don't always know about your past. My father was illegitimate. He didn't know who his father was. So any kind of knowledge certainty is cut off there. I'm pretty sure my father and his mother were born in Wayne County, Mississippi. And I'm pretty sure my mother's parents were born in Mississippi. But I couldn't begin to tell you who my people are beyond those simple facts. And I'm not even sure about that. That's the plight of people who aren't landed aristocracy. I heard my mother say not long ago they live hand-to-mouth. They struggle in their life and they do good to put food on the table. So they're really ill-equipped when it comes to organizing themselves politically.

I live in a trailer. I have got a barn behind my trailer. That's just a barn for my cows. I've got four Jerseys. Three Jersey cows and a Jersey bull. That's where I keep my puppies, under there. I have ten bluetick coonhounds. I have two puppies I am not counting in that number. I've got six Great Pyrenees.

One route to my home is the road where my mother's mother lived. There is squalor there that you won't see anywhere. There is nothing that looks any worse in Haiti.

I've been coming down here to this farm ever since I was about seven or eight years old, when my grandparents first bought this property and built the house. My mother lives next to me, in the two-story house that I speak of. Her home is a very nice home.

I had a pretty regular childhood. They integrated the schools when I was about in the fifth grade. My recollection when I was a kid in school, the classrooms, the hallways, they were quiet places. A school is a place where you go and study and it's supposed to be quiet. Slowly after integration everything seems to be very loud. And I think that is a function of Africans just being basically, you know . . . their natural tendencies come out—they are loud people.

My father was killed in a car wreck when I was eleven.

I talked about Madison Avenue before. After I finished school that was the job I sought and obtained. I was working for IBM, the computer company, in the capacity of a systems engineer, which is somewhat of a technical sales job.

Anytime you would open your mouth in New York they would look at you kind of funny. They would say, "Where are you from?" and draw attention to it. Some did it in a friendly, nice way, and others were rather malicious in their views of Mississippians.

Aged nineteen, I went to Paris for one year. I was studying French at the Sorbonne. Mitterrand had just been elected, and I recall running through the streets of Paris going from one bonfire to another, because they didn't like the policies he enacted as president. They turned over those little French cars and set them on fire. But we don't have that kind of activist group here in Mississippi.

You ask about my wife. I have spoken about all of this on the radio in a very open way. There is nothing that I don't talk about. My lack of a woman. My ex-wife. My mother. My ex-friends, who have abandoned me because of my political views.

My wife was a beautiful Swedish-German woman that I met when I was working for IBM in New York. And being a young, insensitive husband, I screwed that relationship up. That was my fault.

We were married a year.

Did I have an affair? No, no. Really, a lot of it had to do with us moving multiple times with IBM and her ending up in Atlanta, unhappy, and me being insensitive to her unhappiness. Those young brides, there's a make-or-break point in there where you have to treat them right. And if you don't act right, you can lose your girl. And I didn't act right, so I lost my girl.

I have run for Congress three times. I was ignored by the media. But I did capture people's attention with the large trailer I pulled around. Had the Confederate battle flag on it. This was when I was arrested for pointing my finger at that black cop. She said I pointed a loaded .357 at her, when in point of fact all I did is point my finger at her.

I did not have a good showing at the polling booth.

I didn't move here into this trailer until 1996, when my grandfather got so old he couldn't see well enough to go to the doctor and I had to come home and start shuttling him and my grandmother, really, basically, taking care of them. And that turned out to be a fifteen-year, sixteen-year job.

My grandparents have both now died. The death of my grandfather is a rather recent event. And now I have to go out and get a real job. I existed off of their pensions. I was able to stay here and care for them. They didn't have to go to a nursing home. That was really my job in large part, even though I have engaged in organic farming here and I have done Internet radio.

I am working now on finding another girl. I have put in a concerted effort—I have joined dating sites and I am diligently pursuing an attractive female as we speak. But honestly there are two things holding me back. Number one, I have very high taste in regard to women. Number two, I have a lot of baggage in regard to all this public speaking. Most pretty girls, most people in general, I don't think necessarily want to be associated with somebody who is so out there and so vocal on such a controversial subject as race.

I soon will be fifty-two years old.

Jim Makes a Call

Jim begins dialing a number, live on air.

"Well, if it's meant to be a straight book," Jim says, "and you are looking for somebody who actually knew Barrett, I have a friend in particular, to this day, who sings Richard Barrett's praises. And I don't understand him and I am a little, to be honest with you, worried about him. His name is Joe McNamee. One second, Mr. Safran."

Jim gets through to Joe.

"Joe. I am on air now," Jim tells him. "I have got this writer from Australia, and he is writing a book, so he says, about Richard Barrett. And he is Jewish. He is not a friend of . . . He is not a, you know . . . He is not one of us, Joe, is all I can tell you! But he comes across as real nice and he has got a reputation for playing pranks on people. What would you have to say to a Jewish book writer on Richard Barrett, who is in Mississippi right now?"

"Well, I got nothing about . . . I got nothing against Jews," says Joe, "other than what they are doing to us over here. Me and Richard was long-running buddies. Richard was really my attorney."

"Why did you need an attorney?" I ask.

"Trying to have my voice, my opinion," Joe says. "And now'days they claim you can't say nothing."

Joe says he struck trouble fighting to keep the Confederate flag at Ole Miss football games.

I ask him what he knows of Richard's life before he came to Mississippi. Joe says he knows nothing—it never came up.

"Hey, Joe." Jim laughs. "Let me tell you the prank he pulled on Barrett. He came down here and got a saliva sample from Barrett and he went and contended he found out that Barrett had African ancestors."

"Oh yeah," says Joe. "I know who I'm talking to now. He came to Barrett's Spirit of America. Yeah, that was a bad day. I don't even want to talk to him. He's crazy."

"Well, he's back here in Mississippi, Joe," Jim says, quite delighted.

"Were you there, Joe?" I ask.

"I was there," Joe says darkly. "I remember all the lies you come up with. You were buddy-buddying up to us, then turned on us like a goddamn snake."

"But Joe," says Jim, "Mr. Safran and I have had a very congenial conversation thus far. And one thing that he was critical of Barrett was in Barrett's misleading. So maybe Mr. Safran felt justified. Mr. Safran pointed the finger and, Joe, I think he's kind of right about this. Barrett would tell white Mississippians, 'Y'all come to this event, it's for the Spirit of America,' when in fact it was something totally different."

"But Jim, you just wasn't there," Joe splutters. "He got up and said Richard was half-black!"

Jim laughs.

"Well, one difference, Mr. Safran," Jim says, "between me and Joe is Joe contends that he never suspected Barrett of being bad."

"Well, I'm not saying that he is a good guy," Joe says. "I am saying that I never seen anything about him being queer. I don't believe anyone can come out and prove he's queer. And I was 'round him all the time."

"Did you always notice he was around young boys?" Jim asks.

"Yeah, I did. That didn't look good," concedes Joe. "I heard on the radio—but you have to understand this was a black radio station—that he was running around with dresses on in his neighborhood. But I know three people who lived in the neighborhood and they never saw it."

"But Joe, wouldn't you admit that in terms of being a regular Southern guy, Barrett was the opposite? He didn't come across as one of us."

"No, he didn't," admits Joe. "I talked to his sister." (I reach for my ballpoint again.) "And his sister said the reason he came down here, he wasn't getting no attention in the North. So he came down here where he could get some attention. From the news media and all. That was what Richard liked."

"Joe, you said you knew his sister?" I say, excited.

"I didn't know her," Joe says. "I didn't even know he had a sister till he died. I spoke to her over the phone. I never even met her. She did say that Richard had a girlfriend for ten years. And I didn't know Richard had a girlfriend. That's what looked bad."

I ask Joe how he contacted the sister.

"Well, she really contacted me," Joe says. She did that through the executor of Richard's will. Joe doesn't have this man's name or number at hand, but he might be able to find them.

"Let me get off the phone, because I am at work right now," says Joe.

"Good-bye, Joe," says Jim. "We got to go and eat some catfish here one of these days."

Joe hangs up.

"Promise you won't hang up when I say this," I say to Jim. "But because you didn't get back to my Facebook message, because you didn't reply to that, and because I had come here and I wanted to interview you and I didn't have your phone number, yesterday, I drove to your farm."

"Well, that's no problem," he says. "You see my coonhounds? Did you see the bee yard?"

"I saw the dogs but not the bees. So have you got that costume that you wear so you don't get stung by the bees?"

"I do. You are welcome to come down here. We will go collect eggs and I will show you my birds and you could see my pack of dogs and my bee yard."

"Oh, I'd love that," I say, sealing the playdate.

"I'm ready to get out of here. I am getting hungry. I got to get in my push-ups and sit-ups."

Jim finishes his glass of orange juice.

"This is Jim Giles, and you're listening to *Radio Free Mississippi*."

Jim pulls up Rammstein, and I shut my laptop.

I'm pumped about the sister lead. My favorite bits in the true crime books are when you find out all about the baddies as little kids. And in my months Googling Richard, I'd seen no mention of any family member. I put this note alongside the boy with a bomb. And what I saw at the Spirit of America Day. These pieces form a strange picture. Richard seems both a buffoon and a danger, someone running his own agenda for his own curious, confidential ends.

I look out the window of my room.

I decide that when I do the movie of the book I'll have a scene where there's a mix-up. People spy Jim in the distance on his farm in his bee-keeper suit and think it's a Klan uniform.

The Footage

Something's occurred to me. My footage is probably the last film of Richard alive.

The Voice of Black Mississippi

There is no component of this bed that doesn't squeak. The frame squeaks, the mattress squeaks, and the sheets squeak. To get to the bed that squeaks I must cross the carpet, which squeaks. And to step foot on the carpet that squeaks I must open the door, which squeaks. Like a lyre-bird mimicking its environment, my asthma wheeze, which I swear used to be more of a whistle, has become a squeak. I shuffle to the kitchenette and begin preparing my third bowl of cornflakes for the day.

The silver laptop's talking again, this time with the rasp of an older black man, Earnest McBride on *The Empowerment Hour*.

Earnest is also contributing editor of the *Jackson Advocate*—"The Voice of Black Mississippians since 1938." The paper comes out weekly and has a smaller print run than Jackson's mainstream *Clarion-Ledger*. I'd called Earnest from Melbourne. He said to get in touch when I arrived and he would sort out contacts for me.

"As you know," Earnest rasps, "we at the *Jackson Advocate* were instrumental in getting involved in freeing a young man who had been, for no reason at all, locked away in seclusion, in isolation. Locked away from his family and all incommunicado for five days. And he was being charged as an accessory to the murder of Richard Barrett. But this young man just happened to be the common-law brother-in-law of the main suspect, Vincent McGee."

I swallow two Tylenol, squeeze my head in the kitchenette sink, and wrap my lips around the spout.

"May I add a footnote on the character of Richard Barrett," Earnest continues. "Lot of people—even black people, some of the black leadership—are coming out after his death and saying, 'Oh, Barrett really wasn't a real racist, that was just a public facade.' What they don't understand is that Barrett was sincere—probably one of the sickest psychopathic racists that would have come into this state. He was born in New York, grew up in New Jersey. He had beaten a woman within an inch of her life!"

I jerk my mouth from the spout, ripping my gum, grab for my notepad, and scribble *beat a woman.*

"And that was one of the reasons why he was compelled to leave New Jersey. Richard came here in '66. The political power brokers at the time, they embraced Barrett. They sent Barrett out to every white high school in the state of Mississippi to spread his poison. They gave him entry. They gave him letters of introduction to the high school principals. So Barrett was able to take his message of white supremacy and take it to these children. And these children are grown-ups now, forty, fifty years old. The age of Haley Barbour, today's governor. He probably heard him back then."

I tickle my suddenly numb gum with my tongue and keep scribbling. This Richard doesn't sound like the goofy outsider Jim Giles described.

"This man was sick! And some suggested there was some type of a homosexual overture in his approach to McGee. I kind of doubt it. But that would be a part of the whole schematic, a part of the sickness. They hate people so much, but at the same time they want to despoil them, they want to rape them, they want to bring them down to the basest level they possibly can. I just wanted to make it clear that I have no doubt whatsoever about Richard Barrett being a sincere racist. I interviewed him two or three times. And there was no . . . none of this, *Oh, he's just faking it, in real life, one-on-one, he's a nice guy and all.* No, that's not true."

I spit into the kitchenette sink. My saliva is swirled with red like a peppermint candy. So Jim Giles thinks Richard wasn't a racist but was gay, and Earnest McBride thinks he wasn't gay but was a racist. I wonder which one he was to Vincent McGee.

I call Earnest. He tells me to drive over on Saturday morning. There's a Civil War reenactment happening an hour out of Jackson that he wants to cover. And he has no car and he needs a lift.

Saturday Morning

Last night a Jackson pothole burst my tire, and my mood. A warning shot to my kneecap. *Get out of here, boy.*

This morning, I cruise through a Jackson historic area called the Farish Street Entertainment District. It looks like a million dollars in the moonlight. But in sunlight it's a slum. Shop fronts with the guts knocked out. Facades collapsing. The "Entertainment" refers to things that happened long ago. Duke Ellington and Louis Armstrong played in the now-shut-down Crystal Palace Ballroom. Robert Johnson recorded blues tracks at the no-longer-there Speir Phonograph Company. Trumpet Records, closed. Ace Records, closed. Two small eateries are still here. Above one is the tiny office in which civil rights activist Medgar Evers typed a letter on a sheet of cream paper before driving home to a waiting Klansman. For a state obsessed with its history, they don't seem to look after it too well.

The funeral home is still running. (It's the very one where Medgar Evers found himself that night.) The Alamo Theatre used to host Nat King Cole and now hosts community theater. The black letters running across the front read MIMIC: A STAGE PLAY IN HONOR OF DOMESTIC VIOLENCE SURVIVORS.

I blump over potholes and pull up outside the *Jackson Advocate*, a squat cement box with no apparent windows. As I walk to the red front door, the air tastes like gasoline and stings the little cuts on my fingers.

What Did Kant Say?

Earnest is pacing up and down, his ear to the phone, his free arm flapping. He is tall and aging, maybe in his sixties. His pale blue suit pops against the yellowing front pages that wallpaper the office. As he's talking, I take in some of the headlines: PRISON AUTHORITIES DENY INMATE FACING AMPUTATION IS REALLY SICK; ENVIRONMENTAL RACISM: DEATH FROM EVERY DIRECTION!; FINDING UNCLE TOMS TODAY.

"Two p.m. Central Standard Time today!" Earnest brays into the phone. "Mr. Jefferson is accepting presidency of the Confederacy! Ha-ha!"

What does that mean? While Earnest's mouth is on the call, his fluttering hand carries on a second conversation with me.

Get the car ready, say his fingers, mimicking twisting keys in the ignition.

Staple those sheets on the desk, says his palm, splatting down in thin air.

He waves a phone memo at me: *Malinda Adams, NBC Nightly News.*

"Yes, Malinda!" Earnest chuckles into the phone. "I just wanted to let you know so you won't be left out, behind a curve, when you hear that the Civil War has broken out! Ha-ha! Bye-bye."

"What's happening?" I ask, confused.

Earnest tells me this year is the one hundred and fiftieth anniversary of the Civil War.

"The first year of the five-year war. The good people of the South and the Confederacy are only going to celebrate four years. They're going to celebrate their four years of glory, which were not really glorious at all. But they're going to ignore the fifth year because that's the year that they got their butts kicked, mostly."

"Who's Mr. Jefferson?" I ask.

"Jefferson Davis! He's the president of the Confederacy! Abraham Lincoln's enemy."

White Mississippians are holding a reenactment of Jefferson Davis accepting the presidency on the steps of a courthouse in Vicksburg. Earnest wonders whether today Jefferson Davis will read out *all* of the Mississippi declaration of secession or dodge around the awkward bit that endorses slavery. If he does read it out, Earnest wants to challenge him. If he doesn't read it out, Earnest wants to attack him for whitewashing history.

"They're pretending history," Earnest says, "and so we're going to go over and I'm going to play the role of a faithful reporter in 1861. I'm going to assume the persona of someone who is on the scene, a freeborn black man. I just want to let him know that we have every right to fight and kill anybody who proposes to keep African people in slavery."

"But who's going to play Jefferson Davis today?"

"I don't know. It's reality," Earnest says.

Earnest tucks too many *Jackson Advocate*s under his arm and carries a whole cardboard box of them toward the door as I follow, bewildered.

"You know, John, we might just be dreaming that we are in the twenty-first century, but in reality, we're in the nineteenth century, we're facing this crisis. You know how people fantasize when they have a crisis? They want to get out of it. We're caught up in a crisis!"

"We're in the nineteenth century?" I ask, floundering, as Earnest's white leather shoe pushes open the door.

"What did Kant say? Reality is perception."

Soon, I'm wiggling the car through the historic district.

"Hi, Chokwe!" Earnest shouts into his phone. "I have John, who's come all the way over from Australia looking into the Richard Barrett case. Would you call me back?"

I feel better that Earnest gets the answering machine, too. Chokwe and Precious teamed up to pinch the Vincent McGee case from the white public defender. They (and Earnest) think there is a race aspect to the case that will be ignored if left in white hands. They think the whites will explain the crime as a garden-variety fight over money rather than a white supremacist attacking a black man and the black man having to defend himself. "Hello, Tina!" Earnest shouts as I curl onto the highway to Vicksburg. "I'll put you on. An investigative reporter from Melbourne, Australia!"

Earnest hands me the phone and tells me to speed up. I'm driving too slowly for a highway, he says. "It's Tina McGee. You know, Vincent McGee's mother."

Jesus!

This is crazy: It's too early to be talking with the killer's mother! I don't feel ready for this. *Shut up, John, this is a gift, talk to the mother!* But I don't know what to say. I suction my ear to the phone.

"Hello?" I try.

"Hello," Tina says quietly.

"To the left!" Earnest shouts, thrusting his finger to the left lane. "Over there!"

"Um . . . have you seen Vincent since he's been arrested?" I ask Tina.

"They will not let me see him!" she yells. "They will not let me see him! Eddie Thompson will not let me in!"

"Over there!" Earnest says. "John, you need to pay attention to your driving."

"Who's Eddie Thompson?" I ask Tina.

"He the Rankin County jailer!" she says.

"Left!" shouts Earnest.

There's quadriplegia in my future if I don't get off the phone, so I'm grateful when Tina tells me I can pop by her house anytime. We hang up.

I indicate to change lanes but turn on the wipers instead.

"You said on the radio Richard had beaten up a woman," I say.

Earnest tells me old Mississippi spy agency files were unsealed in the 1990s. He says the story is in there, but he can't remember the exact details. I can't write down *spy agency*, but it's the sort of thing I won't forget.

"Were you born in Mississippi?" I ask Earnest.

"Yes, Vicksburg," he says. "You know about Vicksburg?"

Although it's where I'm driving to, I don't. Earnest tells me if I want to understand Mississippi, if I want to write a book about this place, I need to understand that town.

The Ballad of Earnest McBride

Vicksburg is forty miles from Jackson, right up against the Mississippi River. Earnest's father ran the print shop there. He'd print the local newspaper and jazz club posters, with art deco Negroes and copy like so: *Boots & His Buddies—At the Cotton Club Ballroom. From 9.30 p.m. until the milkman comes.*

Earnest found an old *New York Times* when he was young. It told him the very word *jazz* came from his town. Some drummer called Chas, some mishearing when the crowd would click and say, "Chas, Chas."

In 1955 Earnest read something else in the paper. A black guy visiting from Chicago, Emmett Till, had whistled at a white woman in a Mississippi Delta grocery store. He was found three days later in the Talla-hatchie River, tied to an industrial fan by barbed wire, with a bullet in his head. Emmett Till was fourteen.

Earnest McBride was fourteen.

"That was a major teaching point in our lives," Earnest tells me. "Those of us who were getting out of puberty at the time."

Earnest was supposed to scoop poop from the chicken coops behind the print shop, but he preferred to read. In *Jet* magazine he read about the Klansmen just outside Vicksburg. *Jet* told him the Klan were not just lynching but castrating black men.

"The notion that someone's going to castrate you, or even take your life, if you had sex with a white woman, that really got home to us."

Teenage Earnest was a caddie at the Vicksburg golf club. There had been a break-in at the club, and all the caddies were taken down to the police station. In a mildewing room, a white policeman took Earnest's hand. He rolled his black fingers on a black inkpad, then onto a finger-prints card.

The policeman and Earnest were chatting, all cheery. Then Earnest spotted a bottle on the shelf behind the man. The policeman took the bottle down so Earnest could take a closer look. It was a black finger floating in formaldehyde.

"The way he expressed it," Earnest says, "was it was the finger of a Negro."

"A finger of a *what*?" I say, instinctively looking at my own fingers on the wheel. "A Negro? So he was sort of, like, threatening?"

"He was just sounding friendly. 'Hey, look at this finger of this dead Negro that I have. What do you think about that? Ha-ha!'"

"But he would have gotten it off someone already dead. It's not like he would have gotten it off a live person?"

Earnest seems annoyed I'm not keeping up.

"What I'm saying is that the finger had come from some black man who had been lynched. The policeman was probably from the group that lynched the man and made sure that he got his souvenir."

"Christ," I gasp.

Back then Earnest also worked at a convenience store. The owner was a man named Tom. He had an arm he couldn't use. It had been crushed and was just hanging there. Tom was high up in the White Citizens' Council, a white supremacist group.

"I remember seeing the white woman there, the wife of Tom. She's sitting on the backseat of the car. I was just looking at her and she was looking at me. I'm walking toward her, toward her car."

In a dark homage to Emmett Till's whistle at the white woman at the grocery store, Earnest stopped at her window, spat on the ground, and walked off.

"I quit working for white people in the tenth grade. No more! I'd been exploited and insulted too much."

Young Earnest began reading about the Civil War. And a certain battle began changing the way he thought about being black and being a Mississippian.

The Battle of Milliken's Bend

Milliken's Bend is in Louisiana, opposite Vicksburg, Mississippi. The Mississippi River cuts between the two. In the middle of the Civil War, over a thousand black men guarded supply depots along Milliken's Bend. They were ex-slaves who had pulled on the Union uniform to fight the Confederates who had owned them.

Meanwhile, in Vicksburg, white Union soldiers were shooting and starving the Confederates. So the Confederates in Louisiana planned to capture Milliken's Bend. They could then send supplies and men across the river to break the siege.

One night, thousands of Confederates crept toward Milliken's Bend. There were twice as many Confederates creeping as there were ex-slaves waiting. The ex-slaves were ill equipped and untrained, but those Confederates had them manacled not long before, so there was a certain frisson added to the air.

When the Confederates charged the Union line, the ex-slaves shot their muskets and held them back. The Confederates regrouped and charged again, this time more successfully.

But the ex-slaves didn't surrender.

In 1863, guns took a long time to reload. Even if you were losing, your opponents could only kill so many of you as they closed in. Most battles were won when one side lost its nerve and surrendered or ran away. Something unusual happened at Milliken's Bend.

When the Confederates came close enough, the ex-slaves launched into hand-to-hand combat, slicing with bayonets and bashing with musket butts. The Confederates bludgeoned and bayoneted back. A wreck of men, black and white, piled up on the terrain.

The Civil War street fight ran on for ten hours. Eventually, two

Union gunboats cut up the Mississippi, paused behind the ex-slaves, and fired. The Confederates fled, and the ex-slaves chased after them. One captured his former master. It was over. Milliken's Bend remained in Union hands. So, black soldiers won one of the most important battles in the Civil War, Earnest tells me. The Battle of Milliken's Bend helped win the Siege of Vicksburg, and *that* battle won the entire war! But people just don't know their history. Or they spread lies about it. According to Earnest, over at the museum in Vicksburg, a museum official denies black Union soldiers fought at all! In the Vicksburg National Military Park, another official denies black troops their glory. And Earnest has seen the new park historian dressed in a Confederate uniform, performing a monologue, *real tears* streaming from his eyes as he moans how the South has been treated.

But worse is that there are blacks who don't think the Civil War is their history. Idiots, Earnest tells me, who refuse to see that their ancestors weren't just the slaves but the soldiers who helped free black people and defeat the South.

White Southerners still trying to win the Civil War. Black people thinking of themselves as helpless figurines in someone's (or God's) bigger plan. This, he tells me, is Mississippi.

Vicksburg

Like historic Jackson, Vicksburg is decaying, ivy slithering over crumbling white walls. I roll the car down steep and lumpy roads. Up against the Mississippi River, the abandoned Yazoo and Mississippi Valley Railroad Station is fronted by six white columns mighty enough to front a plantation mansion, but it's a beautiful corpse. One red wooden carriage goes nowhere on the track behind it.

Outside a gas station, a black man is sitting on a red box. He's the only person I've seen since pulling off the highway. Twenty meters after we pass him he rasps phlegm and I can hear it. That's how quiet Vicksburg is.

The casinos ended up winning the Siege of Vicksburg. There are five here, and they are the only things new and shiny. We're one hour early for Jefferson Davis accepting the presidency of the Confederacy. Earnest points me to one of the casinos, a "stationary riverboat" floating in the Mississippi.

"I'm staying in Vicksburg a couple of days so I can catch up with my girlfriend," Earnest says as we burrow into the casino. "You should have dinner with us."

I ask him how long he's been with her.

"Well, I've known her thirty years," he answers, "but only lately been dating her. I've been waiting for her to mature. She's fifty now, but she still thinks I'm too old for her." Earnest is sixty-nine.

His girlfriend used to weld in a factory but lost that job, and now rips beaks and claws from chickens.

"So you've never been married?" I ask.

"No."

"No kids?"

"No. Well, there's only one that could be, but I don't know."

Like Jim Giles, Earnest is an old man who seems a bit lonely.

Electronic bleeps and blips and bings dance through the air. The poker machines try to outsparkle the belt buckles squeezing in the Mississippian bellies.

We stop in front of the Kitty Glitter poker machine. A white kitten is wearing posh earrings.

"Look at the people!" Earnest urges. "Take a census!"

This is the most integrated I've seen Mississippi. Unlike, well, everywhere, there's a jolly mingle of black and white. Fat blacks in cowboy hats yabber with fat whites in cowboy hats.

Earnest isn't impressed. Considering the demographics of Vicksburg, considering these whites are all from out of town, this room *says something* worthy of our attention.

I'm confused about what Earnest is getting at. Not least because I don't know whether he thinks blacks at a casino is a good thing or a bad thing.

"I rallied against this casino for five years in the *Jackson Advocate*," Earnest says. "Then I came in because I was writing a story. And I decided to put five dollars in a machine. And I won eighty. And I was hooked."

Hooked?

"So you gamble a lot?" I ask.

"Oh, yeah."

"How much have you lost?"

"A lot."

"Ten thousand dollars?"

"Oh, more than that."

"More than ten thousand dollars?!" I squeak. Jesus, I chose ten thousand because I thought it was so ridiculously high and he'd be able to chuckle, *No, no, don't be silly, John.* "How much?" I try again. "Fifty thousand dollars?"

"Oh, more than that."

Lord, I said fifty thousand because I thought *that* was ridiculously high. We go higher and higher until we settle on a seventy-five-thousand-dollar loss over thirteen years.

Earnest pulls out his wallet and turns to Kitty Glitter.

The Old Court House

We were an hour early to Vicksburg, but because of Kitty Glitter, we're late to the big event.

A hundred and fifty years ago, the real Jefferson Davis bellowed from the steps of the Old Court House. Fifteen minutes ago, reenactment Jefferson Davis did the same. Now he's slipped off. The whole square is empty. Earnest has missed his chance to confront the president either reading out or failing to read out the awkward slave bit in the Mississippi declaration of secession.

"Why do white people always have to be on time?" Earnest laments.

Inside the courthouse, though, colors swirl. Pink heads are squeezed into top hats and bonnets. Buttons threaten to pop on the army jackets of tubby Confederates. Several hundred folk have turned up dressed for 1861.

Awkward eyes glimpse Earnest, the only black man here.

"John! The stairs!" snaps Earnest. We dart up the wooden staircase.

A hundred or so more folk have flocked to the second story. Behind the deep rows of bonnets and gray felt caps pokes Jefferson Davis's head. Families are lining up to get snapped with the president of the Confederacy.

Earnest is dizzy with giggles.

"This is my friend John," he tells a family. "He's from Melbourne, Australia. He says he wants to see what Jefferson Davis was really like."

This de-awkwards things. It makes more sense to the folks that there's a white Australian in their midst than a black Mississippian.

Jefferson Davis is flanked by four plump Confederates, all lips quivering and eyes nervous as Earnest worms closer to the president. Jefferson sports a black wig and cloak, and a glued-on beard hangs for dear life to his chin.

"Something I want to tell him!" Earnest says to me, smiling like hell.

"What are you going to tell him?"

Earnest spins from me to the president of the Confederacy.

"Mr. Jefferson Davis!" Earnest cries. "I represent the United States Colored Troops! First Mississippi Infantry! And we defeat you at Milliken's Bend!"

The tubby Confederates protecting the president don't know what to do, their sweaty hands fidgeting on their bayoneted rifles. Jefferson Davis, however, remains composed.

"Well, that's okay," says Jefferson Davis.

Earnest tries to blurt out more—*Jefferson Davis owns a plantation! One of his slaves gets him back years later!*—but Jefferson Davis pats Earnest along like Snow White at Disneyland and welcomes the next in line.

Still, that was pretty much a *Race Relations* stunt. I liked how Earnest snatched victory from the jaws of defeat after he'd missed the president's address on the steps. I like to think I would have done the same in similar circumstances.

"John, let's get out of here." Earnest chuckles. "Now don't put no shit out that says Earnest McBride sold out to Jefferson Davis and the Confederacy!"

"No, no, no. I won't," I reply as we escape down the staircase, the crowd closing behind us.

The Elastic Band Retracting

I've been thinking about this. I'm not 100 percent sure what it means. But it feels relevant.

I'm in grade five, so what's that . . . I'm eleven? Mum, Dad, my sister, and I drift through a market or expo. (The Queen Victoria Market?) There are cheap books about pyramids and World War II. There are Michael Jackson cassettes with a white glove glued to each. Shirts have to be fished from up high with a hook on a stick.

And there it is. A sleeveless T-shirt, the entire front of which is a Confederate flag.

The leather-faced man at the stall fishes it down.

Was it just the colors? Did I see it on a toy racing car at a friend's? If you were a Scientology auditor forcing me to suck deep into the innards of my mind, I'd say it was Billy Idol's "Rebel Yell." In fact, there's a photo of me on my knees in the family living room with my hair gelled up, re-creating the *Smash Hits* cover propped up next to me. Billy Idol holds the Confederate flag taut; I'm holding my Confederate T-shirt in tandem.

(There's another photo of me from around that time sucking on a chocolate malt, on holiday in rural Victoria, Australia. Pinned to my denim hat is a tin badge—the Confederate flag. Did that come before or after the T-shirt? I'm also wearing a blue Michael Jackson sweater my mum knitted, causing a fashion/race faux pas.)

Because it's sleeveless and large, I keep wearing the shirt as I grow. It becomes a type of Linus blanket and a conversation point: *Can you believe I've had this since I was eleven?* I can't remember what I thought of the T-shirt when I was obsessed with rap, from the age of fourteen to the end of high school. I don't recall the rappers on my cassettes addressing the flag controversy. Public Enemy, Run-DMC, LL Cool J, they're all New Yorkers. Maybe worrying about the flag was just a Southern thing.

What was I thinking when I wore it to university? University was nonstop dress-ups and dabbling with beats and punks and yippies and anarchists. I briefly pinned a yellow Holocaust star to my jacket, too.

I do recall Malcolm the hippie at the ad agency, my first grown-up job, aged nineteen. (Yes, I'm still wearing the T-shirt eight years later.) I'm a copywriter, writing brochures for car dealers. In the office next to mine is a small-framed vegan who insists there is no connection between his small frame and his veganism. One night we spray-painted *Free East Timor* on the bridge reaching over a freeway. He heard the foreign minister would be driving past in the morning.

We usually riled each other with sarcasm, but when he saw me in the office in the T-shirt he waited till I was alone and approached. He said gently, like I was an innocent *Dukes of Hazzard* fan, "Black people see that like a swastika."

What *was* I thinking? I'm pretty sure it was about dancing with white liberal taboos. There weren't many (or any?) black people around me then. I'm pretty sure I didn't want to upset black people.

And then there was this weird moment. I'm out at a restaurant. Pretty swish, a birthday dinner, for one of the girls at the ad agency. Across the table is one of her friends—a black girl. If the Scientology auditor forced me to cough up more detail, I'd say I *think* her family had come from South Africa. She keeps eyeing my shirt and comes over after cake.

"Love your T-shirt," the black girl says. She's serious. She then brings up the politician considered by many the most racist in Australia. "I mean, I don't agree with everything Pauline Hanson says, but she's right. You can't just have nonstop immigration."

What an unpredictable response to my barely thought-out provocation.

Was Richard Barrett doing a version of the same thing? An outsider, coming down to Mississippi, mucking around with things he didn't fully understand, for some obscure reason of his own? Until he ended up way out of his depth?

Just before leaving for Mississippi, I did a massive cleanout of my study. I found a clipping I'd torn out of an Australian newspaper in 2001: SOUTH'S FLAG RISES AGAIN IN MISSISSIPPI. The article says Mississippians had just voted to keep the Confederate symbol on their state flag, the last US state still hanging on to it. Above the headline is a photo of three people flapping giant state flags. They're standing on the side of the road—in Rankin County.

I feel I've been tied to a piece of elastic my whole life that's finally pulled me to Mississippi.

3.

THE MURDER

The Murder House

Today I'm going to go to the house where Richard Barrett was murdered. There are tingles dancing up my arms as I drive. Is that because I'm worried someone has moved in? Or just the general death vibe of the house?

I stop and fill up at the Texaco Outpost in Pearl even though there's more than enough gas in the tank. It's a chance to calm myself. I catch myself pressing on the pump and releasing it in sync with my deep breaths. A kind of makeshift yoga exercise.

Richard lived in Pearl, but so deep in rural Mississippi, it's "unincorporated Pearl," basically out of town. On a practical level that means when you're knifed and left to burn inside your home, the Rankin County sheriff's department comes to poke at your corpse, not the Pearl police.

Ten minutes from the Texaco, the only store I've passed in unincorporated Pearl, the Stepford Wife tells me to slow down.

I'm dead on the corner of Highway 469 and Richard Barrett's road. The sign on the church on the corner says THE WEATHER NEVER CHANGES IN HELL. The trees don't block the sky in this part of Pearl. Instead, the sky is wide open and golden plains roll out everywhere.

I curve in and slowly, slowly roll down Richard's road. One foot ever so gently presses the brakes, the other ever so gently accelerates. Brake, acceleration, brake, acceleration. I realize I'm tippy-toeing.

Each house sits deep in a golden field, far from the road.

I roll by a white mansion that could be owned by a Colombian drug lord. Then a gap of gold. Next along, a soot-covered mobile home, one God's breath from collapsing. A gap of gold. A cheery little cottage that looks like a gingerbread home. A gap of gold.

A rat hole with dead refrigerators piled in the driveway.

A gap of gold.

Then the Murder House.

The road is too narrow to park on the side.

Mississippi chuckles. *If you want to poke around the Murder House, you're going to have to park in the Murder House driveway!*

My hands roll right. I creep over into the driveway, waiting for someone to appear from somewhere to stop me.

I pull my Flip video camera from my pocket and push the red button. "This is it. This is, um, Richard Barrett's house. Where he was murdered."

The dashboard, like an arsehole, makes a *bing bing bing* as I open the door. It's the loudest sound in the street.

The crummy little house squats deep in the field. "Crummy little" is how the investigators described it in a newspaper article. It's not much larger than the double garage beside it. Redbrick with a red roof, and a white line of gutter. Same with the garage, and the two together look weird, like a couple out in matching tracksuits. The house is not new enough or old enough to mean anything.

Judging by this and Jim Giles's trailer, white supremacy doesn't make you rich. But Richard was a lawyer—doesn't that make you rich?

I teeter toward the house, past police tape lying shriveled in the grass like shed snakeskins. I press the red button on the Flip again.

"Looks like there's still that, um, that red ribbon that the police put out: *Fire Line. Do Not Cross.*"

There's no "next door" on either side of the house. A golden plain to the left, woods to the right.

My nose is touching the Murder House. Iron bars run down the windows, and I push my face between them. A lush old armchair sits alone in a room, framed by clean white walls. Nothing else.

I head to the white front door. I knock.

The armchair doesn't get up and answer.

I glide around the side of the house. The crunch of dead grass is the only sound on offer. Even the wind has shut up. I squeeze my ear against the electricity meter and hear a whirl. Rumors of this house's death have been exaggerated (by me).

A bit spooked that the house is still alive, I skip around the back.

"Broken glass," I whisper to the Flip.

I crunch over the glass to the window whence it came and squeeze my face between the bars.

The lush old armchair sits with its back to me—the house is so small, the armchair can be not far from the front window and not too far from the back window at the same time. I press my face harder to the bars and dart my eyes left. I catch sight of bottles of cleaning agents in a kitchen framed by clean white walls.

I plod on, over glass and grass. Tipped against the rear of the garage are six white tubes. They're the size of me, plus half of me more. I knock my knuckle on one, and metal clangs.

"I don't know what these are," I tell the Flip.

What am I meant to be doing now, anyway? Looking for clues? Clues to what? The murder? What does "finding clues to the murder" even mean? A gun in the water tank? A bloodstain? They've got the killer already! Clues to who Richard was, I guess. And what might have happened here the night he died. Things that won't make it to court. Things that tell me what it might have been like.

I've full-circled the house and now I'm back out front. A twinkle from some tall dead grass out in front of the Murder House catches my eye. I walk over to the twinkle and pull the Flip from my pocket again.

"Holy moly. This is the bed."

A metal skeleton, rusted and blackened, lies stretched and twisted in the tall grass.

Vincent McGee stabbed Richard and then tried to burn everything. Did he drag Richard's bed outside to set him on fire? No—more likely the firemen pulled it out. Why? Was Richard on the bed? I don't know.

I'm in full snoop mode now. Snooping is scary, but fun. I once broke into Disneyland for a TV show, climbing a back fence.

My fingers are now pulling me somewhere else, to the mailbox. They unhook the latch and crawl in. The box is stuffed with drugstore catalogs. And one envelope: a power bill addressed to Vince Thornton. He was Richard's sidekick at the Spirit of America Day. Maybe Vince paid the bills. Maybe Vince owned the house.

That double garage is begging to be snooped in. I wander casually down the driveway. With a quick peek back at the road, I thread my fingers under the roller door and heave.

No luck; it's locked.

There is a crackle of pebbles behind me. Hell! I whip my head around, still squatting. An SUV, king-size and dark green, is slowly creeping past.

The SUV brakes.

It rolls back and turns down Richard's driveway, blocking my car.

I spring up.

The SUV door opens. Out steps a small black woman in a pink tracksuit. Her hair is gray. She stares me down.

"Who are you?" says the woman.

I reverse-psychologically confidently stride toward her.

"I'm a writer." I fumble through my pockets. "My name is John. Here, I'll get you my card."

"Oh," she says. "I thought you might be the Realtor."

"The Realtor?"

"Yes. I want to buy . . . Well, my friend wants to buy this place."

I'm not in trouble (I think). I lower my voice like a funeral director.

"You know what happened here?"

"Oh, yes."

The woman in the pink tracksuit tells me she lives not far from here.

She had seen Richard stroll along the street, picking up trash, but had never spoken to him. She'd had no idea at the time that he was a white supremacist.

"I never seen anybody over here unless it was someone doing maintenance. Either air-conditioning man or something of that nature. But I never seen anybody visit him." She points her chin to the house. "It's a nice-looking house." The sun squeezes through the clouds, and she squints. "Some ladies, we went out to lunch and we were just talking. And one was like, 'I wouldn't want to live in that house!' And I said, 'He's gone! What can he do to you? Not a thing, not a thing.'"

A sunbeam bounces off her silver bangles and nearly takes out my eye.

"If I hadn't just bought a house," she says, "I'd try to get it, you know?"

"How soon after you heard about the murder," I say, "were you kind of going, *Ah, now there's a house on the market?*"

"Well, I was so caught up with what happened, I wasn't thinking in terms of that. I was just so shocked at what had gone on, you know. He was such a reserved person. The one thing I thought—there may be a retribution from Klansmen for killing him. I thought the Klansmen would come and terrorize the neighborhood. That was my thinking, because someone had killed one of them."

"Wow."

"But when that didn't happen, I sort of got to thinking, *There's a nice-looking house.*"

She wishes me luck with my book, climbs in her SUV, and disappears.

I find myself at the tip of the property, where the driveway meets the road. I press the red button on the Flip and hold it out as a periscope.

Up the street, past the woods, the Flip catches a tiny black car in a tiny driveway.

"I think that's, er, Vincent McGee's house," I tell my Flip. "Or Vincent McGee's mother's house, at least. That was only a few places up. Could be that one there. I don't know. To be honest, um, I'm here on my own, so I'm a bit timid. There's no one here to egg me on. I sort of feel like I'm already pushing my luck, for some reason. It's pretty, um . . . it's pretty quiet. Holy moly. Anyway, um, bye."

How the World Works

There's a New York professor called Harold Schechter who writes about true crime books. I've been reading him to figure out what I'm meant to be doing.

True crime stories are morality tales that explain how the world works, he says. That's why people read them. They always reflect the time in which they were written.

True crime stories from Puritan days say the killer fell victim to the devil. That's how their world worked.

Then Freud came along. Suddenly every killer was playing out a fantasy to kill his mother or father. That's how their world worked.

The new trend—reflecting our progressive times—blames the killing on "the system." The killer was a victim of racism or poverty or social isolation by capitalism.

Schechter's point rings true. When I tell my Aussie friends about my case, *everyone* automatically assumes Vincent is a victim of Deep South racism. With little information they're certain he's been locked up unfairly by rednecks. He is even a hero for snuffing out a white supremacist. This is basically *Django Unchained*.

I want this to be the case. I'd *love* this to be the case. After all, I'm the Race Trekkie. But there's already a niggle tickling my brain. That the way this world works is more lumpy and awkward.

The District Attorney's Office

Except for the dead cat in that flower bed over there, the little town of Brandon is impeccably well kept. Neat little shops and dollops of flowers.

This is the administrative center of Rankin County. So from where I'm slumped against a pole across the road, I can see that the district attorney's office and the courthouse sit in the one sandy building. Behind the sandy building stands the county jail. I'm gobbling chicken gizzard nuggets from the gas station.

A puff of smoke floats out of the mouth of the black policewoman sitting in her police car in front of the sandy building. Next to the police car, a Confederate soldier statue juts out his chin. Chiseled beneath him is the Confederate flag and the inscription TRUTH CRUSHED TO EARTH SHALL RISE AGAIN. The telling feature isn't the soldier or his old message, but what's at his feet. Fresh flowers poke out from four black urns. This isn't a dead relic left standing, it's a living shrine to revere the men who nearly everyone agrees fought to keep the slaves. Every black person on his or her way to court must pass this shrine, with yellow flowers freshly arranged by a living white Mississippian.

An officer with a Polish name too long for his badge mans the metal detector at the entrance. Two white women scratch and shake next to him, CONVICT stamped on their shirts. This is part of their reintegration program.

Waiting for the old gold elevator, I kick my shoe into the carpet and type *gizzard* into my smartphone dictionary. Jesus Christ.

District Attorney Michael Guest

Michael Guest eyes me like my presence in his town is a bigger mystery than any case that has crossed his desk. Why has an Australian flown over for this? His pink cheeks and aqua eyes glow. He's Caucasian even for a Caucasian, with the face of a boy-band singer hitting forty.

One fat file labeled *Richard Barrett* squats on his desk. The edges of photographs temptingly poke out. I eye them like I might a custard tart.

I start with my go-to question, because it opens things up and I'm obsessed with people's families.

"Are you and your family long-term Mississippians?"

"We are. We have lived . . . I married a girl, I went to high school here. My parents moved over here to Rankin County when I was elementary age. I was actually born in New Jersey. My dad was in the military and he was stationed up there."

"That's where Richard Barrett grew up," I say. "New Jersey."

"He and I have something in common," responds Michael Guest.

I pull out my Flip camera, and Michael Guest speeds up his rocking in his big leather chair.

"Some of the things . . ." Michael says, wary eyes on the camera. "Because the case hasn't been to trial, there may be some questions I can't answer at this point."

"So, what happened?"

"As far as the crime itself?"

"Yes, as far as the crime itself."

Michael slows down his rocking.

The Crime Itself, in the Words of DA Michael Guest

Mr. Barrett lived in a rural Rankin County community. The defendant, Mr. McGee, lived several houses down. And from what we've been able to put together, the defendant would often do work for Mr. Barrett. Not so much as full-time employment but yard work, things of that nature. And on the day of the crime, Mr. Barrett had picked up Mr. McGee. He had taken him over to another county to do some yard work. Apparently there was another house that Mr. Barrett had over there.

Mr. McGee had basically worked for him all day. And that evening Mr. Barrett had dropped Mr. McGee off at the McGee house and had returned home.

At some point that evening—some time, nine, ten o'clock, somewhere around in there—Vincent McGee walked down to Mr. Barrett's residence. He returned home sometime later. His parents saw him. He was covered in blood.

He left his residence and went to a cousin's house in an adjacent county. The next morning, he returned back to Mr. Barrett's residence. He then set fire to the residence. That is when law enforcement became involved. They received a 911 call about a house fire.

Law enforcement responded there to the house—mainly the fire department, but also local police there to assist, to direct traffic, things of that nature.

When the fire department arrived, the house was not fully engaged, but fires had been set on two ends of the house. So there was a lot of smoke. The fire department entered the residence and attempted to see if anybody was inside. When they did, they found the body of Richard Barrett—there in the kitchen. He was there on the floor. He'd been stabbed—and I want to say approximately thirty times. A large number of times. And he had a belt that was wrapped around one of his hands. Mr. Barrett was removed from the house.

They immediately notified the deputies, who were outside. As soon as the fire was under control, of course, at that time Mr. Barrett's residence was declared a crime scene. Law enforcement noticed that there was a gas can—a plastic gas can—there outside the residence. And based on the origin of the fire being in two different ends of the house, in two bedrooms, they immediately suspected arson, in that whoever killed Mr. Barrett then set the house on fire in an attempt to cover up the murder.

They began speaking with the people in the area, the neighbors. And one of the people who lives there in the community stated that the previous night they had seen Mr. Barrett's truck at the defendant's residence.

So law enforcement went down to the house to try to see what information they could get from Mr. McGee and/or his family. And when they arrived there at the residence they saw the top to a gas can in the carport area. They had an open carport. And they also saw shoes, and on the bottom of the shoes there was soot.

And actually no one was home at the time. So they applied for a search warrant to begin a search of the residence.

At some point, Vincent McGee's mother returned home. They began questioning her. And during the questioning of Vincent's mother she admitted Vincent had come home with blood on his hands and said that he had killed Mr. Barrett the previous night. And so at that time a warrant was issued for Mr. McGee's arrest. The family shared with law enforcement that they believed that he was at a location in an adjacent community in Pearl. Members from the sheriff's department went to that residence, found Mr. McGee at the residence, and placed him under arrest for the murder of Richard Barrett.

Michael's Big Leather Chair

Michael's voice is always even and calm. His face and hands reveal little. But his big leather chair speaks of what's inside the man. His level of unease can be measured by the tempo of his rocks. From total calm (no rocks) to high anxiety (rapid squeak-squeak-squeaks) and all levels of unease in between.

The bed frame in the long grass outside Richard's house drifts into my mind.

"The fires in the bedrooms," I ask, "were they started in the beds?"

"Yes, sir," says Michael Guest. (Minor rocks.)

"And did he try to actually set Richard on fire or just the house?"

"Now let me just look here and see." Michael prizes open the fat file, careful to make sure I can't peekaboo. "I think he did suffer some burns on his body. The autopsy report talks about injuries, multiple stab wounds, blunt force injuries to the head. It also shows approximately 35 percent of the body surface area did contain burns, the singeing of the eyebrows, eyelashes. Soot was deposited in the mouth and the nasal cavities from the fires. But did he directly set fire to Mr. Barrett? I do not know, Mr. Safran."

"So what did Vincent say when you arrested him?"

"After an arrest was made, Mr. McGee agreed to speak with law enforcement. He waived his rights and has admitted the killing. He made several statements, I believe there are actually four, on various days, and in all of the statements he admits to killing Richard Barrett. Some of the details around the killing changed from statement to statement. The first statement that was made was he went down there that night to get on Facebook because Mr. Barrett had a computer. When he was down there at the house, Richard made some sexual advances toward him. Then Mr. McGee just snapped—kind of went crazy."

"What kind of sexual advances?"

The big leather chair speeds up.

"I think Mr. Barrett just basically had gone up to him . . ." Michael stumbles. "Let me see, I'm going to try to get a little information."

He opens the fat Richard file. I perform yoga contortions with my eyeballs, trying to peek in.

"Out of interest, can I photocopy that or is that private?" I say, trying not to sound like a salivating rodent.

"At this point," Michael says, "since the case hasn't gone to trial, we can't release any of the report or anything at this time."

"I understand," says the salivating rodent.

"The interviews are videotaped," says Michael, nose in the fat file, "but the report just says that Barrett began to make sexual advances toward him. He told him to stop. Barrett would not stop, and then they got into a struggle. Mr. McGee pulled a knife out, the first thing he could find, and began stabbing him with it. Almost a temporary insanity type of thing—not really sure what he's doing. The next thing he knows, he's got a knife, which he grabbed off of the kitchen counter, and begins stabbing him to death."

Michael says the fat file holds no more color or detail about the sexual advances.

"As he begins to be interviewed other times," Michael says, "the story begins to morph from being one of sexual advances to being one where he's upset over the amount of money that he was paid. That he gets to the house, he begins confronting Barrett about that, that Barrett refuses to pay him the money. That they then begin to struggle and that he then stabs and kills him."

"So in the second statement, he's taking out the sexual element?"

"That's right. The only time he brings up anything regarding a sexual assault—" Michael stops himself. "A sexual *advance*—I guess it wouldn't be an assault—was during the first statement. Also during the second statement, I believe that he admitted to stealing items from the residence. We learned that Mr. Barrett's wallet is missing. Vincent also in later statements states that, after he kills Mr. Barrett, that he takes not only the wallet but also takes a gun and a knife."

"Do you have an opinion on which version is true? Was he repelling a sexual advance? Or was he out to rob?"

"If we believe that he went down there because he was upset about not being paid and that he was there trying to get his money, that to me more closely fits the facts of the case. Because we know that he did in fact kill him, and he did in fact take his wallet and any money that he had. He did in fact also take items of property from the house, being a gun and knife, things of value that he could later, if he had not been apprehended, resell to get the money back, that he believed he was owed. So to me the facts tend to more closely fit the second and subsequent versions of events that he gave."

This, it must be noted, is the version you need if you want to thread a lethal injection into the arm of Vincent McGee. If Vincent flipped out over a sexual advance and killed Richard, says Michael, the most he can get is life. He'd be eligible for parole at age sixty-five. Even if Vincent flipped out, killed Richard, and then, as an afterthought, decided to steal the wallet, gun, and knife, it's still life with parole at sixty-five. The only way Vincent can be killed by the state is if he killed Richard for the purpose of robbing him—a capital murder charge.

"Why do you think he changed his story?" I ask. "Because an attorney told him to? Or do you think just there was some personal thing, like he is embarrassed that people might look at him . . . that he was involved in some gay thing?"

"I have two theories," says Michael. (His rocking speeds up.) "One is that, like you said, that he didn't want it to be known that this white supremacist is trying to be engaged in some sort of sexual relationship with him, and that he was embarrassed by that. On the other side, did he come up with the first story, the sexual advance story, because Mr. McGee has been through the legal system before? Does he know just enough about the legal system to know that *if I say that it wasn't during a robbery then that's going to lessen the charges*?"

Michael says perhaps Vincent morphed his story to something closer to the truth because he thought his sexual advance version wouldn't hold up. He's rocking pretty quickly now, wanting to ride on from the sexual aspect. I ask him about the other thing that complicates the simple robbery/murder story he wants to tell.

"You dismissed pretty early on that it had anything to do with being a hate crime and the fact that Richard was a white supremacist, Vincent was a black man. Why are you so sure of that?"

"A lot of that is again based on the statements that Mr. McGee has made. He at no time ever has said, you know, 'I killed Richard Barrett because he was a white supremacist and I was aware of his politics and I was aware of who he was and what he did,' and, you know, that that was the motive. You know, they were neighbors, they had lived in the same community together. I mean, Vincent had worked for Barrett before."

Why does Michael assume people who are neighbors can't hate each other? No one hates me more than my Jewish neighbors back in Australia. But more than that, the black boys who were hired to blow up balloons at the Spirit of America Day, they knew what it was. Just because Vincent lived next door to Richard and worked for him doesn't mean he was necessarily oblivious. Living near to and dealing with Richard might have just made Vincent hate him more.

I tell Michael what Earnest told me. That Chokwe Lumumba and Precious Martin have taken over the case precisely because there is a race dimension. A racial dimension they felt the white public defender was dodging.

Michael's lips and eyes go all confused.

"For them to make that an issue, I believe that Vincent McGee would have to testify at trial," Michael says. "He would have to take the stand, and he would have to now give a different version than he's previously given. And so now you are looking at a *third* version."

Michael thinks Vincent springing a third version would color him shifty to the jury.

"Did Vincent out-and-out say he had no idea about Richard's white supremacist history?"

"I don't recall exactly what he said about his history. There is just a handful left of those folks who are still in the white supremacist groups. They don't receive a lot of publicity. They kind of—thank goodness—slowly died out. And so while there were some people that were quite aware of who Richard Barrett was, there was a great deal of people who had no idea."

Michael stops rocking and stops talking like a public official. The cadence of coffee-shop gossip blends into his twang.

"Some would have thought it strange," he says, "that here we have a white supremacist who is living in a mixed neighborhood. You know, it just really didn't fit the bill for what you would consider your hardcore white supremacist. You know, generally those people, they want to have very little dealings with people of another race. And a lot of them, they don't want to live in the same neighborhoods, they don't want to send their kids to the same school. And so while Richard was involved in that movement, there were other aspects of his life that really didn't tend to fit what you would or what I would consider to be a hardcore white supremacist."

Does he mean that Richard wasn't a real white supremacist—that he was an agent, like Jim Giles says? Or is he getting at something else? His rocking's slowed down; perhaps he's not riding away so fast, now that he's done his duty and stated the formal case. Maybe he wants me to do a little digging.

"Do you think," I say, leaning a little closer, "there's any chance that Richard and Vincent were engaged in a longer-term sexual relationship? You know, where Richard paid Vincent?"

"You know, the only person that would know that would be Vincent McGee," says Michael, playing it as straight as he can. "Now, you know, Richard kind of kept to himself. He had moved down to Mississippi from up north many, many years ago, so he has no family here in this area. You know, we weren't able to find anyone who was extremely close to Richard."

"What about in New York or New Jersey? Did you speak to any of Richard's family in any other places?"

"We've not been able to talk to anybody. And no one has come forward and contacted us, as a family member of Richard. We know that he's never married, didn't have any children." If I ask Michael whether that's code for *gay*, I'm worried he'll clam up entirely.

"So what happened to his estate and who took care of his property?"

"I don't know. I believe that he had a will, but I don't know where the estate went upon his death. We always like to let the family members know where the case is at and get their input. And so basically this is an odd case because we don't have close friends, family members, those people that we can consult with in this matter."

So, even the measly few people I've discovered as Richard's connections have gone to ground in the face of the DA's inquiries: Vince Thornton, who introduced Richard at the Spirit of America Day, and whose name was on the bill in Richard's mailbox; Joe McNamee, the man present at my prank who I spoke to on Jim Giles's show; and Richard's sister, whom Joe spoke with but did not meet. Michael Guest has his secret file, and I have mine.

Now Michael pulls out two pages from that fat file and takes me through Vincent McGee's criminal history. Whether or not there's a sexual angle or a race angle to the murder, there's no question Vincent has a bit of a dodgy past.

Five years ago he assaulted a couple of law enforcement officers. For this, he served one year in prison. Not long after he was released he was arrested again for grand larceny. So, both a history of violence and a history of robbery. Vincent was meant to serve five years for the grand larceny.

However.

For whatever reason—Michael doesn't know—Vincent was released early. And within two months of his early release, Vincent was shadowing over Richard Barrett in his kitchen with a knife.

I decide we've become chatty enough for me to ask the big question.

"Even if Vincent did steal from Richard and that was his motive, don't you, as the district attorney, have discretion to *not* seek the death penalty? Why did you go for the death penalty?"

The big leather chair rocks very fast. His face and eyes soften, like the thought of snuffing out a man's life weighs heavily on him.

"You know," Michael says, "what we did is we indicted with the death penalty to keep that option open."

I'm wrong about our chattiness. Michael won't say any more on the matter. The conversation is clearly finished.

"Just one final question. Tina McGee said—that's Vincent's mother—said she's not allowed to visit him in prison. Is that true?"

Michael's eyes and lips squeeze into confusion again.

"The family should have access to him. I would be surprised if the family would not be allowed to see him while he is here in jail."

Halfway down the corridor to the elevator, I can still hear the pacy squeak-squeak-squeak of Michael Guest's big leather chair.

How the World Works, According to Mark

A local lawyer called Mark is waiting for a client outside the entrance of the courthouse. His white hands grip a leather satchel.

"All my family is originally from Mississippi," he tells me. Nevertheless, and not consciously, he refers to Mississippians as *they*, not *we*. He and his parents lived in New York for long stretches, so he's an insider and an outsider.

I tell him I just chatted with Michael Guest and his squeaky chair.

"The district attorney is elected every four years," he tells me. "He doesn't want to lose a case this high-profile. There are a certain number of folks out there who are still ardent segregationists. They were supportive of Richard Barrett. If he allows Mr. McGee to be acquitted at trial, he will lose those people's votes."

Mark thinks Michael Guest will try to pry a guilty plea from Vincent.

"Honestly, I don't think Mr. Guest wants to go to trial. And the reason he doesn't want to go to trial is that there is that very slim, but possible, group of folks that would be on the jury pool that upon hearing of Mr. Barrett's solicitation for sex would be so offended, they'd say, 'He got what he deserved.' There is a possibility that Mr. McGee could be acquitted."

I notice that Mark doesn't think there's a chance that a Rankin County jury would be sympathetic to a black man. He just thinks that there's a chance that they'd hate gay people even more.

Mark knows of both Precious Martin and Chokwe Lumumba.

"Precious tends to be a more even-keeled-type person. Chokwe tends to want to cast everything in racial terms. He has a reputation for viewing every black defendant as innocent and every white victim as guilty of racism and therefore deserving of whatever happened to them. In this particular case he is absolutely correct. Mr. Barrett actually was a racist. Even a blind squirrel finds a nut every once in a while."

Still, while Chokwe's routine kills in black Jackson, it could fizzle here in Rankin County, says Mark.

"What's Vincent's Hail Mary pass," I ask, "that gets him minimal jail or no jail?"

"I think the best that Vincent can hope for is to find other individuals that have had the same experience that he did with Mr. Barrett. That they were propositioned and/or threatened by Mr. Barrett with physical harm if they had not engaged in some sexual relations with him. If he can find somebody to corroborate his version of that story, that is the type of thing that could possibly destroy the prosecution's case."

Richard Barrett was running his fingers down my producer's back within hours. Jim Giles and even the DA think Richard was leading a double life.

I'm thinking there must be someone in Mississippi with a story.

Chokwe at Martin Luther King Day

Except for a French news photographer checking out the legs of high-school girls, everyone at the Martin Luther King Day parade is black. I've been threading through the crowd for an hour—not even one knot of white Mississippi liberals, and nothing like those white kids in dread-locks who would rock up to an Aboriginal march in Australia.

Navy-blue black men toot golden tubas. Army-green black kids rat-a-tat drums.

Marching bands and marching girls and marching bands. Endless. Each regiment has the same shtick: Go along for a bit with tradition, then break it on down with the band going hip-hop and the girls doing booty shakes.

Everyone's pretty joyless considering it's a parade. No winks and secret smiles. Few seem to be into it on its intended level, and Mississippi doesn't do meta, so no one's enjoying it because it's kooky.

I, however, am loving it.

Freemasons! A silver sedan slides past, marked 33° MOST WORSHIPFUL GRAND MASTER. KING HIRAM GRAND LODGE. The silhouette of the Grand Master waves from behind the tinted glass.

Obscure Freemason spin-offs! A black sedan follows, marked GRAND MATRON—ELECTA GRAND CHAPTER. ORDER OF THE EASTERN STAR.

Perched on the head of the old Grand Matron is a fascinator that looks like a large exotic bird about to eat her.

Can it get any better? Yes, it can.

Shriners! A purple tractor creeps by, steered by a man in a blazer with a fez atop his head. The tractor is pulling a purple car marked IRON CAMEL JERUSALEM SHRINE #1. In the car, the Grand Poobah nods his fez-topped head.

I'm impressed, but, standing beside me, Earnest is not. Who are these black idiots appropriating the ancient rites of white secret societies? He's also not sold on the beauty pageant winners rolling past on SUVs. They're not independent competitions, he says. Rich fathers just make up some pageant name and award their daughters the trophies.

Earnest is in a foul mood for another reason, too. He arrived at the *Jackson Advocate* office this morning to find a small team furiously pulling out one page from each of the four thousand copies of this week's paper. An obituary had been printed with a photo of the wrong woman. A living woman, as it happens. Earnest's Vicksburg article, culminating in him sticking it to Jefferson Davis, was printed on the back of the obituary. The long piece covered his passions: It celebrated the black soldiers at Milliken's Bend, attacked present-day black Mississippians for not understanding the past, and had a go at the curator of the Vicksburg museum. Now no one in Jackson will read it.

"The owner is so scared of any legal action," Earnest hisses.

He had smuggled out one copy of the banned *Jackson Advocate*. It was obviously tense enough at the office that when passing it to me he added, "When you come back to the *Advocate*, you can't bring it with you."

A man in a porkpie hat and long winter coat skids through the crowd.

"Chokwe!" shouts Earnest, suddenly perked up. "Chokwe!"

Chokwe connects the *Chokwe!* with Earnest. His body, face, and silver mustache droop.

This has been a recurring theme among black Mississippians. Earnest spots you and you droop. It happened a couple of times in Vicksburg (once with a barman, once with a jazz-activist), and a few times here in

Jackson, once with Earnest's own sister. I think it's because he's got his theme and he sticks to it. I don't mind that, because I've got mine, too.

Chokwe has been dodging my phone calls. He droops further when Earnest tells him I'm *that guy*.

"I'm only *co*-counsel!" Chokwe says. "Precious has not spoken to me!"

Precious and Chokwe work at different law firms. Chokwe says he has only agreed to help on the case with the proviso that Precious handle the bulk of it. He hasn't had time to look into the case himself. He's been focused on the Scott sisters.

I tell Chokwe that Precious isn't returning my calls, either. His eyes say, *So?* It's feeling awkward. So I don't ask why it is—seeing as Vincent's death penalty trial is starting in less than a month—that he and Precious haven't worked out who's doing what. I don't ask what defense they've got worked out, because they clearly don't have any defense worked out, beyond their usual routine.

The vein in Chokwe's temple is purpling deeper the longer he's trapped with us and my nonquestions. As a circuit breaker, he tells me he'll hook me up with a woman from the Vincent McGee Defense Fund.

Chokwe fastens his porkpie hat and slinks away into the crowd.

The Woman Fighting for Vincent McGee

Pollution and sunshine compete in front of Chokwe Lumumba's law firm. A skeleton of a dog hobbles past, following a black woman sweating diabetes. Opposite the law firm, a vast concrete plain is sprinkled with debris. And in the center is what looks like a soldier's watchtower in war-torn Beirut. Then my brain cracks the puzzle. The "watchtower" is actually an elevator shaft. It's the only thing left of whatever was there.

This is where Chokwe comes to work every day.

Inside, Vallena Greer grips her handbag in Chokwe's boardroom.

"Is that sound or pictures, too?" she asks, pointing at my Flip camera.

"Video, just so when I'm transcribing . . ."

She pulls a comb from her handbag and combs her already neat gray hair.

Vallena is the founder of the Vincent McGee Defense Fund.

"Are you and your parents originally from Mississippi?" I ask.

Vallena slowly strokes her hair a few more times and puts the comb away.

"Yes," she says. "Yes, originally from Mississippi."

Jim told me his white story, Earnest told me his black one. Vallena tells me how things get tangled when you're both in Mississippi.

The Ballad of Vallena Greer

I was born in Sunflower County in 1946. My father was half-white. He was whiter than I am, with straight hair. And we got away with stuff that regular black people wouldn't.

I remember once my sister and I were walking in the street, downtown shopping, and there was a group, it was about eight white folks. And usually black folks had to step off the sidewalk and let them pass. We didn't know. So we just walked straight through, and one of them— I think the male in the group—bumped my sister. He wouldn't move. They were facing each other and neither of them would move. So when he bumped her, she elbowed him. And he called her—what did he call her?—"You goddamn whore." And she said, "You po' red dog." This was unheard-of for a black person to say to a white person.

So we went about our business. We were coming back down the street. There was this black man sitting at a booth, he was a shoe shine. He said, "Did one of you girls just hit a white man?" I said, "Yeah, she did." And he said, "Go home, because he just went to a store and bought a knife." And my sister said, "Is that all he got? A knife?" She was a lot like my father.

So we went home. When we got there, there were these police cars there at the house, so we walked in and Dad said, "Don't say a word, go in the house." So we went in the house, and the next thing we knew the police were flying out, because my dad just pointed his finger and stood up to them. So that's how my dad protected us. A full black person could never do that.

When I got married, I was twenty-two years old, and my husband was from Carthage, Mississippi. The Klan was real bad there. I didn't know it, because I never been to that part of the state. This was in probably 1970. And I think they were trying to integrate, they had integrated, but the white folks had not accepted it.

I didn't know anything about *back door*: The whites go to the front door and the blacks go to the back door. Because most of the places Dad took us to were black-only places. So we didn't never experience that. So when I got married and moved to Carthage, there was this little hamburger stand. They had a window in the front and had a window in the back. And in the back was just mud, you know, just nasty. And in the front it was nice and clean.

So, my husband pulled out in the front parking area. I just got out and went to the front window and ordered my food. And so I noticed the lady was slinging the food, and slinging real mad. I thought, *She must have had a hard day, a bad day, or something.*

So, when it was time, she lifted the window, and she pointed. She said, "Your food is ready." She said, "You need to pick it up in the back." So, okay. "Look," I said. "No, I am not getting my shoes dirty, no, ma'am. Why can't I get it here? No, I want my food here."

So she gave it to me out the front window. So I said, "What is your problem?" I didn't know.

My brother-in-law was about thirteen years old and he was with us. So he was so excited. He went back and told his father, "Vallena went to the front window and was served at the front window!" He said, "When I go back, I am going—I am going to the front window!"

So anyway, he went back, he went to the front window and he came back crying. He said, "They threw ice all over me."

My mother was full black. She used to participate in all the civil rights demonstrations. She participated because she told us her mother—my grandmother—was killed by Klans.

My grandmother had a Bible. The Bible had black pictures in it, and the Klans were destroying all the Bibles that had a black picture in it. And my grandmother was hiding the Bible. Before she hid the Bible, she took the Bible to church to show it to the black pastor and she said, "This is the true Bible."

The pastor went back and told the Klans.

Yeah, he was black. But you had what we call Uncle Toms. They want the white man to like him. So, he told the white man that she had the Bible and they came to get it.

Okay, so anyway, the Klans came to the house. Mom, she was very young, said they came to the house on horses. She said she remembered eight horses carrying. Eight horses. She said they heard them coming, the horses galloping in the dust before they got there.

And the children went and told their mother—my grandmother—that they were coming. And my grandmother hid up under the house with the Bible. And my grandmother wouldn't come out and the children wouldn't tell the Klans where she was.

And the Klans started beating them. The Klans had . . . my mom called them "billy jacks." She said they were sticks. And she said the Klans were on the horses and they would run past and hit them with the billy jacks. "So you better tell us where she is or we are gonna kill."

And so she come out, but she didn't have the Bible with her. She hid it under the house. And they start asking her where was the Bible. She wouldn't tell and so they just run by her, run over her, with the horses and hit her, beating her in the head with the billy jacks.

After, she just passed out on the ground.

And the youngest child, I call her Aunt Beatrice. It was twelve children to my grandparents and Aunt Beatrice was the youngest. And I never knew why Aunt Beatrice had a scar across her forehead. It was about the size of my finger, and she was crossed-eyed. And Mom said that Aunt Beatrice ran up and said, "Stop hitting my momma! Stop hitting my momma!" So she ran up and tried to save her mom. And they hit her, they struck her across the head, and knocked her into some barbed wire. They had to untangle the barbed wire off her and then she had the scar across her forehead.

Eventually one of the children, one of the older brothers, went under the house and got the Bible and gave it to them to keep them from beating the mother and them.

And my grandmother, as a matter of fact, she died. She died in 1945, because I was born in 1946 and she died a year before. And she died from injuries to her head.

Vallena and Vincent McGee

"Richard Barrett, he was a Klan," Vallena says sharply. "He was the biggest snake, biggest crook, biggest terrorist that you don't want to see."

It seems to me she's been tied to a piece of elastic her whole life, drawing her to this event, too.

"How did you end up getting involved with the Richard Barrett and Vincent McGee case?"

"I was in Dallas with my job, training with the Chamber of Commerce. And one of the employees from Mississippi, she came to me and said, 'Have you heard the news about the Klan who's been killed in Pearl? I understand that it's a teenager, a young black guy, who killed him.' So, of course, I was concerned. And especially when I found out it was Richard Barrett. So the first thing that came to my mind was, *What did he do to the teenager, the black young male who killed him?* Because that's just unheard-of, a young black male killing the Klan. So I never thought of it as a murder. I looked at it as a killing."

Vallena knew it was going to be a heavy trial and Vincent was going to need funds for a good lawyer. She had her eyes on Chokwe. She had known him a long time and knew his history of helping poor people.

"So I called Chokwe and I said, 'We are going to raise the funds, would you be interested in taking the case?' And he said, 'I will think about it, but see what else you can find out about the case.' So I decided that we would do our own investigation to find out exactly what happened."

Vallena and her friend organized to drop in on the McGees. Vincent's immediate family, and some of his extended family, squeezed in on the couches in the living room.

"So we asked them actually what happened," Vallena tells me. "And I wanted them to be real open, because in the back of my mind I just know the history of Klans murdering and hanging and terrorizing a young black man has to do with the white woman. That's most of the history, I think. So, all the time I am thinking, *It's got to be a white female somewhere involved in this.*"

What Tina Told Vallena Happened the Day of the Killing

Tina McGee and Alfred Lewis, Vincent's stepfather, are relaxing on the benches in their front yard.

A black pickup truck rolls into their driveway. Out slides the white man from three houses up. Tina had seen him now and then, mainly pedaling his bicycle up and down the road. But she doesn't know him, as such.

The old white man says he keeps a property about an hour away, in a town called Learned. He needs some help painting and raking and cutting grass. He had seen her son drifting about the street. Would he like the job?

Tina smiles. Since leaving prison, Vincent has just been loafing around the house with the blinds down, watching television. And that was over a month ago. This is good work. This is a prospect.

"Vincent!" yells Tina McGee.

After a hot day of work in Learned, the black pickup rolls back into the McGee driveway. Vincent slides out and Richard drives back to his own home, three doors down.

One hour later Richard has made his way back to the McGee front yard. Tina is out on the bench.

Richard tells Tina he has a computer. Would her son like to pop on down? He could teach Vincent how to use the computer.

Tina is really liking this Richard Barrett. She's never known his name before, and she's never heard it before. He knows Vincent is fresh out of prison. Yet here he is, putting that to one side, to give the boy a hand in life. You need to know how to use a computer these days to get a job.

Richard leaves. A short while later Vincent wanders down to the crummy little house.

Not too long after that, Vincent comes home and bursts in the door. He's crying and his clothes have been torn. He has blood on him. And he says to his stepfather that he has hurt Richard, and that's what happened, and he says that Richard tried to rape him, and they got in a struggle and he killed him, or—

Vallena interrupts herself.

"No, I don't think he said he killed him," she tells me. "I don't think he knew he was dead. He said he *hurt* him, to the stepfather. And the mother said she never knew anything was happening, she was just sleeping in the other room."

Vallena says she looked around the McGee living room, where, just weeks before, a bloody Vincent had stood.

"They still never told me about the question that I was most concerned about," Vallena tells me. "And that was, *was there a white female somewhere in there?* We talked to them about three hours, me and my friend. And as we were wrapping it up, and about to go, I think it was the sister of the mother, said to Tina, 'You need to tell Vallena.' And I heard it whispered: 'You need to tell her.' So I turned and said, 'Tell me what?' And I said, 'You need to tell me whatever it is you think this is.'

The White Female Somewhere in There

Vincent had been dating a white girl six years earlier, Tina told Vallena. The girl had invited him to a party. Some money went missing. It was Chinese money, or some other foreign money. Not a whole lot, just a few dollars.

And they blamed it on Vincent. They blamed it on Vincent because the girl had cousins and uncles unhappy with her dating a black boy.

The police charged Vincent with grand larceny and he went to jail. And officers who had ties with the white girl's family beat Vincent in his cell. Vincent defended himself, just put up his arms to block their blows. For this he was charged with assault on a law enforcement officer.

For the theft, coupled with the assault, Vincent was sentenced to five years' jail.

"I said, 'I knew it had to be a white girl somewhere,'" Vallena tells me, "'because they just do that.'"

Vallena left the McGees' house for her car. Soon her friend came from the house, pulling Tina's sister behind her.

"And the sister said, 'I don't know if you needed to know this or not, but Vincent's first cousin is married to a white lady.' And she said that two weeks ago, before the incident with Richard Barrett, that the Klans went to their house and cut three dogs' heads off, okay, and threw them upon the porch and spray-painted *KKK* on the house."

I squint my eyes and my temples hurt. I run back in my head what she just said. I'm finding it hard to take it all in in one go.

"So after that I pretty much had what I was looking for," Vallena tells me. "A motive. A motive for Richard to do bodily harm to the defendant. Because that's the history of the Klans. That's what they do. They burn crosses in the yard to try to scare you off. And if that doesn't work, the next thing you know you end up hanging in a tree and you committed suicide. But if you look at the background, the young black male that committed suicide had some kind of run-in with the white female, and it never fails. So that was the information that I needed to get back to Chokwe. It was just like Emmett Till."

The murder of Emmett Till isn't scorched in Earnest's psyche alone.

"So," I say, "you think it's possible that Richard, through his Klan connections, knew Vincent's cousin was married to a white woman, and they knew that Vincent himself had dated a white girl? And that's why he attacked Vincent?"

"Yes."

"Do you think Richard just physically attacked Vincent, or also sexually attacked him—tried to rape him?"

"That, I don't know. It might be rape, because they always try to take the manhood of the black man. They either cut his penis off or they try to turn him into a girl."

"Lots of people are saying, though, that Richard might have been a repressed gay person and that's why—"

"I don't think so," Vallena interrupts. "I don't think he was gay, because if I'm not mistaken, I think the Klans have some kind of issue with gay people."

"But, you know, people can be secret about it. But in this case . . ."

"I don't think so."

"So this was like a war, when you try to sexually humiliate your enemy?"

"That's what I am thinking. Like I said before, when I heard about it in Dallas, the first thing I thought about: *Did he have a white girlfriend?* And most of the time, if you find out they were humiliated by a Klan, there is a white female in the background somewhere."

On the way home I try to work out the questions the trial's got to pick through. Did Richard attack Vincent, or did Vincent attack Richard? Was Richard killed because of something Richard did, or something Vincent did? Did Richard make a pass at Vincent, and if he did, was it because he was attracted to him or wanted to humiliate him? Or is the sex angle really about a white girl, not a white man?

Everyone seems to think it was about more than just a robbery, except the prosecution, who want to keep the death penalty on the table. For Michael Guest, race is a third version of events, after the sexual advance and the robbery. But for everyone else, it's the first.

Precious, the Otter

I'd read in Melbourne that Vincent's lawyer was named Precious Martin. *Precious must be a woman,* I thought, because in the film *Precious* she was a she. But a niggle tickled my brain: *Precious may be a man's name, too.* The first three pictures on Google Images were of a man named Precious, a woman named Precious, and an otter named Precious.

So, since then, Precious Martin has been an otter in my head. Striding around its law firm in a waistcoat with a fob watch tucked in its pocket. He's remained an otter even after I found out he was a he.

But Precious won't return my thrice-weekly phone calls, even though I've got footage to offer and am a potential witness to Richard's behavior. He sees the phone memo *John Safran called,* screws up the memo in his little paws, adjusts the spectacles on his snout, and continues on to the tearoom. For a while I thought it was because I was white, but Earnest has tried a couple more times, too, and can't get anywhere.

Who cares, Precious? Chokwe's right, you don't need to talk to me. Avoid me all you want. I'll be waiting for you, to see whether you've done your homework. I'll see you in court.

In the meantime, like Vallena, I'm conducting my own investigation. I've heard enough secondhand stories to be ready for something firsthand.

The House of McGee

I knuckle the front door of the redbrick home, three doors up from the Murder House.

The heavens have thrown a fierce sun across the land this morning.

I knock again.

A 1980s boxy van, a Vandura 2600 Starcraft, is embarrassing itself on the front lawn.

I knock again.

I've told Tina I'm coming.

"Hello?" I say. "It's John."

"Who's that?" says the house.

"John Safran."

"What?"

The voice is not from behind the door. I peek right. A black hand, then arm, is forcing itself through a taut red curtain, as if the curtain is giving birth to the limb. The hand is clenching a can of Budweiser.

"Side door!" says the hand.

I go around the side and through the door there. Inside, my pupils dilate furiously, desperate for light. Black people are moving through a near-black room.

Thick material blocks every window. The only light source is a small TV, beaming blue.

My eyes slowly adjust. The arm of a green velvet armchair glows through the dark, then the whole chair. Then the people. A boy in a white singlet and shorts leaves up a hallway. I'm left with Sherrie McGee, Vincent's sister. One hand is clenching a Budweiser, the other is clenching a Bible.

"Mama!" screams Sherrie McGee.

She scuttles up the hallway, leaving the Bible open on a coffee table. I poke my nose close.

"And they journeyed, and the terror of God was upon the cities that were all around them."

Tina McGee

Tina McGee, mother of Vincent and Sherrie, sits down in the green velvet armchair.

I jot down *Tina McGee*, my handwriting tangled like wire, the best penmanship I can offer in the dark. By the way, why are we in the dark?

Jersey Shore smolders in the corner, casting a little blue on Tina McGee. She offers me frightened eyes.

"Is it okay if I tape this?"

"Yes, sir," she says softly.

"It's not for broadcast, just so I can transcribe it later."

"Yes, sir."

You never really get used to a black person calling you *sir*, I think to myself.

"So, I guess my first question is, what happened with the crime? What actually happened? Between Vincent and Richard?"

"My son was incarcerated, and he got out and Richard was riding his bicycle up and down the road and he seen my son out in the yard and he stopped right here." Tina points through the wall to the front yard. "And Richard asked him did he want to work for him and my son say yeah, and he went to work for him."

"So, just a pedal bicycle?" Vallena had said a truck, and I wonder whether the difference makes any difference.

"Yes, sir," she says. Maybe the truck came later. "And he had brought him home afterward. And that night he come pick him back up and took him down there to his home to get on his computer. And Vincent had told me that he made sexual advances toward him. And pulled a knife on him and stuff like that."

"So did Richard pull a knife on him or did he pull a knife on Richard?"

"Richard pulled the one on him."

"Wow."

Richard in his crummy little house menacing Vincent with a knife. That scene didn't appear in the district attorney's version. Or in Vallena Greer's. I stop worrying about small differences in the stories now that there's a big one. The Richard I met boasted unconvincingly about "stomping" an anarchist and looked down the wrong end of a gun—can I imagine him actually pulling a knife on anyone? But Richard had been in Vietnam, and Earnest said he'd beaten up a woman, so perhaps I can.

"So after that," Tina says, "I don't really know. But that's what my son told me, that he pulled it on him. So what happened in the house I really don't know, but he had to defend himself."

"Were you here when Vincent came back?"

"He came in crying, and said that a man was trying to—like I told you—molest him, and he pulled a knife on him. And I don't know what happened down in that house because I wasn't there."

"Did he have any blood on him?"

"I didn't see any blood."

"Did he tell you the nature of the sexual advances?"

"No, sir."

"Had he been working for Richard a long time?"

"No, sir. He worked with him one other time when he was younger, as I recall. Something like five years ago."

Five years ago Vincent was sixteen, seventeen. There is a three-year jail stint between the two times he worked for Richard.

The door at the end of the hall opens and shuts, exploding light into the room like a camera flash. Tina's face lights up, and I'm startled by how young she looks.

"Have you gone to see him since he's been in jail?" I ask Tina, who has quickly returned to being a shadow.

"They haven't let me see him. He been writing letters; they will not let his letters come through."

"Really? Because when I talked to the district attorney he said you would be able to see him if you wanted to."

"No, sir," she says, warming up to anger. "I called—what's his name?—Eddie Thompson. I think he's the captain. And he said I had to get a special visit. And he said he would give me one sometime this month. He said he had a lot he was doing right now, but I have called trying to get a visit and they would not let me have one."

"So, Alfred Lewis—"

"That's me," says the darkness.

Lord! How long has he been there? I twist to the voice of Alfred, Vincent's stepfather. My eyes focus to a silhouette of a slouched man on a couch.

"Hello? Hello," I say. "You were here when Vincent came in on the night?"

"I was lying on the floor, watching the Cavaliers. Yeah, the Cavaliers and the Mavericks was playing."

"So what did you tell Vincent?"

"No!" he snaps. "The *Spurs* and the Mavericks was playing for the play-off."

"Okay. What did Vincent say? Was he crying?"

"Yeah, he were crying a bit. And holding his stomach like that."

I can't see the "like that" in the darkness.

I know Alfred led the investigators to Vincent's hideout. I realize this topic—betrayal—could be a raw nerve.

"Because you knew Vincent was in trouble, were you scared to tell the police where he was? Or were you, like, *We've got to tell the truth*?"

"They asked me. I told them where Vincent was. They needed direction where he was, you know?"

Obviously not a raw nerve. It occurs to me that Vincent's cousin's still in jail as an accessory, but Alfred, who drove Vincent away, is not.

"Were you close with Vincent?"

"We were close," Alfred says. "Real nice. In the room, lifting weights in the morning time. We'd mostly stay in the house watching TV."

"Did Vincent look at you as a father?"

"Yeah, he had good respect."

"What about Vincent's real father, who was he?"

"JD," says Tina, a little reluctant about where this is all going.

Tina tells me she was on and off with JD for eight or nine years, but he left when she was pregnant with Vincent, her only child by him.

Up the hallway, the door opens again, shooting a blade of milky light into the room. I make out a wooden cabinet, with just one china teapot, behind Tina. The door shuts and the cabinet disappears.

"He was in jail twice before," I say. "Why was Vincent in jail twice before?"

"People told stories on him, say he did something he didn't do. I didn't have money to get a lawyer, and they just really railroaded him for something that he didn't do, that they didn't prove, they just gave him time for it."

"The first time would be something to do with the police, like threatening the police?"

"No, sir. Two police had jumped on him and they said he jumped on the two police."

"Sure, and the second time had something to do with stealing some property or whatever?"

"Mexican money," she says. "He was going with a girl and he had spent the night with her. She was a white girl, and the mother had some Mexican money that was stolen. And they say he did it, but he was not the only one in the house, and they did not get any Mexican money off of him."

"Vallena said that for that particular crime, they wanted to get him because they were very angry because he was going out with a white girl."

"Yes, sir. I think her uncle or her brother was in the police force, and they was mad because he was dating a white girl. And I reckon that's why they laid that on him, the Mexican money. He wasn't going to Mexico. What would he need with Mexican money?"

"What was her name, the girlfriend?"

"Daisy."

"Daisy. And what's her surname?"

"I don't know."

"Was Daisy his first girlfriend?"

"I doubt it."

"You doubt it." I realize I'm beginning to sound like a lawyer, and Tina is the reluctant witness. "And was that his only white girlfriend?"

"I can't really say."

Tina's eyes drift over to *Jersey Shore*.

"It's said Vincent said to the police he didn't know Richard was a famous white supremacist."

"No one did."

"So you'd never heard of it?"

"No, sir."

"How long had you been living next to him?"

"I don't know when he moved down there, but I been here eight years."

No wonder Jim Giles believes Richard was a police agent. He was either the world's most tolerant white separatist, or he had something else going on.

Once again the door at the end of the hall opens and shuts, nuking the room with light, then snapping it back to black.

I feel footsteps vibrating the floorboards. The steps are coming down the hall. The steps are getting closer. The virgin-white singlet and shorts float back into the room like a ghost and fall into the couch next to Alfred. It's Justin McGee, Vincent's younger brother.

"Another thing people said about Vincent," I say, meaning that I read this on an Internet message board, "was the tattoos on his face showed he was in a gang called the Vice Lords."

"He wasn't in no gang, no, sir, no," Tina says. "Not in no gang. He never did no gang stuff. He weren't in no gang." Tina touches the bone under her eye. "He had teardrops for his brother that passed when he was, like, a month old, and a butterfly on his face. I don't see that's no gang thing."

"His brother died?" I ask.

"Yeah, that's why he got the teardrops he had on his face."

"How did his brother die?"

"Crib death."

"A crib death? So that's, like, a gang thing?"

"No, that's a baby death. Crib death."

My face heats up. I realize I processed *crib* as *Crips*, the black street gang. *Nice one, Safran, you dickhead.*

"My child was not in no gang." It seems very important to her that I understand this.

I peek at my notepad for more questions, but I can't see my notepad. I guess I could ask why we're sitting in the dark.

"What do you know of Vincent's lawyers?" I improvise. "Precious and Chokwe. Have you spoken to them?"

"Yes, sir. Chokwe, he want to get a continuance on the trial because he said he already got something on when the trial is s'posed to start."

"Have either Chokwe or Precious said what they are going to argue in court?"

"No, sir, I haven't heard anything about that."

"Because Chokwe and also Vallena, they are saying there is, like, a racial component to this. Do you think Richard took the knife to Vincent because he didn't like black people?"

"Yes, sir."

"Is it just that Richard was very messed up in the head, so even though he didn't like black people, and he wanted to hurt Vincent, he was also sexually attracted to him?"

"Yeah."

I think this might be called leading the witness. I change direction.

"Is it scary knowing that one of the possible consequences is he gets the death penalty?"

"Yes, sir," she says flatly.

"Did you know that because Vincent changed his story it made it more damaging for him?"

"No, sir, I didn't know that."

I tell her what I was told. When it was a sex attack it was murder, and jail at most. When Vincent changed it to a fight over money, it became capital murder and the death penalty. I ask her why she thinks Vincent changed his story.

"Scared, that's all I can say."

"He was scared?"

"That's all I can say."

Because that really is all Tina says, I end up leading again. "You mean the police tried to make him change his story?"

"Yes, sir."

For the first time, Justin McGee, in his virgin-white singlet and shorts, butts in.

"He didn't want people to think he was gay. That's what I think."

"Sure," I say. "Because even if he was involuntarily attacked, maybe people in the community would think he was gay?"

"'Cause they had it all on the Internet," Justin says. "They thought it was a relationship that went bad or something."

"Do you think that it could have been that, Justin?"

"That's what I think."

"You think it was a relationship that went bad?" I blurt excitedly.

"Nuh-uh!" says Tina.

"No," Justin corrects me, "I think that's probably why he *changed his story.*"

"Okay, sorry," I say. Christ. Do I really want that badly to add gangs or sex to race? Still, to clarify: "Do you think there's any chance he was in some relationship with Richard? You know, Richard paid him for sexual favors or anything like that?"

"No, sir!" says Tina. Passion courses through Tina's voice on this particular topic, like nothing else we've discussed—not the prison visits, not the gangs, not even the death penalty.

Justin smirks.

"Fair enough," I say. "And also—because of the violence of that crime—he wasn't violent when he was growing up, or anything like that?"

Tina shakes a no.

"So were you quite surprised when you heard that he stabbed someone? He stabbed him, like, thirty times."

Shock bolts through her face.

"Thirty times?" she says.

"I've heard between sixteen and thirty times," I say.

Tina can't hose down her shock. She seems to have forgotten I asked a question. I feel bad about having said it so bluntly. But I'm puzzled. Haven't the police spoken with her? Hasn't she read any reports about the murder her son's accused of? Hasn't anyone told her what happened? The best thing I can do is move on.

"I'm trying to get a picture in my head of who he is," I say. Vincent never replied to my Facebook message, but I want to get a sense of him for the murder in my mind. "I've never met him. When did he leave school?"

"He left school," Tina says, "he got the tenth grade."

"When he was young, did he have interests? Like, was he into sports or music, or anything like that, or guns?"

"Basketball and stuff like that . . . sports."

"Did he follow a particular team or did he like any particular player?"

Tina shrugs.

"And what about, like, movies? Did he like a particular sort of movies or particular actors?"

"He liked regular movies."

"And what about music?"

"He liked regular music."

"Did he spend lots of time in other places, like a bit of an explorer, an adventurer, so even when he was young, he would kind of go off and just do his own thing for days?"

"He was a homebody."

"So what did he do at home all that time?"

"Watch TV."

"What were his favorite TV shows?"

"Regular TV."

Tina's shut me out, maybe still dealing with the stabs. I ask a couple more aimless questions, and then realize I'm done. Who can complain about a mother wanting to think the best of her son? I crack my neck and thank Tina and the silhouettes of Alfred and Justin.

Tina says I can come back and ask more questions anytime I want. Despite everything, I think she even means it.

The Clobbering Sun

The sun clobbers me on the short walk from the side door of the house to the car. It's pushed its heat into the concrete, too, so I'm hit from above and below, through my soles.

I burn my palm on the car door, opening up and sliding in.

I realize sitting in a dark room with this sun sealed off is probably the most sensible thing to do on a day like today.

I'm kind of irked that Tina came more to life defending her son against the charge of homosexuality than anything else that came up. My entry point to understanding this murder has been race, Race, RACE!

But is this really a homophobic crime? Bad news for the Race Trekkie if it is.

If Vincent killed a white supremacist, fighting racism, he can be the hero in that story. If Vincent killed a gay man for hitting on him, that doesn't work anymore. I wanted the narrative to be me and the brave McGee family against "the system." I wanted to be hanging with the black activist lawyers, but they've cut me off. Worse, I got on smashingly with Jim, the white supremacist.

This story isn't working out like it should.

4.

WHAT WAS RICHARD BARRETT THINKING?

#1 WAS RICHARD A RACIST?

Hey Joe

I pluck a scrap of paper from my wallet. Smudged across it is the phone number of Joe McNamee—the friend of Richard's who I offended with my antics at the Spirit of America Day and who Jim conferenced in during our radio interview.

If I want to know whether Mississippi's most famous white supremacist was a real white supremacist, or an FBI agent, or gay, or Klan, or violent, or just unlucky, I need to talk to his family and friends. Joe McNamee would be both rolled into one: an old friend who has spoken with Richard's sister.

My brain has been scratching around for days, trying to figure out a hustle. How can I get Joe to talk?

I punch in his number.

"Murble murble murble," twangs a Southern man through the phone static.

"Hello? Joe?" I say. "It's John Safran. We spoke on the phone the other morning!"

"I don't need to speak to you," he coldly twangs.

"The reason I want to talk is because I'm writing about Richard Barrett and people have only been saying bad things about him and I need someone to say something good," says the salivating rodent. The reverse psychology hustle was my best bet.

"I don't need to talk to you," Joe says, and hangs up.

The knot in my neck tightens. Damn. Damn, damn, damn. Richard's sister is the closest I can get to Richard. And Joe is the only way to her.

More Than One Way to Skin a KKKat

A big gray cube throws a big gray shadow over the colorful cars parked alongside it. This is the William F. Winter Archives and History Building in downtown Jackson.

Military records from the Civil War are bound in crimson. Newsletters from the Daughters of the American Revolution are bound in blue. Microfiche film is spooled up in cold white drawers.

The old man behind the pick-up desk flicks a speck of white lint from his tie. He pushes two fat manila folders across to me. He widens his eyes and pokes out his lower lip when he reads the label on the folder: RICHARD BARRETT.

"You know him?" he says quietly.

"No, no," I say.

I feel he's hankering for gossip.

"Did you?" I say.

He darts his eyes around.

"He used to come in here all the time," he says.

"Oh, really?"

I feel his gossip is like a kitten. Best to let it come to you in its own good time rather than leaping at it and scaring it away.

"Him and a fat man," he says. "I'm talking about the 1970s. He'd go obsessively through the press with pictures of young athletes. The school newspapers and such."

"No way," I squeak in my softest library voice.

"Young male athletes," he says.

"No way."

"He was polite on the surface, but he was abnormal."

"Abnormal?"

"He would look through all these pictures. And he and the fat redneck would say, 'He should get a scholarship. Let's give him a scholarship.' But it was a scholarship with strings attached."

"What do you mean, strings attached?"

"You'd have to be with his way of thinking."

"What do you mean, he'd look obsessively at these pictures?"

"He was just strange."

The kitten has run away, and the more I ask, the vaguer he gets. Still—I'm excited by this sighting of an unguarded Richard.

I schlep the two fat folders to the photocopy machine.

There's Richard's FBI file, released under the Freedom of Information Act after his death, with some names blackened out. An old-fashioned typewriter bashed out the early pages—they go back to Richard's arrival in Mississippi. The FBI was hardly liberal. They would infiltrate black groups, but white supremacist groups were also seen as antigovernment and spied on.

There's Richard's local law enforcement file. In the 1960s the men in uniform weren't necessarily anti-Klan. In fact, the men in uniform sometimes flung their police caps off at night and pulled on white hoods. Still, they kept an eye on Richard.

There's Richard's Sovereignty Commission file. The commission was a Mississippi spy agency petulantly set up in the 1950s. The United States Supreme Court had just ruled segregation illegal. Mississippi's most powerful politicians told the people of their state to ignore the ruling. In this moment, they pulled together the Sovereignty Commission to keep tabs on black civil rights agitators. When an odd New Yorker drifted into town, they expanded their objectives. They'd kept tabs on black civil rights agitators and Richard Barrett.

I feed ten dollar bills into the photocopy machine.

The Photocopies

My motel room looks more crack den than motel room. Three plastic bags blurt garbage in the kitchenette, and the rest of the floor is covered by the spy agencies' files, arranged in little stacks, squeezed between tangled shirts and underpants.

I flip through the first impressions of the New Yorker who drifted into Mississippi in 1966.

> **Federal Bureau of Investigation**
> **United States Department of Justice**
> **Jackson, Mississippi**
> **June 1, 1967**
> **RICHARD ANTHONY BARRETT**
> **RACIAL MATTERS—KLAN**
> A confidential source advised on October 27, 1966, that Richard Barrett, a white male, age 23, in the past few months, went to Natchez, Mississippi, and contacted ███████. The purpose of the contact was for Barrett to ascertain if ██████ knew the names of a couple of men in each county in Mississippi whom Barrett could contact in an effort to have them join some type of hate-group he was trying to form. ███████ told Barrett he could not assist him in his request.
> Assistant Chief of the Mississippi Police Department advised he had received information that Barrett had two large flags hanging in his room which he claimed were given him by Governor George Wallace of Alabama. Barrett has received mail from "Voice

of the People," address unknown, condemning Negro servicemen in Viet Nam.

An article in the *Natchez Democrat* newspaper indicates that Richard Barrett recently returned from Viet Nam where he was wounded twice in action and received the Purple Heart twice.

Barrett was interviewed by Special Agents of the FBI, at which time he advised he is a "racist" and gives talks frequently concerning segregation and talks concerning Viet Nam. He says he believes in segregation and feels that segregation should some day be the law of the land, and it is his objective to organize an organization with this objective in mind.

Barrett continued that he is not a member of the Ku Klux Klan or any other organization and would not identify any of his associates nor state whether he was or was not acquainted with any members of the Ku Klux Klan. Barrett refused to discuss in detail any of his activities insomuch as he felt the FBI was becoming a national police agency similar to the Gestapo.

Because I'm a Moron

Because I'm a moron, something that should have sprung into my mind a while ago has just sprung into my mind now.

The FBI are not the only ones who saw Richard in full swing.

There is also me. And I have the footage.

The *Race Relations* story showed my first night in Mississippi (the Nationalist Movement headquarters) and my second night (the prank at the banquet). There was a whole day in between. On this day the film crew and I had to pretend we were shooting a serious documentary, to build Richard's trust, so he'd allow me to speak at the podium at the Spirit of America Day banquet. All this footage was immediately dumped on the cutting room floor. I've never watched it back.

I grab my laptop from the kitchenette counter. I serve myself cornflakes in a teacup, the only remaining clean dish.

I click on a file of this lost footage. Tiny John Safran pops up on the
screen. Tiny John is rambling through a park.

The *Race Relations* Cutting Room Floor Footage

In the background, a lone council worker with a leaf blower strapped
to his back drifts through a park in downtown Jackson. In the fore-
ground, I'm squinting at the camera, and wind is huffing into my lapel
microphone.

"It's not the giant skinhead rally I was expecting," I hiss to the camera.

This morning, in this park, Richard Barrett will be declaring open
the Spirit of America Day. There will be a day of activity culminating in
the evening banquet, where I hope to zing Richard with my African
DNA speech. For my prank to work to optimum effect, I need a big and
dangerous crowd here. Preferably skinheads. Richard does pitch himself
as the father of the American skinhead movement.

Cameraman Germain spots Richard's black pickup truck parked on
the street. Richard is pulling a cardboard box from the trunk. I nick on
down to help.

Richard lugs the box and I schlep the flagpole, thrown over my
shoulder like a cartoon hobo. The Mississippi state flag is three thick
stripes and one awkward corner where the Confederate symbol sits. I
cheekily unfurl the flag as I walk, so Germain can capture the Confederate bit. So things look a bit dangerous. A swastika would be better, but
this is what I have to work with.

"What kind of people will be coming?" I ask. "Young people? Old
people?"

"All sorts!" Richard says. "Vince should be down there."

"Lynch?" I ask.

"No, Vince."

That's how much I want a race war for my TV show. I'm hearing *lynch* for *Vince*.

Vince is Vince Thornton, his Nationalist Movement second-in-command.

"I was on the Negro radio station this morning," Richard says, plodding and squinting, "talking about the Spirit of America Day. He actually ended up agreeing with me."

Negro almost makes up for the lack of swastikas.

"I said, 'I'm coming down to the park with a Japanese camera. But I'd like to have one made in America.' The Negro said, 'I agree with that.' He said, 'That's what Obama wants to do.' I said, 'Well, I called for it first, so Obama's stealing it from me!' And he laughed. And I said, 'Also we'd like to have Americanism, where America means something. Pride.' And he agreed."

"You're sounding all about togetherness. You're sounding very anti-racist."

"That's your words. Ours is about nationality. One nation. Pauline Hanson–style."

The KKK Grand Dragon in *John Safran vs God* also name-dropped Pauline Hanson, telling me how great she was. It's weird how in Australia she became a *Dancing with the Stars* contestant, pitched to the audience as the lovable eccentric, while being racially inflammatory enough to be revered by US white supremacists.

We reach the park's amphitheater. Cement arches around a small wooden stage.

"And then, on the Negro radio station, he said the Black Caucus is not happy with the Spirit of America Day. I said, 'When they have a Black Caucus meeting, they have Patti LaBelle. If I insisted on them putting on Loretta Lynn, they'd say no!'"

"So," I clarify, "if they can have a blacks-only event with black singers, why can't you have a whites-only event?"

"Well," he says, "we prefer to say red, white, and blue."

Tiny John Safran in the park looks annoyed at Richard's response.

Giant John in the motel room hits pause on his computer. He's annoyed, too. He's sure he's heard this routine of Richard's some other time. Giant John takes another sip of cornflakes tea and spools through the footage. There it is. The scene of the prank. The ballroom. Richard is setting things up for the Spirit of America Day. Tiny John is about to lure Richard into blowing up a balloon for a saliva sample.

"We're honoring our country and our young people," Richard tells me when I ask what the point of all this is.

"Is it *all* athletes?" I ask.

"Mm-hmm," he says.

"But," I say, "I thought it was just white athletes?"

"Well, we say red, white, and blue."

"So you're bringing people together?"

"No," Richard says definitively.

One more Nationalist, with tarantulas for eyebrows, stands nearby.

"Hello," I say to the man. "I'm John Safran."

"Well, hello," he twangs. "I'm Joe McNamee."

Giant John in the motel room nearly spits out a mouth of cornflakes tea. *That's the guy.*

"I hear some people have been complaining about this event," Tiny John says.

"They are. 'Cause it's all-white. That's what we're about," Joe says, as pleasantly as giving me directions to the post office.

And it makes me realize that Richard makes my skin crawl not so much because he's a white supremacist, but because he's a lawyer.

He gets no Purple Hearts for bravery in what he says. He knows just what to say to plant ticking bombs while covering his own arse.

The Mississippi Department of Public Safety
State of Mississippi
April 24, 1967
SUBJECT: RICHARD BARRETT

On the night of April 14, 1967, Richard Barrett addressed a group of approximately 35 people in Pearl, Mississippi. He was accompanied by a hillbilly band and four white males who apparently were acting as bodyguards.

A week later, Barrett addressed a group of 61 people at the private school. A KKK member apparently sponsored this meeting. This meeting was attended by two Investigators. These Investigators were followed and kept under observation by three unknown white males during the entire meeting.

A collection was taken which apparently netted approximately $50.00.

Barrett speaks about Governor Wallace sending him an Alabama State flag to Vietnam and of displaying it over his hut.

He then becomes very emotional in telling how a group of Negro soldiers tore this flag down and destroyed it.

He tells of Negro soldiers being yellow and scared to fight and of all soldiers losing their morale when they are integrated. He states that after he was discharged from the Army, he visited Governor Wallace at which time Wallace gave him a new Alabama flag.

Subject usually speaks for an hour and one-half and tends to ramble.

Back in the Park

Richard screws a gold eagle to the top of the flagpole at the amphitheater in the park.

"This is the flag of Mississippi," Richard tells me, "recognized as a Confederate flag. It's a flashpoint for patriotism and Americanism because of the people who opposed it in a vote in 2001—the Communist Party, the Black Caucus, and the homosexuals."

Opposed by homosexuals! Giant John writes on his yellow notepad.

"When I was young in Australia I used to wear a T-shirt with the Confederate flag on it."

"Really?" he says happily. "This flag was worn when they tore the Berlin Wall down. It was flown in Vilnius when they kicked the Soviets out. It has a freedom spirit all over the world."

"Do skinheads have that spirit?" I ask Richard. (*Are there going to be skinheads at this banquet or not, goddamn it!*)

"They do have that spirit," he says. "We have a camp for them."

"You have a camp for skinheads?" I say, my lisp so happy, it sounds like a tweet.

"I don't want to get into it today, because this is not that day, but come in October and we'll have you around. Where the car was yesterday."

He means his Nationalist Movement office in Learned. Christ. Even *that* he can't just say straight out. But maybe if you'd been followed by the FBI for forty-five years, you'd become a little evasive, too.

"What would I learn in skinhead camp?" I ask.

"Well, I don't want to distract from the Spirit of America, which is today, but we have twenty acres out in the country and we have target practice, legal practice, education, physical training."

"Whites only?"

"Red, white, and blue."

Richard mounts the flagpole in the flag stand.

"I want to make plain we don't want to secede from America," Richard says. "Or fight the Civil War again."

This sounds to the untrained ear as if Richard is being moderate. *He doesn't want to secede! What a guy!* But to a Race Trekkie, this sounds like Richard being a rat fink. Most Southern white supremacists *do* want to split from America. To them the Civil War was an invasion, and they would love to fight it again. This is why Jim Giles has Richard marked down forever as a New Yorker, a Northerner, a Yankee. But I still don't really get it—it sounds as though Richard wants to avoid trouble. What sort of white supremacist wants to avoid trouble?

People dribble in to the park and stand about the amphitheater. What I first think is the start of a crowd is actually the end of the crowd. The five high school boys chosen as Spirit of America Day honorees pick at their ears and noses, with mums, dads, and aunts by their sides. Everyone looks a little thrown. Are there even twenty people here?

Two beauty queens touch up their hair by the side of the amphitheater. Kimberly, a Miss Hattiesburg Outstanding Teen, looks bitter at the shitty turnout. She'll be singing the national anthem. Richard offers her a megaphone. She winces and pushes it away. This crowd will be able to hear her without that.

Just when I've given up hope of skinheads, I see him. A tubby shorn-haired boy with a Confederate tie, one of the five honorees.

I shuffle over to the boy's mum.

"I really don't know how my son was nominated," the pink and cheery woman says, "but we got stuff in the mail."

"So you're friends with Richard?" I ask.

"No," she says. "This is the first time I've met with him."

I try the boy himself.

"Not sure what I'm getting this award for," he says. "This is the first time I've been nominated. I don't really know what it is."

"You friends with Richard?" I ask.

"No."

Sometimes a cigar is just a cigar, and sometimes a "skinhead" is just some guy who went to the barber and asked for a number two.

I nose about the crowd. I can't find one person who knew Richard before today. Not one parent clued in that he runs the Nationalist Movement. All the boys just got something in the mail and are flattered to have won a sports award.

Richard's bony fingers hand out Confederate flags to the parents.

"They said we couldn't bring these flags along to the football games." He laughs. "Not allowed to bring sticks into the stadium!" He's selling these folks a "safety bylaws gone mad" story, while it's really a "racially charged Confederate flag" story. I bunch up with the families and look up at Richard. He's standing behind the podium, giving a speech about how "new" isn't always "new and improved." It means one thing if you don't know he's a white supremacist, and another if you do. Then, as I stand there, it whacks me in the head what Richard has done. He's constructed a fantasy-reality: He's the charismatic leader hammering out a political speech from behind a podium to a crowd waving flags. Everyone else thinks they're at a high school sports award ceremony hosted by an eccentric.

The beauty queen sings a sour "Star-Spangled Banner."

Richard tells us it's time to march to City Hall to plant a flag.

> **The Sovereignty Commission**
> **SCR ID # 6-72-3-22-1-1-1 (July 27, 1971)**
> **RICHARD ANTHONY BARRETT first came to our attention as the result of a full-page article in a newspaper. With the article was a picture of Richard Barrett with his college diploma under his arm, going in to return same to the president of Rutgers University, New Jersey. This act was prompted by the fact that Barrett disagreed with the communistic leanings of one of the faculty members. Barrett made this return of his diploma into quite a publicity stunt.**
>
> **Barrett has appeared in many high schools, mostly rural, his theme being "Victory in Vietnam, Victory over Communism, and Victory under God." In his speeches he usually addresses and puts emphasis on male students who are members of the local high school football team. He usually asks for contributions from the students to help finance his cause. He has upset parents of the students as a result.**
>
> **Typical of Barrett's activities was an incident when he attempted to take a patient from the Veterans Administration Hospital, Jackson, a wounded Vietnam veteran who had lost both legs, and transport him to Washington, DC, to exploit him in some type of racial or Vietnam demonstration.**

Barrett is constantly attempting to organize the young people in Mississippi. A source commented that Barrett appeared to be operating in the same manner as Hitler operated in Germany prior to World War II. It was this person's sincere belief that Barrett is a Nazi.

Richard Barrett's "America's Victory Force" sponsored a banquet in Arlington, Virginia. It was highly publicized with the fact that both speakers would be members of Congress. After some $6,000 worth of tickets were sold, neither speaker appeared. There were many questions as to where that money went.

The latest venture of Barrett's part was the organization of "The Spirit of America Day."

Barrett had drawn up a scheme whereby he had made Mississippian football player Archie Manning the Honorary Chairman. His name was printed on "Spirit of America Day" official stationery. This was to gain as much as possible from the publicity, a very routine procedure followed by Barrett. He used identical tactics in setting up "America's Victory Force," placing names of prominent generals, admirals, and other top-ranking officers on the stationery.

Barrett does an excellent job of getting around where prominent people are congregated, and having a friend take a picture which reflects him being a part of the gathering. He is spoken of as a first-class con artist and he takes care of himself in fine fashion. He is fantastic on getting newspaper publicity.

City Hall

We thread through the Greek columns fronting the building and pass a plaque: BUILT 1846–47 BY SLAVE LABOR, OF HANDMADE BRICK. USED AS HOSPITAL FOR BOTH UNION AND CONFEDERATE SOLDIERS DURING WAR BETWEEN THE STATES.

After winning the demographic war in Jackson, black officials removed the Mississippi Confederate flag from City Hall. Every year Richard marches on City Hall and replants the flag.

Richard has presented this flag ceremony to the families as a genial part of the Spirit of America Day, as recognition of the day by City Hall. But it's nothing of the sort. It's in fact civil disobedience *against* City Hall.

Richard drifts in with his dupes. It's a risk. What if the City Hall folk kick up a fuss? What will he tell the families?

Richard makes no eye contact with the four black security guards, three with bodies so wide, they slosh when they walk. Awkward energy glitches through the air. The guards know what's going on, but for some reason no fuss is made—maybe they've decided it's easier just to let him do his thing once a year. A female guard ushers Richard through to a mahogany and leather room that looks like a courtroom. She asks if he wants the air-conditioning on. She has concern in her eyes for one of four reasons, and I can't tell which:

1. She's a black woman nervous of a white supremacist.
2. She's nervous because she thinks he's mentally ill. (I'm serious.)
3. She sees an old, frail man and is being slightly maternal/respectful.
4. She's determined to do her job right in these weird circumstances.

I'm the last into the room after all the families.

The shield of the City of Jackson hangs over three leather chairs. Seated there, like aristocrats, are Richard Barrett, Vince Thornton, and Kimberly, the beauty queen. The US flag is planted in a gold flag stand next to them.

I join the families sitting on pews facing the three while Richard reads out a letter of well-wishes from the governor of Tennessee. It sounds generic even for a form letter. *Please accept my personal best wishes for all of your future endeavors.*

A silver beard tickles my shoulder. One of the boys' fathers has leaned forward. He asks me if I know who this guy Richard is. He's never heard of him, but he's already picking up that he's a bit odd. I still have a prank to do, so I feign naiveté.

Richard has left his leather chair and is lurching over the five boys in the front pew.

"The city here has taken down the Mississippi flag," he whispers. "And one of the parts of our ceremony is to put it back. So is there one of you who would like to bring the flag here?"

"Okay," says one of the boys, a peach-fuzzed Justin. Richard ushers Justin from the room.

Vince Thornton stands from his leather chair and raises his hand. He asks us to raise our hands and repeat after him.

"I pledge allegiance to the flag of Mississippi and the sovereign state for which it stands, with pride in her history and achievements, and with confidence in her future, and under the guidance of Almighty God."

Richard ushers Justin back into the room. He marches an awkward march with the state Confederate flag, as if he's been pushed into an improv theater game. Justin plants the flag in the gold flag stand alongside the Stars and Stripes. Richard takes photos with his Japanese camera. Justin's photo will be printed up in Richard's newsletter and posted on his website. Justin will be the face of the white race fighting back against the black race.

Outside I ask Justin why the City of Jackson removed the flag in the first place.

"I really don't know," he says. "Mr. Barrett might know."

This is two-way theater. The families think Richard has the support of City Hall; City Hall thinks Richard has the support of the families. Everyone's both an audience member and an unwitting actor in Richard's play. (This year is extra-meta. Everyone, including Richard, is also an unwitting actor in *my* play. And the crew and I are actors in Richard's, too, making him look newsworthy in the eyes of the families. This is a race war written by Charlie Kaufman.)

And it won't end when the day ends. The security guards will no doubt tell their black friends that a bunch of white supremacists marched on City Hall this week.

Kimberly is smiling at Richard's camera.

"Why'd Jackson get rid of the flag?" I ask, all faux-naive.

Kimberly's antennas go up. She twigs straightaway.

"There were different . . . racial issues." She rubs her nose on the word *racial*.

"It just looks like a normal flag with normal colors," I say.

"They said it represented slavery so they wanted it gone," Kimberly says. "I don't feel it represents slavery or says that Mississippi is a racist state. I just think it's our flag and I am proud of it."

Within minutes Kimberly's mother has cornered my producer: "I want to know what you're doing! I want to know what this is for!"

So not every white Mississippian was naive that day.

LETTER FROM LAWYERS FOR ARCHIE MANNING

Law Offices of Lyon, Crosthwait & Terney
100 Court Street
Indianola, Mississippi 38751
March 18, 1971
Mr. Richard Barrett
P. O. Box 3333
Jackson, Mississippi 39207

Dear Mr. Barrett,

I have recently learned that your foundation is listing Archie Manning on its board of trustees as honorary chairman. It is my understanding that Archie has not consented to the use of his name and serving on the board of trustees as honorary chairman.

Therefore, as his attorney and at his request, I would appreciate your removing his name as honorary chairman and from your board, and refraining from the use of his name in connection with your foundation.

Thank you.
Very truly yours,

Frank O. Crosthwait, Jr.
Lyon, Crosthwait & Terney

The State Capitol

Giant John spools the footage forward.

Richard has taken us to the House of Representatives. A politician with golden hair has just introduced a resolution commending the Spirit of America Day and its honorees. The politicians look up to the public gallery and applaud. The boys and their mums and dads look down, cheeks turning pink. One mother smudges off a teardrop of pride.

Richard's out of sight. He drifts in a circle outside the doors of the public gallery with a dizzy smile, consumed in his fantasy. He'll *just* get away with this if he doesn't show his face to the legislators. Showing his face may tip the black legislators over the edge. They might bellow and point their fingers at the public gallery. They might shout words like *white supremacist* and make a scene that will be hard to explain to the families. A new side of Richard the double-dealer: He's attracted to risk.

"Unbelievable building," I say to Richard. Golden light washes over four stories of marble in the State Capitol.

"Built in 1903," Richard says. "The same year that they had electricity come in. So they wanted to splurge on lights."

"And what happened in there?" I ask Richard.

"Well, we defeated all the opposition," he says. "And that's good. That's a victory."

The families and I didn't see any politicians opposing, so it must have happened before we were ushered in by Richard.

"And there was a round of applause," I say. "Was that for you, or the Spirit of America boys, or both?"

"For the Spirit of America and the people who represent it. Not the sore losers." Richard is giddy with glee. He's pulled off his State Capitol show for yet another year.

"Who are the sore losers?" I say.

"There's one over there," he says, pointing his liver-spotted nose at a black politician.

"Can we meet the sore losers?"

"*You* could. You know what I say: I'm not going to get in a spray competition with the skunk." Richard's mouth, eyes, and hands are all smiling. "I have a feeling they may not be too spry at this point."

Richard glides down the staircase of the State Capitol.

"All right, we're headed for the banquet," Richard calls back. "We'll see you out there."

"And when did you want me to say thank you?" I call down. "The start? The end? Or the middle?"

"Oh, I'll find a place. Probably when I get up."

"And then I'll come up and just say thank you?" I say, trying to seal the deal.

"That'll be great," he says.

Weasel #1 continues gliding down the staircase.

Weasel #2 smiles at cameraman Germain.

Germain & Craig

"This is fucked," says Germain, wincing. A mother of one of the chunkier boys had sobbed with joy to him before. "He's never won a prize before," she cried.

Director Craig grabs my arm. "You have to do a piece-to-camera," he tells me with a disgusted look in his eye. "You have to say the families don't know what's happening. That Richard's duped them. We can't put them on TV like this."

I've spent a decade with Craig and Germain. We've hung with evangelical hucksters, Holocaust deniers, and terrorists. I have never seen these two scrunch up their faces like Richard has made them scrunch up their faces.

What Richard Did Next

A 1967 telegram in the FBI file is headed RICHARD BARRETT INTERNAL SECURITY.

Soon after the FBI first interviews him, Richard ducks out of Mississippi and heads east. He ends up in North Carolina, where he tries and fails to organize a parade in support of the war in Vietnam. Rumors circulate that he's a member of the American Nazi Party. He ends up holding his "Victory for Vietnam" parade in Natchez, Mississippi. (Natchez is where those white Southern mansions in your head are, with columns and Scarlett O'Hara fainting out front.)

Bad reviews come in from the FBI. "The source stated the parade was not well organized and was a complete flop. There were approximately twenty-five automobiles in the parade with two people in each car, making a total of fifty people in the parade. Several individuals participating in this parade were members of the Ku Klux Klan."

The FBI have high standards. I would have killed for that level of turnout when shooting *Race Relations*.

"The general consensus of the people he comes in contact with is that he is a 'nut.'"

Two days later, Richard disrupts the Poor People's March, organized by a black civil rights group, by turning up with a parody sign: *Fight Poverty. Go to Work.*

The crowd rips up his sign, and the police arrest Richard for disturbing the peace. The Jackson office of the FBI asks J. Edgar Hoover, director of the FBI, to place Richard on the Rabble Rouser Index. Hoover calls for an investigation of Richard, but "as he is nationally unknown at this time and has precipitated no racial violence to date, the recommendation is turned down."

But Richard's on the up.

Soon after, a predawn explosion blows a chunk out of the Soviet Embassy in Washington, DC, and shatters windows across the street. Richard is a suspect. Agents poke around Jackson; they clear his name.

Then two months later: "Barrett's whereabouts were ascertained during the pertinent period in the case of the assassination of Rev. Martin Luther King, Jr."

The FBI is struggling like I am struggling. Nobody can work Richard out. Is he somebody or nobody? Is he dangerous and important? Or a fantasist? If he is a fantasist, that doesn't rule out he was a danger to either Vincent McGee or himself.

Even a fantasist can conjure things into the real world and then lose control of them. One of the things Richard did next attests to this. It involved a man named Edgar Ray Killen.

The Ballad of Edgar Ray Killen

Edgar Ray Killen was a Southern Baptist minister and Ku Klux Klansman.

In 1964, two young Jewish New Yorkers are in Mississippi. They are rallying blacks to register to vote. They've met up with a young black Mississippian, also a civil rights activist.

The three activists have already annoyed law enforcement, many of whom are Klansmen. A black church was razed to the ground in Neshoba County. The three are seen poking around the site, trying to find evidence of Klan involvement. If you've seen the film *Mississippi Burning*— the film that's shaped the way Mississippi is seen around the world and which is based on this case—then you know what happens next.

The activists drive from the burned-down church in their station wagon. They're stopped by a deputy sheriff (and Klansman). He says they were speeding and throws them in jail.

The deputy sheriff then meets up with Edgar Ray Killen. Killen has a plan.

That night, the three are released from the jail. The deputy sheriff tells them to leave town. They drive off.

Edgar Ray Killen has arranged for two carloads of Klansmen to follow them. The Klansmen pull over the activists on a dirt road as they're leaving Neshoba County.

The two New York Jews are shot through their hearts. The young black man is beaten (probably with a chain) and shot three times.

The Klan may run the show in Mississippi in 1964, but they've overplayed their hand killing two white New Yorkers. Liberal America notices they're missing. Mississippi law enforcement doesn't seem too motivated to find the civil rights workers—they're also the Klan, after all—so Democratic president Lyndon Johnson becomes involved. Overruling the wishes of Mississippians, he instructs the FBI director to send in agents. They comb the land and dredge the lakes.

The three are found buried in an embankment dam. Their car is found burned out in a swamp.

What this means for white Mississippians: Federal troops have infringed on the independence of Mississippi again, just like in the Civil War. So Mississippi officials refuse to pursue or prosecute Edgar Ray Killen or the other Klansmen.

Murder is a state crime, but the federal prosecutor gets lateral. He charges Edgar Ray Killen and seventeen other Klansmen with the federal crime of depriving the young men of their civil rights.

He still has to prosecute the case in Mississippi in front of white Mississippian jurors. Seven Klansmen are found guilty and none serves more than six years in jail. But the jury can't reach a verdict on the mastermind, Edgar Ray Killen. It seems one juror just can't bring herself to sentence a preacher. So Edgar Ray is released, and that's that.

Well, that's that for forty years.

If you want to catch Edgar Ray today, you'll have to do so in Unit 31, Mississippi State Penitentiary, Sunflower County. For this, he and his wife, Betty Jo, blame Richard Barrett.

The 2004 Mississippi State Fair

The annual Mississippi State Fair celebrates the best of Mississippi: its food, its music, its culture, its history. In 2004, Richard decides a fair like this needs to celebrate Edgar Ray Killen. He prints up pamphlets. Richard's going to organize a stall and tells everyone the man himself will turn up to shake hands and autograph photos.

For a few years, a new case against Killen has been bubbling away on low. Among other things, a schoolteacher and his students teamed with a reporter to dig up new leads, new evidence, new witnesses. But Killen has kept his head down, and keeping your head down counts for a lot in Mississippi.

Richard's stunt cascades everything into the sunlight. Black people want to know why this Klansman will be goose-stepping up and down on their family day. And the national media starts to file stories: *Here are those Mississippi yokels, still trying to lynch blacks.* A white sheriff calls for the reopening of the case against Killen.

Soon eighty-year-old Killen is arrested on three counts of murder.

This time the Neshoba County district attorney and Mississippi attorney general prosecute the case. Mississippi itself has been forced to act.

After a delay—Killen somehow breaks both his legs chopping wood—the trial starts. Killen rolls up each day in a wheelchair. Then someone says they spotted him after court just walking around. Others say they saw him driving a car. The judge had let Killen out on bond because he thought the old man couldn't get far in a wheelchair. Now Killen has to spend his nights in prison for the remainder of the trial.

The trial lasts one week.

Then there's almost that cathartic moment for Mississippi, but not completely. The jury—nine white, three black—don't accept that Killen murdered the boys. But they do agree he masterminded the killings, recruiting and organizing the Klansmen on that day in 1964. He gets sixty years for manslaughter—twenty for each civil rights worker—to be served consecutively.

Here's the thing: Edgar Ray Killen says he knew nothing about the stall at the Mississippi State Fair until law enforcement started ringing. He says keeping a low profile served him well and he would never have turned up at the fair. He certainly didn't give Richard permission to set up the stall or use his name. Richard just printed the pamphlets and rang the media.

Instead of promoting the white supremacist heritage of Mississippi, through his vainglorious bumbling Richard managed to get the state's most famous white supremacist locked up for life.

The fantasist lost control of what he started.

Richard Barrett was a real racist, but always on the fringe of trouble rather than ever caught at its center. So how did he end up getting in the worst trouble possible? Could Richard have made the first move—pulling a knife on Vincent, or pulling down his pants—or is it more likely that he just tried to weasel the wrong guy?

Documents will only take me so far. To find the people who knew him, I need to get out of my motel room and go deeper into Mississippi.

5.

WHAT WAS RICHARD BARRETT THINKING?

#2 WAS RICHARD GAY?

Just Suspicious

Jim Giles is driving me to White Haiti. That's what he calls the poorest white area in Rankin County.

Now that I can see him, Jim is a youthful-looking fifty-two: tall, short blond hair, and a strong straight back. Back at the farm he maintained better posture with a heavy sack of chicken feed on his shoulder than I did with nothing to weigh me down. He seems very serious but not unkind, softened a little by a baby-blue Windbreaker.

While I'm waiting for Joe McNamee and Vince Thornton to return my calls, I've been talking white supremacist history with Jim. Among other things.

"Real strange figure," Jim says of Richard. "Definitely the radar went off with him—with me and him. Every time I turned around he was calling me."

"You think he was hitting on you?"

"I think possibly."

Jim can't point to an unambiguous instance of Richard hitting on him, but says it was just a feeling he got.

"I think his interest was in males," he says as we drive on. "I don't think he was interested in girls. I am without a girl, but I am pursuing them."

"Why don't you live in the house with your mother?" I ask. "Why do you live in a separate trailer next to her?"

"Well, I mean, I'm a grown man, I'm not really expected to live with my mother," he says.

"Oh yeah, I guess so, but you're living on the same plot of land . . ."

"On the family property, but that's much more appropriate. Do you live at home?"

"No, I've got my own home."

"Why don't you live with your mother?"

"Well, my mother's not alive, but besides that, I know what you mean, but it's, like, you are living right next to her."

I'm doing this for a reason. On *Radio Free Mississippi*, Jim has been moping recently that girls are turned off by his trailer.

"I just wonder," I say, "if on these Match.com dating things, if you could bring her back to a house . . . you know?" I'm thinking of this rich Jewish frenemy of mine. In university he'd had this decked-out, funky apartment that he'd insinuate was his, when it was his parents'.

"That would be misrepresentation. I would never, I wouldn't do that," Jim says, at his most serious. "I would much rather have a girl really recognize that I live in the trailer and it's okay with her. I could see some people doing that, I get your drift there."

An idiot carrying a plank of wood walks out into traffic to cross the road. Jim is forced to swerve. We both chuckle.

"I bet he's not American," Jim says. "I bet he's Hispanic, what do you bet?"

Wood Plank Man's hat was pulled down, and we swerved past fast.

"We'll never know," I swerve, too. "So how does it work on Match

.com?" I ask. "You just like each other's photos and profiles and then you, like, e-mail each other or something?"

"Exactly. And you can propose to meet. And I did actually meet with one, I had my first date with her via Match.com on Saturday."

"Last Saturday? No way!"

"Yep, just the day before yesterday."

"Wow. And hang on, where did you . . . Why did you like her enough to meet up with her?"

"Well, I mean, she was an attractive girl, her profile picture was pretty and she was a younger girl, thirty-six, blond, height medium. It didn't go . . . I mean, it went okay, but she was clearly interested in a different type of guy. I think she was interested in somebody with money. She was a Russian girl."

"And where did you go for the date?"

"I brought her to Borders."

"Oh, yeah. Like in the café there?"

"Yeah. And there were two strange guys. It was almost like she had them be there for her personal protection. I may be totally mistaken by that, I might be a tad bit paranoid. Two very conspicuous-looking guys."

"So how did it end?"

"She kind of abruptly said . . . she didn't say it exactly this way, but the gist of it was, she said, 'This is the way it works, we just meet briefly, and I've got to meet somebody back at my home, and maybe we will get together again.' But I think that was her nice way to dismiss me. I was dismissed."

Jim turns to me.

"My problem is," he says, "it's hard to get the kind of girl I want when they see that trailer and they know I am unemployed."

"I'd spin it around," I tell him. "It seems like you're self-employed. When I came to your farm before, I wasn't like, *Here is this bum who is unemployed and doing nothing.* I'm like, *Here is the guy running a farm that's going to build up into a business.*"

Now I feel like I'm running a seminar: Jewish Dating Tips for White Supremacists.

His farm did look amazing and high-maintenance, by the way, with cows and quails and fish and bees.

We enter White Haiti, where the small, flimsy houses look like they would easily be sucked into the sky in a twister.

Jim says he didn't grow up with white separatism coursing through his veins. Progressives trying to deny Mississippi its flag triggered his teetering to white pride. Why couldn't his people have their history? But what really sealed the deal was the 1990 murder of the Parker family. Two black men slaughtered a white Mississippian family. They sliced a finger off the father to steal his wedding band, raped the nine-year-old daughter, and burned down the house. Why didn't Jerry Mitchell from the local paper chase that story like he chased all those octogenarian Klansmen? Why aren't there Hollywood films about the Parkers like there are about blacks who were lynched?

Jim rolls the car up beside a man with three teeth.

"Hey, I'm Jim Giles, nice to see you," he says. The man looks confused. "This fella here, he's an Australian writer, and I'm taking him around and kind of showing him the local place, and showing him how poor, how hard people got it here."

"Oh, yeah," the man says, trying to figure Jim out.

"And my complaint to him, and I'll just ask you, you've heard about all these Baptist churches and their foreign missionary work. How they go to places like Haiti to help people? Have they ever knocked on your door?"

The man seems to want to say whatever Jim wants him to say. But he doesn't know what Jim wants him to say.

"Let me ask you a question," Jim continues. "Did you know that our government gives Israel ten million dollars every day?"

"Nope, didn't know that."

Jim wanted the man to be outraged. But he doesn't seem stressed that the government gives Israel ten million dollars every day.

"Could you use a few nickels?" Jim says.

"Oh, yeah," the man says cheerily. "I don't even need a million dollars, I just need ten grand. I'd be set. I mean, I'd pay all my bills off and be fine, I mean—"

Jim interrupts. "Some of these homes, especially right across the tracks there, you don't see homes like that in Haiti, in the country of Haiti—and I've got a brother who literally goes down there to do missionary work and I've challenged him to do the same thing and help y'all here locally. He doesn't have to go a long way away. Y'all have much crime around here?"

"No," the man says.

Jim, it seems, was relying on the man to say yes. So he shifts gears.

"Has Jerry—do you know who Jerry Mitchell is, with the *Clarion-Ledger*?"

"Yeah, I know who he is."

"Has he ever been down here to report on y'all tough situation?"

"No."

"You know the *Clarion-Ledger* seems to care a lot about black folks, don't they?"

"Yes, sir."

"Do they care about you?"

"Nope."

"Yep. Have a good day."

Jim drives off.

Jim stops another White Haitian, then another, outside their houses. Both are polite, but seem mildly insulted that Jim is presenting their town as a shithole. They don't seem to care that the government is giving ten million dollars to Israel every day, either.

"When I was in university," I tell Jim, "they used to always say that the rich people are pitting the black people against the white people, you know what I mean? When really, both sides were poor, so the working class should just stick together and just fight the rich people."

"I see your point," Jim says. "I think both the poor whites and poor blacks would be aided if we closed the borders and stopped free trade. The thing I see, though, that it's hard for someone like you, who sees the races as equal, is that if left to their own devices, white folks are going to arrange it in a way that tends to be safer, quieter."

Jim says whites left on their own create ancient Rome or modern Berlin. Blacks create Haiti.

"Do you have a lot of, like, white friends," I ask, "or are you a bit of a loner?"

"Bit of a loner," Jim says, "bit of a loner."

"Like, I mean, I'm one, too. But it's interesting. How do you marry the idea that you think white people have some joint connection, some joint spirit, with the fact that you are a loner?"

"That's a good question," Jim says. He doesn't say anything more on the matter.

We return to Jim's farm. He parks near his trailer.

"See that?" Jim says. He points to the dirt road stretched along the front of his farm. A black sports coupe is easing past. Jim says the people in the car are probably visiting his brand-new neighbors. The brand-new neighbors are black. "Why is it creeping like that? It's just suspicious. I mean, it has a right, but it's just suspicious."

Here's how blacks can't win (or at least blacks in sports coupes can't win): I would have thought driving *fast* would have been the provocative speed. I was just on that road and I crept, too, because it's a country road and because there are loose stones and a sharp ninety-degree turn twenty meters ahead. Actually, how does Jim even know there are black people in the car? We can't see who's in the car from here.

"So you can see what I mean," Jim says. "It's just suspicious."

A Fifteen-Second Memory

I've just realized there's a moment, a fifteen-second memory, that's coloring everything I read and hear about Richard Barrett. Maybe it meant nothing. It's mulched up with everything else that happened over the two days in Mississippi filming *Race Relations*.

I walk out of the Diplomat Ballroom, where everything was being set up for the Spirit of America Day. And in the lobby Richard's leaning forward, with his hand on his knee, talking to a boy, a white kid. I'm only drifting by but catch what they're discussing—how Richard will be giving him a lift home in his pickup. The kid's eyes, Richard's eyes—something feels weird and nervous.

Maybe I misread things. But I can't unthink it.

For instance, this fifteen-second memory colors how I interpret a memo from an FBI file.

It's four p.m. on Thursday, October 26, 1967. Richard's on foot. He circles the State Capitol, dragging behind him a United Nations flag in some sort of protest.

With him is ███████, a fifteen-year-old boy. The boy's dragging a Viet Cong flag.

They stop. They squirt lighter fluid on the two flags and set them alight.

> A confidential source who has furnished reliable information in the past advised that ███████ is the son of ███████ of Florence, Mississippi, who is known to have been a member of the United Klans of America . . .
>
> Source further advised that ███████ was extremely upset regarding his son's association with Richard Barrett and has stated that he will not allow Barrett to return to his residence or contact his son in the future.

The Clarion-Ledger

The newspapers in Mississippi still smudge like it's the 1970s. Ten minutes with the *Clarion-Ledger* and black ink will stain your fingers, your shirt, and the tip of your nose.

I'm stretched out on the too-spongy couch in my room. An old man eyeballs me with his wonky eyes from the front page. He is Byron De La Beckwith, Jr. His father, Byron Sr., is the man who fired a bullet into the back of Medgar Evers, killing the black civil rights worker. Two white juries refused to convict him in the 1960s. During the second trial, a former governor of Mississippi strode in, crossed the courtroom floor, and shook Byron Sr.'s hand while Medgar Evers's widow was giving testimony.

Decades later, Jerry Mitchell from the *Clarion-Ledger* niggled and niggled until the case was reopened. In 1994 a black and white jury found Byron Sr. guilty of first-degree murder. He was sentenced to life without parole, and in 2001, wheezy Byron Sr., with a decaying heart, passed in prison.

Now Byron Jr. is teasing Jerry Mitchell, saying that his father may not have been the killer, and that he may be willing to reveal who was, leading to the headline smudging on my hands: EVERS' ASSASSIN STILL AT LARGE.

This is not the first I've read of Byrons Sr. and Jr. The Nationalist Movement website says Byron Sr. pleaded with Richard Barrett to represent him in court in 1994. Richard declined, saying it would muddy his activist work to free Byron Sr. Richard organized a "Free Byron De La Beckwith, Sr." petition, which had Richard booted out of his church. He also produced a video celebrating Byron Sr., which led to the lamest battle in the annals of white supremacy (covered in meticulous detail on the Nationalist Movement website), with Byron Jr. attacking Richard for overcharging him on "dubbing costs."

So the Byrons were no friends of Richard's, but over several decades Byron Sr. and Richard were two of the most prominent racists in Mississippi—professional associates. I ring Byron Jr. He tells me, sure, he'll be happy to meet. He invites me to his auction service business in Aberdeen, a three-hour drive from my spongy couch.

It takes five minutes of abrasive soap to scrub the *Clarion-Ledger* from my skin. I leave my room with glowing red hands.

The Shed in Aberdeen

An enormous tin shed sizzles in the sun. STANFORD AND SON AUCTION SERVICE reads the sign. The items laid across the outdoor tables are grimy: broken and grubby egg timers and waterlogged coloring books.

I ask a woman for Byron Jr., and she points to the dark entrance of the shed.

I drift out of the sun and into the shadows.

Maybe Half an Hour Later

Okay, I'm not up at the shed anymore, I'm at the Wendy's just down from that. Hell! He wouldn't let me tape! Jesus Christ. I have to write this down before I forget.

Okay, here's what just happened:

I walk into the shed. Three white guys—two fat and one regular—are playing cards. One points to an old man in overalls and a cap with a Confederate patch, standing near a table of knickknacks, including Franklin Mint figurines of a black mother reading Bible stories to her children. There was the same one in the *Jackson Advocate* office.

That man is Byron Jr.

"So where are you from?" says Byron Jr.

"Well, I work at the ABC, which is like the BBC in Australia. But this is my own solo project," I say. "I've spoken to people who knew *of* Richard. But I need people who really knew him."

"Well, I knew him," says Byron Jr.

Every cough and word echoes in the shed.

I pull out my little Flip camera.

"Do you mind if—" I say.

"Well, you just hold it there," he says. He tells me he's going to need a percentage of book sales.

I tell him I don't even have a book deal, but that I'm not averse to a payment for his services. Why not? The Rankin County Courthouse is getting a buck a page for transcripts.

He ushers me to the side.

"Well, my fee," Byron mumbles gingerly, "is one thousand dollars."

His eyes tingle. Is he worried he's overplayed his hand?

"Hmmm," I say.

"I don't mind telling you, I told Dr. Phil and Oprah I'd need a hundred thousand plus expenses," he says.

"Hmmm," I say.

"Maybe," he says, "I should have gone through this before you drove here for three hours."

Rather than haggle, I take a different tack.

"Do you know Richard's sister?" I say. (A thousand bucks for Richard's sister is okay, I reckon.)

"No," he says. "I didn't even know he had a sister until the funeral."

"You were at the funeral?"

"No, I didn't go. I didn't know until a few days later."

"Do you know where it was?" I ask. "Or who took care of his estate?"

"No. But Rankin County, their courthouse would have to know. He didn't even leave anything to his sister. He left it to a man, and the will said if that man didn't come forward by a certain date, it goes to the Iraqi government."

"The Iraqi government?" I squeak.

"Richard was peculiar like that," Byron Jr. says.

Christ!

Byron slowed meaningfully over "a man," too.

I'm pretty antsy standing in the shed. I'm pretty antsy because I can't tape this. I've already missed gold for the book, including a rant about Martin Luther "Coon" and the Jewish media.

"I like Australia," Byron Jr. says. "You messed up, though!" He either says we messed up because we let the Queen have the farms or because we took the farms off the Queen—can't remember.

"Australia's still mainly white, though," he says.

He checks me out like one might a girl in a nightclub.

"Look at you," he says. "Blue eyes, hair, skin."

He says he doesn't mind talking, but might stop if he thinks something falls more into the one-thousand-dollar category.

"You know, I'll need someone to help me write my book one day," he says. "But I'm telling you, I'm not going to fly over to California to be on *The Johnny Carson Show* to promote it."

Nervously, I mention the Nationalist Movement web page story about Byron Sr. asking Richard to be his attorney.

Surprise, sur-fucking-prise—this was, says Byron Jr., not quite the truth. "In fact, it was the other way around—Richard was always coming to the jail begging to be my daddy's attorney. We said no. He wasn't screwed together right. He was strange."

Byron Jr. sucks the air between his teeth and then with a spark in his eye describes how a few years ago he threatened to "stomp" Richard if he ever told lies about his daddy again.

"You never knew which side Richard was on," he says. "Or if he was playing both sides against each other for money. I thought maybe he was an FBI informant. But he never told them anything they didn't already know."

A black man is standing a few meters back from Byron Jr.'s stall, looking on.

"Oh, sorry, were you waiting?" Byron Jr. says. He sounds impeccably sincere and polite. "I'm sorry to make you wait."

"My friend has things to sell," the black man says, "and was wondering, do you guys buy or does my friend set up himself here?"

"Both can work," Byron Jr. says. He hands the black man a business card. "Tell your friend to call."

The black man's black female companion is hovering around the entrance of the shed.

"Oh, hello there, young lady," Byron Jr. says. "Thank you for stopping in."

Byron Jr. turns to me.

"See, I do business with niggers," he says. "I don't mind. I just don't want them in my home. They can't come over for lunch."

"Why?" I ask.

"Because they should be on the porch," he says. He points at me. "You can come over for lunch. I'd pour you a cola and a tea. But not the niggers."

He says *nigger* like a bondage dominatrix says *bitch*, with a glint in his eye and a curl in his lip.

"Nothing in my Bible says there should be desegregation!" he says. "There were twelve tribes! Twelve separate tribes!"

"Weren't those tribes Jews?" I say.

"There were Jews and gentiles, but they were separate," he says.

He then rolls through his Jew theory checklist. Including, but not limited to:

He can't accept the Jews because they won't accept Jesus.

If you check the history, the number doesn't add up to six million.

Hitler was queer.

The "Hitler was queer" point provides an opening to ask about *those* Richard rumors.

"Yeah, he was always touching me," Byron Jr. says.

He strokes my arm to demonstrate.

"He'd be, 'Byron, come over here.' I'd be, 'I was going over there anyway, you don't need to touch me!'"

One of the men playing cards chuckles and calls out to Byron, "You goin' to be famous on TV?" Byron is not amused and hisses.

"People think Southerners are white trash. But if you spend time in Aberdeen, you'll see—" Byron Jr. interrupts himself. "Well, there is a lot of white trash here, but there's also blue blood, and you can trace me back to German and English aristocracy."

Byron Jr.'s family has all served in the military, except his son, who is as a consequence the "reject of the family." Byron Jr. doesn't see him.

I glance over the black figurines on his knickknack table.

"Look," I say. "So many black figurines. There's even black angels."

"Well," Byron Jr. says, "I've never been to heaven, but I imagine there's black angels there. You know, 80 percent of blacks are okay. It's just the 20 percent."

What? Eighty/twenty? Is an eight-to-two ratio high enough to go to all the effort of being a white supremacist? Maybe Richard worked on the same proportion.

The Chancery Court

I nod to the stone Confederate as I pass him by on my way to the Rankin County Chancery Court. Filed in its drawers are the last wills and testaments of the people of Rankin County.

I sit on a couch in the clerk's office. I straighten the five pages on my lap.

Last Will and Testament of Richard Barrett

I, RICHARD BARRETT, single and not having ever been married, a resident of and domiciled in the County of Rankin and State of Mississippi, being of good, sound, and disposing mind and memory, do hereby make, publish, and declare this to be my Last Will and Testament.

I express my thanks to my friends and compatriots, who labored selflessly along with me. My regret is that I could not have done more, personally, yet my joy is that we breathed the exhilarating air of the highest climes together. May you and yours complete the tasks I have endeavored to entrust to you, according to the inspiration, if any, which I have given to you.

It is my desire that I be remembered, if at all, as I was in life, only: therefore, I direct that as soon as practicable my remains be cremated without public or private viewing beforehand, and that any ashes therefrom be dispersed and mingled with the soil, unceremoniously. It is my desire and direction that none of my organs, bodily parts, or any part or parcel of my body, whatsoever, be used for any type of "organ donor." It is, further, my desire and direction that no military honors or memorials be conducted for me.

I roll my eyes at Richard positing he'll have to modestly turn down the parade and medals that the Army were pressing upon him. I flip to page two. Richard hands out his worldly goods.

I give, devise, and bequeath all of my worldly possessions to VINCE THORNTON of Collins, Mississippi.

I guess that's why the electricity bill at the Murder House was in Vince Thornton's name. *A man*, said Byron De La Beckwith, Jr., suggestively. I wonder what sort of relationship Richard and Vince Thornton had?

If, for any reason, the aforesaid VINCE THORNTON predeceases me or is unwilling, unable, or disqualified to receive the bequest, hereunder, then I give, devise, and bequeath all my worldly possessions to JOHN MOORE of Brandon, Mississippi.

John Moore? I don't recall him from any Googling or Stormfront posts. I add his name to my list.

If, for any reason, the aforesaid JOHN MOORE predeceases me or is unwilling, unable, or disqualified to receive the bequest, hereunder, then I give, devise, and bequeath all of my worldly possessions to the GOVERNMENT OF IRAN at Tehran, Iran.
Christ!

Well, it's Iran rather than Iraq, as Byron Jr. had claimed, but that hardly turns down the volume on inexplicable weirdness.

Richard adds one more note:

> I expressly decline to include any individual member of my family as beneficiary under this, my Last Will and Testament, it being my intent that the same take nothing hereunder paid.

Curious—he's already left them nothing; why hammer it home? What, I wonder, did his family do to him?

Men Like That

A friend back home bought me *Men Like That: A Southern Queer History*. The writer, John Howard, not only grew up gay in Mississippi, he grew up gay in Rankin County. He thinks outsiders mash together how Mississippians saw blacks and how they saw gays. He says they were two very different things.

Yes, Mississippians thought homosexuality was a biblical sin. But like many other vices, it was accommodated "with a pervasive, deflective pretense of ignorance." In contrast, Mississippians didn't overlook blackness.

The book covers a case from the 1950s in which two servicemen killed a gay man, claiming he had made sexual advances on them. This defense didn't stop "the most extensive investigation the Jackson police department has participated in," according to the city's chief detective. It didn't stop the district attorney pushing for the death penalty. One killer got life, the other plea-bargained down to twenty years.

The same year, Emmett Till was shot in the head and thrown in the Tallahatchie River. Two white supremacists were tried and acquitted of his murder. Soon after, knowing they were protected against double jeopardy, the two struck a deal with a magazine and confessed to the murder. The case was never reopened, and they died old men. A couple of the jurors said they thought the men were guilty but didn't think they deserved life in prison just for torturing and killing a young black guy.

I pull into JC's, a gay bar in Jackson. *Men Like That* is thrown on the passenger's seat like a street directory. I've underlined the gay bars in the book, wondering which have survived.

I *think* JC's has. The squat and gloomy building hides up a street and is trying to act inconspicuous in the middle of a parking lot. There are no apparent windows and no signage. The reason I reckon this must be the place is an old tin drum out front has been painted in rainbow stripes, dulled by age.

I want to find someone who remembers little Richard Barrett skulking into gay bars late at night. Proof that the white supremacist was homosexual!

A nervous bald man in a lime-green T-shirt walks toward the door as I'm walking toward the door.

"You know what sort of bar this is?" he asks gingerly.

"Yes."

"Because some tourists come in and *whoa!*"

A video bowling machine is pushed in a corner. Chandeliers hang from the low ceiling of the dimly lit room. Behind the bar sits an old woman with a hump.

The crowd is thin—two women and three men.

The old woman with the hump tells me she runs JC's. Yes, she answers, she knew Richard Barrett.

"Oh, really!" I say excitedly. But alas (for me), she didn't know him from his skulking into JC's late at night.

"My ex-husband was a police officer, and Richard was always down at the station stirring up trouble. He'd be telling them he'd been appointed by the Ku Klux Klan Grand Dragon to lead a march down the Jackson streets where the blacks were."

"And he wasn't appointed?"

"No, he wasn't. And there was no march."

I droop. I don't need another story about Richard the exaggerating racist. I came to find the smoking gun about his secret gay life so that Vincent has a defense against the lethal injection, and I can show that white supremacists are self-hating frauds.

She says that Richard wasn't wrong about everything, though. Mississippi was better before desegregation.

She writes down a name on a square piece of paper: *Eddie Sandifer*. He is a gay civil rights activist, she says. Eddie knew Richard.

I chat with the other folk in the bar. One man tells me that his gay friends won't come to JC's unless he drives, because someone takes photographs of the license plates in the parking lot and posts them on the Internet. Nevertheless, he agrees with *Men Like That*, that homosexuality here is overlooked "with a pervasive, deflective pretense of ignorance."

"My dad was in charge of the Mississippi softball team," he says. "And the best softball players were lesbians. My mother and father would say, 'Isn't it nice how Shelly and Mary can share expenses?'"

A lot of the people at JC's knew Richard from the news, but no one ever saw him in a gay bar. Most of the conversations start with me asking about homosexuality and them seamlessly easing into complaining about black crime and asking me if the Aboriginals "you have" are as bad as the blacks here.

Mississippi. Where even the homosexuals are rednecks.

Eddie Sandifer

I pull in to a crumbling plaza in Jackson. A dozen flat-roofed businesses, some with 1950s typefaces on their signs, form a horseshoe around the parking lot. DIABETIC FOOT CLINIC, KIRK R. SMITHHART OPTOMETRY, and so on. The plaque screwed to the wall of my destination reads MY BROTHER'S KEEPER. DENOUNCERS OF HEALTH DISPARITIES.

Piled on the reception desk, My Brother's Keeper business cards are stamped in the corner with NATIONAL ASSOCIATION OF PEOPLE WITH AIDS and TAKE THE TEST. TAKE CONTROL. PROTECT YOUR FUTURE. Good Lord. This is an HIV/AIDS clinic!

In an otherwise empty community room, a sick old man sits proud as a mafia don at the end of a long table. Standing next to him, where the don would have one of his men, Eddie Sandifer has a walking frame.

"I was born in Louisiana," Eddie tells me in a husky voice. "My father was there pastoring a church at the time. He was a Baptist minister."

Spread out before him are clippings from his life in plastic sheet protectors. Eddie points to a photo. Three men are at a wedding altar with 1980s haircuts.

"That's one of my weddings I performed in '83. I used to perform before preachers would do it, and I was performing the weddings in Mississippi. Not legal, but weddings. They're both dead now. They died of AIDS."

"Oh, right," I say. "When I came in here, 'cause I didn't know what kind of place this was, when I saw it was an AIDS place I thought maybe you had AIDS."

Christ, Safran.

"Oh, no," Eddie says. "No, I haven't. I get tested all the time. I've never had any venereal disease, period. The clinic, they gave us space here."

"Us" is the Southern AIDS Commission, which supports people with HIV/AIDS. Eddie is the only full-time staff member of the Jackson branch.

In the 1960s, Eddie did a lot of demonstrating and protesting for gay rights. "Now, Richard Barrett gave me some problems."

"What did he say?"

"The things preachers always say. That it's a sin and against the morals of the society. He was always calling my office and bugging me. Or calling people to call me. But he just liked seeing my boyfriend at the time. And other lovers. He tried to recruit them to do things for his group. I have an idea that eventually he was planning on trying to get in their pants. It didn't happen. But I think that was it."

Another encounter, in the 1980s, sticks in Eddie's mind.

"One time when we were on a gay pride rally in the park in Jackson . . . some of his loons came in, carrying their hate signs against gays, into the park. And Richard came from the back way, by the church, and walked down and made them leave. They were his kids from his group and he told them to leave."

"Why do you think he dispersed them?"

Eddie looks at me and blows out a huff.

"I have no idea."

Back in the 1950s, Eddie helped run secret gay parties in a white antebellum home in Jackson.

"It was bought and put together from one of the homes that was being torn down, with big columns, pillars out front going from the bottom, two floors high, that sort of thing."

"And were those parties often?"

"June and December. Twice a year at least. And that's when people would come from Memphis to party and stuff. They couldn't do it up there back in the fifties. You had to bring your own liquor. Liquor wasn't legal here at the time. You had to get it from bootleggers."

"What was the music?"

"Oh hell, I don't remember!" Eddie raises his voice. "See, you're going back longer than half my life."

"Was it jazz or rock 'n' roll?"

"There *was* no rock 'n' roll. It was dance, where you could hug up to each other and dance. Ballroom, two-step, fox-trot, that sort of thing."

I tell Eddie that when I went to JC's bar, the gays slagged off the blacks just like the straights might. There wasn't some sense of solidarity in oppression.

"Back in the fifties," Eddie says, "a lot of homosexuals were racists. The black guys that I invited to the parties, they always came in white jackets in case there was a raid. They'd look like they were working.

But they wound up in bed with the racist white men. The racism ended there."

I tell Eddie about a security guard I talked to at the State Capitol, who pulled a mischievous grin when I told him about rumors of Richard's secret life. "He was talking about gays who are members of Congress," I tell Eddie. "He says they really push it. Like, they don't really have to be that secretive about it. They just can't actually say it. They can't go, *Oh, listen, I'm gay.* But they *can* turn up to political functions with another man, their date, and then don't say it's their date."

"When I was active and on the streets—available—I was the one that got called to go to bed with them," Eddie says.

"What do you mean, active on the streets?"

"I was available. I could keep secrets."

"Oh, really? So you were with members of the legislature?"

"I've been with them, yeah."

Eddie says they had to be discreet, but not *that* discreet. They never had to drive out of town to have flings. Just book a room at the luxurious local hotel.

"We got a room at the King Edward Hotel," Eddie says, "called the Robert E. Lee."

Richard's phrase in *Race Relations* about homosexuality comes back to me: "People can do it, but you don't flaunt it."

The Knife

I pull a knife from the kitchen shelf and slice.

I fold open the flaps on the cardboard box and pull out *The Commission.* In the early 1980s, Richard self-published his manifesto—not available at all good bookstores. I found it online, at a secondhand bookshop in Georgia, while I was looking around unsuccessfully for Vince Thornton's address.

The fat and heavy hardback is uncomfortable to hold lying back in bed. I roll over. What's this going to tell me about what Richard was thinking?

A quick flick reveals much of the book to be Richard pounding his fist, about culture, the law, and race: "The Negro features a hypertrophy of the organs of excretion, a more developed venous system, larger teeth, a thicker cranium, and less voluminous brain as compared with the White race." And so on. But it begins not with Negro craniums and Confederate flags. Richard first talks about his childhood.

Richard was born on February 18, 1943, into a family squeezed into a small apartment, a block from Broadway. Irish Catholic families filled up this wedge of New York City.

Richard would peek out his second-floor window and take in the crowd. Still quite young, he sensed something new was rumbling through his city.

A massive influx of the foreign-born suddenly disrupted school, as it rent the neighborhood apart. Uneasiness became tension, which became fear, as vandalism and crime erupted everywhere. The newcomers could not speak English. I detected a haughtiness, a slovenliness, which irritated my classmates and teachers, too. In no time at all, one could hear Yiddish more than English spoken in many public places. Little corner stores became kosher. Kidnappings and murders were mentioned in hushed whispers, chilling us all to the bone. It was as though a curtain had rung down and the entire scene had been transformed to another act, to a whole new cast, to an unrecognizable scene. The school across the street was burned to the ground, leaving me with such a feeling of sickness and sadness that I could not bear to look on the ruins. A Jewish hall was erected in its place.

Jim Giles also said he was distressed by the noise of black kids at school. Jews, Puerto Ricans, and Negroes roll in and white families split town. The Barretts flee to New Jersey, a suburb called East Orange.

How clean and fresh was this new air. Houses were one- and two-family types, close together, with small, well-cropped lawns and lots of trees. Here were largely Anglo-Saxon working people of English descent, some Irish, and a few traces of very old Dutchmen. There was singing and stickball and sleigh rides.

But Richard's father drinks too much and angers too quickly. Once an assistant to the American military attaché in Moscow, he now sells machine parts. Richard, however, still respects him, understanding that this "downgrade" twists him to this state.

My father was a stern disciplinarian, a devout believer that to spare the rod was to spoil the child. He often read to me on his knee and we spelled and recited together. My sister, Geraldine, was born when I was four.

I scribble *Geraldine* on my yellow notepad and read on. Richard's childhood in the fat book doesn't match the story he tells elsewhere. Richard typed up a pamphlet when he first came to Mississippi: "Richard Barrett. Soldier for the People." He writes of himself in the third person:

Before joining the Army, Barrett did farm work and painted signs to put himself through Rutgers College in New Jersey. He had no family to help him. His mother and father left him when he was young, and his grandfather helped raise him until he died.

His mother and father don't abandon him in *The Commission*, nor does his grandfather raise him. But "left him" feels like more than just something made up for effect. So does "helped raise him." Is Richard really saying no one really raised him? "Until he died," rather than until the job was finished. Is Richard saying that whatever the reality, as far as he was concerned, he was abandoned? Such a person might well hate crowds and noise and want to live in the woods. He might well not have family or friends and keep his secrets impossible to find.

Sunset Terrace

When Richard moved from New Jersey in the late 1960s, he found himself in Sunset Terrace, Jackson, where he stayed until he moved to the Murder House. I ramble into the same street over forty years later, in search of anything he might have left there.

The street is a horseshoe cut into the woods. I can tell some people aren't home by the cobwebs spun on the door handles. Although sometimes you can't see the door handles because the grass has swelled so thick and high. Some doors bear the sign THIS PROPERTY HAS BEEN DEEMED VACANT AND SECURED PER THE INSTRUCTIONS OF YOUR LOAN SERVICER. Pinned-up bedsheets are as common as curtains. But like elsewhere in Mississippi, it's every man for himself, so these dilapidated houses are shuffled in with respectable ones and big flashy ones. So it's hard to know what kind of place it is. Except in one respect: When Richard fled from here to the Murder House in the mid-1990s, he made it a media event (well, he got a Jerry Mitchell article in the *Clarion-Ledger*): "After fighting against integrated neighborhoods in Jackson for three decades, white supremacist Richard Barrett is leaving because his own neighborhood has become multiracial."

Richard's old home stands here today, the weatherboard painted yellow, the lawn freshly shorn. A *Welcome* heart hangs from the front door.

I knock just below the heart. No one answers.

The black kids across the street tell me a light-skinned guy lives there now.

"Light-skinned, like white?" I ask.

"No, light-skinned black."

The black kids have never heard of Richard. They throw up names of old people who might remember him: Mrs. Yates. Mr. Strickland.

I plod up the street, trying to figure where to knock first. The heat is socking me out and glistening my face. My glasses slip off my nose. Now and then a dog, which I don't trust has had his shots, pelts out and yaps, the only sound besides my breathing. As the horseshoe curves around I see a big old white house in the distance. Pine trees have sneezed brown pins all over the roof.

Standing on the front lawn, with his top off and his hands behind his back, is a white man. He's watching me.

"Hello!" I say.

"Creepy old man . . ." he says.

"I'm not a creepy old man."

"*I'm* the creepy old man," he clarifies. He gives a warm, self-deprecating laugh. It should be noted this is the first incidence of self-deprecation I've come across in Mississippi.

The Ballad of the Creepy Old Man

"I'm Curtis Rumfelt. *Rum* and then *felt*," he says as I scribble his name on my yellow notepad. "I've been here so long, I'm older than a lot of people in the street now," he says. "I used to be the youngest kid in the neighborhood. Ha-ha!"

The youngest kid now has gray hair, gray eyebrows, and gray chest fluff. His laugh is the laugh of a hurt man, chuckling at his own supposed flaws before a bully gets in.

"Really?" I say. "You've been here that long?"

"Our family built this after World War II." He points his big nose at his big white house, keeping his hands behind his back. "It was my grandparents' house. My father's family."

Curtis's grandfather was a drifter, so his family moved a lot. When they arrived here in Jackson, two of the kids died—Curtis doesn't know what they died of, something that people don't die of these days. His grandfather was ready to move again, but his grandmother told him, "I buried two children here in Jackson, I'm not leaving." His grandfather was still a drifter, so he left. She kept all the kids in the big white house.

"I took after him, though!" he says. "Ha-ha-ha-ha! I'm the drinker and the alcoholic in the family, just like he was. But I always ended up back here. He ended up anywhere where he just happened to end up being."

I now point my own crooked nose across the street.

"Were you aware Richard Barrett lived there?"

"Yes," he says. "I first met him when he introduced himself to the people in the neighborhood." Richard would have been in his midtwenties. "And I was just a young kid back then. I was reading and the next thing I knew he was at my bedroom door introducing himself."

"He'd come into the house?" I gasp.

"He was talking to my parents in the living room and then he wandered over," Curtis says. "Have you ever seen the movie Andy Warhol's *Blood for Dracula*?"

"No," I say.

"Okay, well, you'll have to watch it, because then you'll know exactly what he looked like. He was very pale. He was in a dark suit and he had slicked-down black hair. And he was very creepy, even then."

"Did it seem weird or something? Like, *Why are you at my bedroom door?*"

"No. I just looked up, my eyes got bigger, and I thought, *Hello.* He just introduced himself and he turned around and walked back out."

"Did Richard cause any trouble on the street?"

"I don't recall any trouble. Only a few people that I know of actually had ever been over to his house."

Sweat drips off my nose onto my yellow notepad, smudging the ink.

"I don't know if this is true," Curtis says, "but they said he had his mother's . . . all his mother's china, he had the dining room table all set up. He had the table all set up like he was expecting guests over, but nobody ever came. Like a state-visit type of thing. It's all laid out, napkins and everything and the wineglasses and all the plates in the right place for a dinner. Usually you don't keep china patterns out like that because they get dusty, so if they were all ready he must have cleaned them every day. It's all I can figure, because I know this area. You have a window open for more than five seconds, you have to go back dusting everything."

Curtis squints at the sun.

"He would make a good horror movie, wouldn't he?" he says. "Just by himself."

Curtis and I laugh. We're the loudest thing in the street.

"His Nationalist Movement," Curtis says, "seemed to be just him."

"So he didn't seem to have any friends?" I ask.

"Didn't know of any, other than his neighbor right across the street. Wendell. It was just Wendell who was his friend. Wendell's wife didn't want anything to do with him. And his son Bobby hated him."

"Wendell doesn't live there anymore?"

"He's dead."

"Do you know where I could find Bobby?"

"He's dead."

"Did you hear what the killer said," I say, "why he killed Richard?"

"He had various reasons," says Curtis, "and the last thing he said was, 'I did it because he made a pass at me.'"

"More than a pass. He claimed he dropped his pants."

"I guess he thought he could have a good defense if he said that."

"Richard didn't seem like that kind of character to you?"

"Not to me," Curtis says. "And I'm gay."

I ask Curtis if the people around here know he's gay.

"They just don't know," he says. "It never comes up, and I see no reason to tell them. I didn't tell my family till I was in my forties. The worst response was my mother. 'Thank goodness your father is dead.' You don't really like to hear that kind of response."

Curtis laughs and laughs.

I tell Curtis people think Vincent will get a tough sentence because Rankin County is so tough on law and order.

"In their own way," he says.

"What do you mean?"

Curtis doesn't buy Rankin County's good clean Christian routine. He's not talking about racism—it's a place of phonies and hucksters, turning up to church on Sunday and bootlegging Monday. That's its roots, Curtis says. That's its origin story.

I ask him if he'll agree to a snap, for the photo section of the book.

"Sure. My ex may see it," he says, hope in his eyes.

"When did you break up with him?"

"He broke up with me."

"Yeah, but when, how many years ago, though?"

"I was in my thirties," he says. "We had met in Saudi Arabia. I was with the military. He was from Scotland. It was long-distance, and he met some German. His mother was not happy. She was an old 'Brits against the Germans' type."

"She might have been just not happy with him being gay, maybe," I say.

"No," he says, a little wounded. "She didn't like the guy because he was German. She knew me. She liked me."

He tells me he'll go fetch a photo of his ex.

"Hey, could I use your bathroom?" I ask.

"You picked the wrong place."

"Why is it the wrong place?"

"I have absolutely no money. The water's cut off, electricity, phone, gas. I don't have a bathroom to offer you."

He tells me to go see Mrs. Ruby Yates, second from the end of the street. She'll have some Richard stories. And a bathroom. I walk off with a strange feeling tingling through me. I realize Curtis isn't the only one growing old, alone in his grandparents' old place. There's also that guy back in Melbourne.

Mrs. Ruby Yates

Mrs. Ruby Yates is just a nose. A streak of sun lights it up. The rest of her stands in the shadows of her half-opened door.

"I don't know anything I could tell you about him. I mean, every-body on the street knew him, but that was it. He sort of stayed to him-self," says the nose.

I ask Mrs. Yates if there is anything she knew about Richard.

"He did not have a neatly kept yard," the nose confides. "He would let the grass get pretty high before he would get out and cut it. *But he would always cut his own grass.*" She clearly wants me to understand something here. "So the black boy doing yard work at his other house—why was he hired? When I heard that, I said, well, that just don't make sense. Because Richard would always let the grass get high, but he'd al-ways get out and cut it himself."

She tells me I should speak to Tommy Strickland. He has the maroon car parked in front of the green house.

I don't ask if I can use her bathroom.

Tommy Strickland

The five kittens sunbaking in Tommy Strickland's front yard are either adorable or feral, I can't figure out which. There's also a wind chime that won't tingle because the spiders have strangled it with spiderwebs.

Tommy's black-and-gray beard sort of matches the web-covered wind chime.

"I need to go to the store in a minute," Tommy says, shooing a cat from the bonnet of his maroon car. "But yeah, I mean, you know, he was a peculiar person. It's hard to explain."

Fifty-two years ago, Tommy was pushed up and down Sunset Terrace in a stroller. And he's still here, with his own family in the house behind the kittens. Tommy knew Richard. "He was a super nice guy. And to be honest, too, he tried to do recruiting with young men."

"Oh really?" I say, fishing for whether this was recruiting for the Nationalists or recruiting for sex.

"He knew all the kids in the neighborhood. And once we reached a certain age, fourteen or fifteen, he would start tryin' to pump the racist stuff into us, you know?"

Hovering a meter from Tommy is a tanned man without a shirt. All of him droops except his big, taut, spherical belly. It's really quite impressive and hard not to ogle. I ask the owner of the belly who he is.

His cheeks turn pink and bashful, like my Dictaphone is a bit Hollywood and he's not sure he deserves the attention.

"Hee-hee, all right," he says, "I'm his nephew."

"My nephew, James Drew," says Tommy.

James is forty-nine and left Sunset Terrace moons ago. He returned just four days ago to crash on his uncle's couch.

"Did it seem like Richard was a predator when you were growing up?" I ask Tommy.

"Nah, nah, nah," he says, "not when he approached me. He would just be talkin' racist stuff, just to see how you would be back to him; you know, he would play off that. And if you said, 'Yeah, I hate fuckin' niggers,' oh, well, he'd be, 'Okay then, well here, take this pamphlet.' He always had his literature with him."

James Drew cools his desk-globe belly with a beer bottle. A tender red blotch of skin glows below the bottle. James catches me staring at the blotch.

"Yeah, my stepdaddy stabbed me," James Drew says.

I'm not sure what to say to that, but perhaps the reference to knives emboldens me to ask, "Did you know Richard?"

"I was younger, but I remember who he was," James says. "He'd been in jail, too."

"What?" I yip.

"He'd been to jail, too," James says.

"He'd been in jail? What for?" I say.

"Sexual predator."

"Really?" I ask, confused. In my long nights spooling through gossip about Richard on the Internet, I read that Richard was a Jew, a pedophile, and an FBI agent. But nothing about jail. And for being a predator? Is this just gossip he's heard? "How do you know?"

"I was in jail," James says. "When he was there."

"You were in jail with him? What year?"

He turns to Tommy. "When did I go to treatment? '05? '06?"

"Yeah," says Tommy.

"Wow," I say.

"The day, it were really hush-hush. The only way I knew him was 'cause I seen him here in Sunset Terrace when I was young. In the jail he recognized who I was. And he talked to me. He got out within the hour. I mean, he had good lawyers and all that. Got him out of jail and nobody there talked about it."

"I've never been to prison before," I say. "Are you all in the same area or in different cells?"

"I was in a holding cell. Where they book you. They don't separate you when you first come in."

"And what did you say when you spoke to him?" I ask.

"I just said, 'How you doin'?' He mentioned he was in some deep crap." James laughs. "He said that they had got him because one of the boys in the neighborhood said something to the parents. About his advance to him. And I said, 'Well, did you?' And of course he denied it. He said, 'I been set up. I have a lot of enemies.'"

James was released fourteen days later. He flicked through the papers. Richard was supposed to be a big deal. His arrest should have been a big deal. But nothing in the papers.

James was friends with a turnkey at Rankin County Jail. The turnkey is the guard who opens and shuts the doors. Next time he caught up with her, he brought up Richard. Orders came down from the top to let him out, she told him.

"What does 'orders came down from the top' mean?" I ask James. "The jailer? The sheriff? The DA?"

"Something like that would have to come from the governor," says James.

James doesn't know if it was a white kid or a black kid who made the complaint against Richard.

"And you never talked to him afterward?"

"No, never seen him again."

"And why were you in jail?" I ask.

James says he lost his mind. He had found himself darting through a forest at night, in Terry, Mississippi, following three days gorging on drugs. He smashed on a woman's back door, not knowing where he was. The woman telephoned his mother and stepfather, who drove out to the woods and picked up James, then forty-two years old. That night his stepfather slapped him about the ears and called him a fuckup, so James beat him until his head bruised purple. The stepfather telephoned Rankin County police.

James says he accidentally snapped an officer's wrist in the arrest, so they walloped him behind the police car before driving him to Rankin County Jail.

I'm not sure what to make of James's story about Richard now that I know this one.

"I knew a lot of Klan people when I was growin' up. I never become one because I guess kind of I never fed into the hatred part of it. But a black guy's sayin' that he was a predator toward him—that's BS to me. If you knew how much Richard hated blacks, you'd know it made no sense."

But inside (finally, a bathroom!), Tommy Strickland's wife has another idea. We talk in the shaggy living room, where there are several more cats and a daughter.

"If he was a child molester," Mrs. Strickland says, handing me an iced tea, "and if he did target black kids, to me, that's just—I'm real analytical—that's the ultimate insult to you. *I'm gonna rape you and I'm going to hurt you.*"

"So he hates blacks so much, he's going to rape one?" I ask. That was Vallena Greer's angle, too. (Two women, I note.)

"That's the ultimate—to be raped, man or woman—it's the ultimate degradation. *I'm more powerful than you.*"

I drift for three more hours through Sunset Terrace, ping-ponging from home to home. The cement burns through to my feet. I have to wipe the sweat from my face before each bell-ring so I don't look like a sexual deviant/drug addict when the door opens up. As I talk with people, something sneaks into my brain. The Internet commenters, the black and white podcasters, all bluster about Richard's misshapen sexuality. Yet here I stand in Richard's actual world. And none of the young boys in this world—Curtis Rumfelt, Tommy Strickland, James Drew, and others—think Richard was hitting on them, nor that he was a sexual predator in general. They mostly thought him odd or creepy, but not in that particular way.

James Drew's Arrest

In the Rankin County circuit clerk's office, I slide over a sheet of paper with the name *James Drew* neatly written on it.

The clerk punches his name into her computer. She says not only is there no arrest record, there's no James Drew in the system at all.

I'm stumped. Why would James make the story up? Or is he confusing Rankin County Jail with some other holding cell? Pearl, Richland, and Flowood are all towns in Rankin County with police stations and no doubt holding cells.

I call Mark, the attorney I met outside the district attorney's office. I've been calling him whenever I hit a wall. He tells me that around the corner from the circuit clerk's office is the justice clerk's office. If James Drew's case never made it to court, the record of his arrest might be tucked away there.

I duck around the corner.

The clerk here is serving a woman who looks so much like my mother that my head sloshes with disorientation. The woman has big, watery blue eyes. The clerk is sorting out with her when she is going to surrender herself to prison.

My frightened mother drifts out of the office.

The clerk punches in James Drew's name. Soon a printer starts bleating in the corner. She snatches the printout and pushes it over the counter.

James Drew looks up at me, miserable. A cloud of cotton wool is taped to his head. He holds up a board with his name and prisoner number. James was incarcerated in Rankin County Jail when he told me he was.

I tell the clerk I'd like to look up another name: Richard Barrett. He would have been pulled into jail the same night as James Drew.

The clerk punches in *Richard Barrett*. I breathe in and out.

The printer in the corner of the room does not bleat.

There is no arrest record for Richard Barrett, she says. There's no *Richard Barrett* in the system at all.

Richard disappears again.

Sherrie McGee

And it's not just Richard who's disappeared.

I told the McGees when I visited that I was hunting for Richard's book, *The Commission*. Today, Vincent's sister Sherrie called me out of the blue and asked if I'd found it. She wanted to read about the strange man her brother had killed.

So there I was for a second time on the couch at the McGees', lending Sherrie my copy. Sherrie started talking about Vincent.

"You don't know nothing!" Tina shouted at Sherrie from another room. "You come in here!"

Sherrie left the living room. A muffled screaming match pounded through the wall, and Sherrie returned.

"She thinks it's not good if we talk," Sherrie said. "It'll get Vincent in more trouble. I think talking can only be good. Vincent can't get in any more trouble, and people should know it was self-defense."

Tina hollered again.

"Call me later," Sherrie said.

I sat in the diner area of the Texaco Outpost in Pearl nursing a chicken drumstick and rang Sherrie an hour later.

"Can I speak to Sherrie?"

"Not here," said Tina.

"Do you know—"

"She left. She doesn't live here."

"Do you have a new number?"

"No, she just got up and left."

"Do you have an address?"

"No."

Tina Again

I watch again my Flip camera interview with Tina McGee. Her scared eyes. My nosy questions. Her *Yes, sirs*. It's wincey on the page. But it wasn't like that in person. She liked me. She said I could come back.

The Black Bar

Earnest McBride has taken me to a bar by the Mississippi River in Vicksburg. I've driven Earnest to Vicksburg several times when he wanted to see his girlfriend.

"I'm not going to lie, I hate this guy," he says, referring to the owner. "He clears two million a year at this bar, but he'd have to spend five hundred thousand dollars on alimony all over America."

"Is that why you hate him?"

"No," Earnest says. "My mother and brother—he's a minister, he doesn't have a church at the moment, so he's sleeping at my house—they were big in the civil rights movement. And he says my brother made out of town with money collected for the movement. He is a damn liar."

Earnest sips his drink and delivers the unfortunate news that Tina McGee has cooled on me. She thinks I'm out to make her look bad. She's warned her circle of family and friends not to speak to me. Has she warned Vincent? Earnest says he'll write a profile on me for the *Jackson Advocate* to make me look respectable to the black community. That might help turn Tina around, he says.

Earnest has really been on my side ever since he saw me on YouTube in blackface for one of my documentaries. One night I picked up the phone. "Ha! Ha! Ha! You, you, you!" he screamed for ages.

Right after pranking Richard, I had gone on an intentionally clumsy mission to experience life as a black man in America, with convincing prosthetics. I sermonized at a black church and did black speed dating. Now, when we stop for gas and Earnest sees friends, he tells them about my black man adventure and quotes lines from the sermon.

This vodka is stinging my gums.

"I rang the Edgar Ray Killen prison," I tell Earnest. "But they just said they don't allow the media anywhere. Is that always true?"

The prisons in other states have paperwork you can fill out, so they can then turn you down. Not in Mississippi. There's not even a process by which you can be rejected. Really, I'm thinking about Vincent and how I'll get to him.

"They don't allow it," Earnest tells me. "Under the Constitution, the prisoners have a right to be interviewed. To express themselves. One of the Scott sisters was able to do a full hour radio interview from inside the prison. Since that time they just shut it off. In fact, they took away all the cell phones. Prisoners had cell phones they were buying from the guards—contraband."

It's one a.m., and Earnest says we should crash at his sister's in Northern Jackson so we don't have to drive all the way back downtown. This is the second time I'll be sleeping over in his sister's guest room. She lives in a big suburban home. It seems that on every mantelpiece, cabinet top, and table there's a Bible or book of prayers. There's even one atop the toilet.

It's four days until the trial starts. I'm curious as to how it's going to show Richard. Vince Thornton, Joe McNamee, Precious the Otter, even Richard's sister, Geraldine—I'm hoping they'll all show up in the courtroom.

Every time I feel I've got a hold of Richard, he slides off again. I haven't been able to get any sort of consensus on whether Richard might have made a pass at Vincent, and an aggressive one at that. I wonder whether the people who think Richard was gay are using "gay" as another word for "just suspicious." He was queer, bent, but was he literally homosexual? He was a racist, but was he aggressive enough to threaten Vincent? If Vincent's going to have a defense, Precious and Chokwe need to find the leads I haven't found yet—they need to find other young men whom Richard propositioned. But so far in my journey, it's gay people and those who knew Richard as young men who *don't* think Richard was gay.

I fall asleep in a puffy pink bed next to a teddy bear, reading *God's Promises for Your Every Need*.

6.

THE TRIAL

Homework

R ichard is flesh and blood to me. He doesn't creep me out because I read about him and his murder; he creeps me out because I met him, because I was there. That murdered man put his hand on my shoulder.

But who's Vincent? The McGees have cut me off, so I'll need to start my homework elsewhere. Vincent wasn't a public figure like Richard, but he had his archive, too.

The Criminal History of Vincent McGee

The Rankin County circuit clerk's office is a peaceful place to spend some time. The staff members, all female, glide around gracefully and quietly, like it's a nunnery. Leather-bound marriage records, winding back to the early 1800s, fill up one wall of the office.

A black guy in a prison jumpsuit wanders through. None of the office nuns bat an eyelash, so I assume he's not on the lam, it's some rehabilitation thing.

Open in front of me is a red folder that contains the criminal history of Vincent McGee.

This particular Ballad of Vincent McGee begins six years ago. Seventeen-year-old Vincent has just been arrested and pulled in front of a grand jury. A grand jury is a bunch of locals who are phoned up whenever the DA wants and told to drive down to the courthouse to decide if the facts of a case, as presented by the DA, merit a trial. The defendant doesn't get a lawyer to argue back, nor can he argue back himself. So these are the facts of the case according to one side.

RANKIN COUNTY GRAND JURY SUMMARY SHEET

Vincent McGee is charged with: two counts, simple assault on law enforcement officers.

Facts of the case: While on duty at Rankin County Juvenile Detention Center, two officers had reason to approach the cell of McGee. This was because of McGee's behavior inside the cell. McGee understood that he was to be released on this day and no one had come to pick him up. Upon being told that his mother had been notified to pick him up but had failed to do so, McGee became very unruly. Upon opening the cell door, McGee came out of the cell and began to hit both officers with his fist. Because of this behavior, McGee was placed under arrest and charged with two counts of assault on a police officer. During this time McGee threatened both officers and promised them a shot to the head upon his release from jail. He was then transported from the Juvenile Detention Center to Rankin County Jail.

The grand jury agrees with the DA: Vincent needs to go to trial.

Why was Vincent in the juvenile detention center in the first place? The file does not say. Vincent secures an appearance bond of ten thousand dollars from the AAA Bonding Company and walks out on bail. When Vincent doesn't show up for his trial, the court issues a warrant for his arrest and an order for the AAA Bonding Company to cough up ten thousand dollars.

One month later, Vincent has been found. He stands before the judge in the Rankin County Courthouse and pleads guilty to striking the officers. The district attorney asks for, and the judge accepts: *Five years in penitentiary. Four years suspended. One year to serve.* Vincent is pulled into a van and driven to the Central Mississippi Correctional Facility.

For some reason not in the file, Vincent doesn't serve even a year. I know this because eleven months after that van drove him off to prison, Vincent is a free enough man to be driving a truck when arrested again.

ARREST DOCKET

Offender was arrested and charged with grand larceny, giving false information, careless driving, public drunkenness, no driver's license, and no insurance.

Despite these multiple charges, by the time Vincent, now nineteen, is pulled before the judge in the courthouse again, the only charge the district attorney's office is pursuing is the grand larceny.

CHARGE SHEET

Vincent McGee did willfully, unlawfully, and feloniously violate the State Laws to wit: did take, steal, and carry away $300 in Mexican Pesos, $200 in Mexican Paper Dollars, and one silver ring with a value of $300, property of Jamie Reyes.

So this is the Mexican money Tina mentioned, which she denied Vincent stole. I write down *Jamie Reyes*. Rankin County is a small world, I think to myself, eyeing the signatures on the court documents. The lawyer, Vicky Williams, who defended Vincent in the assault case two years before, is now assistant district attorney and prosecuting Vincent.

The judge hits Vincent with ten years in jail, nine years suspended. But the four years for the assault that were suspended before are reinstated, so Vincent is condemned to five years in jail.

Vincent is pulled into a van and driven to the Central Mississippi Correctional Facility.

Vincent doesn't serve five years. I know this because three years later he had a knife drawn on Richard Barrett.

How the World Works, According to Me

I blabbed to a science reporter friend about Vincent McGee. She instinctively pulled together what she knew of the human brain and chemical imbalances to explain why Vincent killed.

Science is not where my mind instinctively goes to explain how the world works. This is where I go: Family is everything.

Without my family, I would have been lost. In high school, I was an awful, tangle-headed student. I would have dropped out of school had my mum and dad not forced me to stay. Later, my dad told me he thought I'd end up like the weird homeless guy in the *Seven Up!* documentaries. Hell, even after I completed Year Twelve, my mother had to remind me, "Don't you have the journalism entrance exam tomorrow?" If she hadn't said that sentence, I would have forgotten to turn up and all the good things that tumbled from that would never have happened.

When I chatted up girls at university, I had a near perfect strike rate of guessing whether the girl grew up with her father or not. I remember my non-Jewish friends coming to my family's Friday night Shabbos dinners. They'd watch my family light the candles, cut the challah, say the prayers, and eat together. Most would respond with a version of: *Why doesn't my family do something like this? Why do I go out drinking on Fridays?*

When I was thirty-one, my mother died out of the blue from a heart attack. It left me disoriented for years. I became obsessed with the writing of prison doctor Theodore Dalrymple, who convinced me the collapse of the family is the collapse of the person.

This is what I brought in my bag to Mississippi. This is the prism I look at this crime through. My brain pulls in everything that confirms this is the story of how the world works.

That's why I keep looking for Richard's sister. That's why my mind keeps rolling back to the facts of the case on the Grand Jury Summary Sheet, describing Vincent in juvenile detention. *No one had come to pick him up. Upon being told that his mother had been notified to pick him up but had failed to do so, McGee became very unruly.* What would be different now if Tina McGee had picked up Vincent that day? Upset that his mother hadn't come to pick him up, he assaulted the officers. And striking the officers rolled him out of juvenile detention into the adult prison system. And from there things kept tumbling down the hill. If Tina had picked Vincent up that day, would Richard be alive? What would the story be if Vincent hadn't had an absent father?

My fingers peel over another page in the red folder and arrive at the killing of Richard Barrett.

Richard Barrett

Precious the Otter becomes present in the paperwork four months after Vincent's arrest, when he takes over the case from the white public defender. Precious files a document telling the court Vincent will be pleading not guilty to the murder of Richard Barrett.

Two months later, another document is filed with the court. But this one has not been typed up by Precious Martin's law firm. This one has been written by hand, with childish strokes and sprinkled with capital *N*'s where there should be little *N*'s and *a*'s where there should be *an*'s. This one demands from the DA:

> All forensic evidence and laboratory results
> All DNA and fingerprint results

All expert witness statements

Any evidence that is in the favorable light of the defendant

The signature squiggled below is not that of Precious Martin, but that of Vincent McGee.

The hand continues on its way for ten more pages and, among other things, wants Mr. McGee's criminal history to be suppressed.

Surely Vincent can't have come up with this himself. Could Precious have dictated it to him? Or written it himself? Why is it not typed?

My fingertips come to the last sheet of paper in the red folder, and I let out a gasp so sharp, the office nuns turn and look.

Two days ago Precious Martin quit. And Vincent is due in court three days from now.

MOTION TO WITHDRAW AS COUNSEL OF RECORD

That Precious Martin wishes to withdraw as counsel.

That Defendant disagrees with Precious Martin's legal advice.

That the crime alleged is of the nature that the death penalty may be applied. Precious Martin has never defended anyone in a matter where the death penalty was applicable, nonetheless where the death penalty was sought, and as such, he does not employ the requisite knowledge, complexity, nor specialization to adequately represent Defendant to that end.

That it would be in the best interest of Defendant if Precious Martin was released as Defendant's attorney of record in this matter.

I skid out of the clerk's office, crouch by a potted plant in the hall, and phone Chokwe.

"I was going through the Vincent McGee file," I tell him, "and two days ago Precious filed a motion to withdraw as counsel."

Chokwe says nothing. The potted plant is making more noise than Chokwe.

"Hello?" I say.

"Precious has filed a motion to withdraw?" Chokwe asks, confused. "Okay, all right, well, that's something you have to talk to Precious about. He has not told me anything about that. I don't know anything about that."

"Oh, really?"

"Look, let me be real clear!" he shouts, like I'm out to get him. "I was asked to do this because it's the kind of case I usually try to help people with. I'm more than willing to help. But at the same time, I made it real clear at the time I was asked to come on this case that I could not handle it by myself. Mr. McGee, he don't have a lot of money at all. So our commitment to the case was with the help of another lawyer. If another lawyer is not on the case, then we're going to have to reconsider that."

I fumble through my little black address book for Vallena Greer's number. This is the first the head of the Vincent McGee Defense Fund has heard of Precious Martin's withdrawal, too.

"Oh, boy!" she says. "Well, as long as Chokwe is on the case it'll be okay."

I suck in a wince.

"Maybe Precious did not like Chokwe's style," Vallena says. "Because Chokwe is the best. There is no better. O. J. Simpson wanted Chokwe, but he was busy on another case with one of the Rodney King kids. Chokwe could have made a lot of money from OJ. But it's not about the money. For him, it's about giving poor the same opportunity as rich people."

I tickle the lump in my throat and mutter the news.

"Chokwe said he only agreed to do the case because he thought he'd have resources," I tell her. "And with Precious leaving, that's the main resource gone. So he'll have to rethink his involvement."

"Oh, boy!" Vallena says. "I'll have to see what's going on. With the

Scott sisters' case, we've been keeping a low profile, but we might have to go full steam ahead. I was meant to be on a civil rights call this morning with Chokwe, but I was at my Bible reading and forgot!"

Maybe the case then goes back to the original white lawyer appointed by the court, a man named Mike Scott. Last time I called Mike, he'd pretty much washed his hands of the whole affair. This time, I ask him why Vincent might have disagreed with Precious's legal advice, but Mike is not telling me what he knows. He tells me if Vincent has lost his lawyers, it is indeed likely the court will flick the case back to him. And that the trial will be delayed several months. I ring the DA, Michael Guest, but he's as elusive as Mike Scott.

A couple of days later Jerry Mitchell rubs in my face that he can get what I cannot, with an update on the case in the *Clarion-Ledger*. He has squeezed two crucial developments from the men I called. Michael Guest tells Jerry he will no longer pursue the death penalty. Instead he will go for life without parole, which means Vincent will die behind bars. He doesn't offer a reason for his change of heart/strategy. And Mike Scott hints that Vincent may claim self-defense at trial.

Mississippi Burnout

Three days later—when the trial was meant to begin—everyone's still in lockdown, and I'm out in the cold.

Eddie Thompson, the Rankin County jailer, agrees to meet me outside the Rankin County Jail. The jail is connected to the courthouse by a caged walkway. Straightaway Eddie winces at my shirt. It's cream and patterned with tiny green Don Quixotes and windmills. No one would blink on a Melbourne tram, but here I might as well have minced in wearing suspenders and a corset. I ask Eddie if I can tag along when the McGees come visit Vincent. "No," he says, and shivers at my shirt like it's going to pinch his bottom. He walks off.

Had Eddie said yes, I would still have had to hustle, with Tina cutting me off, too.

I call Vicky Williams, who represented Vincent in court after he thumped the officers at the juvenile detention center. I want to find out what Vincent did to be dragged into juvenile detention in the first place. But she says that juvenile records are sealed and she's not allowed to tell me.

One of the investigators in the case says I can drop by for a chat. Then he calls back and says the sheriff found out, and now he's not allowed to see me.

No one, and no search directory, will tell me where Vincent's dad is hidden, and I'm out of ideas on how to find Richard's sister. I've gotten nowhere with Vince Thornton and I haven't even tried Joe McNamee again.

Even Jim Giles e-mails me, telling me his mother doesn't want me coming by the house.

Jedis & Juggalos

With the trial now officially delayed for several months, I move on to other work due. I skip town to film a short documentary, *Jedis & Juggalos*. I hunt down Americans who fuse religion to pop culture. Mahmoud lives in an octagonal home in Oregon and sees Muslim messages in *Star Wars*. Jason built a church in Maryland bonding God with the teachings of the Insane Clown Posse. Bill runs an exorcism ministry in Arizona that expels devils brought on by reading Harry Potter and Twilight.

I tell all these men about my true crime adventure. With just the mention of "black man" and "Mississippi," all assume Vincent has been unfairly incarcerated by a bunch of racist yahoos. Mississippi really has quite the reputation. The Sufi Jedi, the Juggalo priest, and the exorcist agree there's something strange about those Mississippians.

Months Later, Two and a Half Weeks Before the Trial

Four days ago, I moved back to Mississippi. I'm not at the motel in Jackson anymore. I've moved into a gated apartment complex in Rankin County to be closer to the trial. I'm stretched out on a lounge chair under the gazebo by the pool. The white columns that prop up Southern mansions have been shrunk and prop up this gazebo, too. The humid summer is now in full swing. My eyes sting from the sweat and sunscreen.

I drove past that billboard at the airport again. YES, WE CAN READ. A FEW OF US CAN EVEN WRITE. Last time, I didn't know what to make of it, I hadn't been here long enough. Now I know it speaks of the state's defensive worldview. I try to think of another place that would greet tourists with a paranoid and passive-aggressive accusation. *You think we're stupid? Is that what you're thinking? Screw you!* I can't. Oh, and I checked. Mississippi has the lowest literacy rate in the United States.

The *Clarion-Ledger* is inking up my hands once more and telling me what I missed while off chasing Jedis. James Ford Seale, finally jailed in 2007 for the 1964 killings of two black teenagers, has died in prison. The Scott sisters, with a release conditioned on Gladys donating her kidney to Jamie, have found out they're too fat for the operation.

A small child in a bathing suit walks by and laughs at my face. His mother tells me I have a *Clarion-Ledger* ink mustache streaked under my nose. I wipe my face with a towel, and my phone trembles on my thigh.

It's District Attorney Michael Guest returning my call. I wanted an update on his preparations. Lucky I phoned. Michael says there may be no trial in two and a half weeks. There may be no trial at all.

Michael says tomorrow morning Vincent will be unlocked from his cell. He'll be led across the walkway that connects Rankin County Jail to the courthouse. He will stand before the judge. And if Vincent follows through on what he has said he'll do, he'll be pleading guilty to killing Richard Barrett.

I'm thrown. On the one hand, it looks like finally I'll see Vincent

McGee in the flesh. Maybe I can pass him a note or something? That's good. That's terrific. On the other hand, if he pleads guilty, there's no trial. Don't I need one of those? Lawyers treading back and forth in front of the witness box, asking sharp questions? Emotional men and women, blurting the secrets of Vincent McGee and Richard Barrett?

The Plea

The ceiling lights bounce off the bald patches in a courtroom filled with male-pattern baldness. The security guard has no hair at all, his shiny globe poking in and out of a side door, waiting for things to start.

We're finally in court. Soon, Vincent will be here.

The two white Mikes—DA Michael Guest and Vincent's lawyer, Mike Scott—laugh with each other near the side door, too. Is that from where Vincent will appear?

I crane my neck and scan the pews. Vincent will not be the only person pulled before the judge today, so it's impossible to tell who, if anyone, is here for him. His mother, sister, and brother are not. Nor his stepfather, nor Vallena Greer from the Vincent McGee Defense Fund.

Is anyone here for Richard? There's a shorn-headed man in an army uniform that's not one from the actual Army. Is he? Is Richard's sister here?

A dozen lawyers buzz like atoms in front of the judge's bench (presently judge-less). I pass time deciding who has a crush on whom.

I'm squeezed between Tim Hall, from the *Rankin County News*, and Jerry Mitchell, from the *Clarion-Ledger*. I guess Jerry Mitchell's here for Richard, in a way, for one last article.

Tim points his old finger at one of the buzzing atoms.

"That's the son of Ross Barnett," Tim says, "the old governor. You know James Meredith?"

James Meredith was the first black person to register for the University of Mississippi, and Governor Ross Barnett drafted legislation specifically to keep him out. President John F. Kennedy, fed up with Mississippi, ordered troops to accompany James to his first day of class, to ensure he got a seat without being lynched.

That buzzing atom isn't the great-grandson of Governor Ross Barnett, or his grandson. He is his son. In Mississippi, the incomprehensible past feels just one remove away.

There's a side door on either side of the judge's bench, and Mike Scott ducks in and out of them like a Marx brother, until the bailiff comes out of the stage-right side door and says, "All rise! The Circuit Court of Rankin County is now in session. The honorable William E. Chapman III is presiding."

Judge Chapman whooshes in from the same stage-right door, wrapped in his black robe. His feet cannot be seen, so he appears to float across the floor. As he sits, air puffs up his black robe.

"Thank you," Judge Chapman says. "Whoever's cell phone it is, get it off!"

Judge Chapman reads though a roll call of lawyers like it's school. One lawyer is absent, and Judge Chapman grouses.

"Her grandma died," explains a lawyer.

"All right," says Judge Chapman. "We're on 22157—*State v. Vincent V. McGee.*"

Chains chink from the darkness behind the side door stage left.

The shackled feet of Vincent McGee wiggle themselves into the courtroom.

Vincent's suave face pulls into the light. His eyelids hang heavily. Satan's beard pokes from his chin. A thin, wiry mustache frizzes out. On his cheekbone drips a tattoo of a teardrop. The teardrop heads toward what first looks like a blemish, but is a blotch of a butterfly tattoo. Beneath it all he still projects something urbane, like he could hang in the Rat Pack with Dean Martin and Sammy Davis, Jr.

Vincent *chink-chink-chink*s across the courtroom carpet to the lectern facing Judge Chapman. A security guard adjusts the microphone for

Vincent's plump lips. His hands aren't cuffed together; they're cuffed separately to a chain wrapped around his waist. This chain pulls in a baggy yellow jumpsuit, revealing a slender young man.

"If you'll raise your right hand, please, sir," Judge Chapman says. (So that's why Vincent's hands aren't cuffed together.) "Do you solemnly swear and affirm that the testimony you will give will be the truth, the whole truth, and nothing but the truth, so help you God?"

"Murble," says Vincent.

"Pardon?" says the judge.

"Yessir," says Vincent.

"Do you understand," says the judge, "that you are now under oath and your answers will be sworn answers under penalty of perjury?"

"Yessir," say Vincent's plump lips.

"You were born on February 17, 1988?"

"Yessir."

"Your social security number is . . ."

The last three digits are 666, matching his devil's beard.

"You completed eight years of school and obtained a GED certificate?"

"Yessir."

"Are you under the influence of any drugs or alcohol?"

"No, sir."

"Have you ever been treated for any mental illness or disorder?"

"No, sir."

Judge Chapman may have rolled through this a thousand times with a thousand men in colored jumpsuits, but he sounds stern and emotionally present, gravely conscious of where Vincent's words will lead him.

Vincent is harder to work out. All we can see is his back. He rolls his square shoulders now and then like a boxer warming up. Or maybe like a crazy person on the train. Lifting my butt from the pew and craning my neck, I can sometimes make out a slice of his face. He seems to be staring into the distance even when looking at the judge. When he drops his eyes to his shackled feet, his long, feminine eyelashes bat up and down.

"Did you read and sign your petition to enter a guilty plea?" says the judge.

"Yessir," says Vincent.

"As count one: You did, without authority, willfully, unlawfully kill Richard Barrett, a human being, without malice, in the heat of passion but in a cruel or unusual manner by the use of a dangerous weapon and not in necessary self-defense. Do you understand those elements?"

Insomuch as neck muscles can talk, his suddenly sinewed neck suggests he's agitated with this description.

"Yessir," says Vincent. So maybe Mike Scott's hint that Vincent would argue self-defense was part of the same game as Michael Guest's death penalty. The negotiations are done.

"With respect to count two, those elements are: You did willfully, unlawfully, maliciously, and feloniously set fire to a dwelling house—the property of Richard Barrett. Do you understand those elements?"

"Yessir."

Judge Chapman moves to Vincent's third crime.

"You did willfully, unlawfully, feloniously, knowingly, intentionally, and burglariously break and enter into the dwelling house of Richard Barrett, with the intent to commit the crime of arson therein. Do you understand those elements?"

"Yessir."

"Do you understand that you have a right to a trial by jury," says the judge, "and each of the twelve jurors must be convinced beyond a reasonable doubt of your guilt before you can be found guilty and sentenced?"

"Yessir."

"Should you choose to go to trial," says the judge, "you would have the right to confront and cross-examine witnesses who would testify against you and the right to subpoena witnesses to testify on your behalf. Do you understand those rights?"

Vincent pauses from his reflexive *yessirs*. His eyes take a peek at the heavens. His shoulders rise and lower as he breathes in and out. He looks at the judge, this time really looking, not staring into infinity.

He squeezes a soft and rueful *yessir* from his lips.

"Do you understand I can impose the maximum sentence on each crime?" says the judge. "That is, twenty years on the first one, twenty years on the second one, and twenty-five years on the third one. All of those consecutive would mean you'd be sentenced to a term of sixty-five years in the penitentiary."

"Yessir."

Judge Chapman twists to District Attorney Michael Guest.

"What's your recommendation?" Judge Chapman asks.

Michael says his office is recommending the maximum, sixty-five years.

Judge Chapman twists back to Vincent.

"Is that the recommendation you expected to hear?"

"Yessir."

"At this point," says the judge, "it's not too late to stop the hearing. But it will be if I accept your guilty plea. And I want to be certain that you want to plead guilty. Do you want to plead guilty?"

"Yessir."

And that's that. Vincent is sentenced to sixty-five years in the Mississippi Department of Corrections.

Vincent's head droops forward like he's beginning to deflate.

"The court costs, fees, and assessments in the amount of $846 will be waived," says the judge. "Anything further?"

"No, sir," says Michael Guest.

"No, Your Honor," says Mike Scott.

"All right. Good luck, Mr. McGee."

A sorry-looking Vincent exits stage right, disappearing into the shadow behind the door.

The Press

For his first court appearance, when I was still in Melbourne, the police tightened Vincent into a bulletproof vest. This was to be Rankin County's trial of the century: Perhaps a Klansman would stand up from the pew and pull a pistol from his sock. No bulletproof vest was strapped on Vincent today.

For his first appearance, CNN, MSNBC, and the other national news channels planted their tripods on every square foot of carpet in the courthouse. The party is thinner today: Tim and Jerry from the two local newspapers, an Associated Press stringer, and true crime writer John Safran. A local TV crew stumbles in at the end, when it is all over.

We bunch around District Attorney Guest in the marble hall outside the courtroom.

"Sixty-five years is a long time," I say. "So what was his motivation for accepting that?"

"You know," says Michael, "if he would've gone to trial and if the jury would have convicted him of capital murder, he would've had no chance to ever get out of jail. With this plea, I would say it would be highly unlikely that Mr. McGee will ever leave the state penitentiary, but he would be eligible for parole at roughly seventy-five years old. And so, if he is in good enough health and is able to live that long, then he would have a chance to, you know, walk the streets a free man again."

My brain kicks around this explanation. It doesn't make any sense to me. How could Vincent have been persuaded that the best he could hope for was to get out of jail at seventy-five? Why wouldn't he work up his defense and go to trial? The death penalty had been taken off the table months ago, so that wasn't hanging over him as a threat. But perhaps it had served its purpose as a bargaining tool.

I recall what local lawyer Mark told me. The chance of Vincent's being acquitted by a jury was slim, but not the maddest thought. A jury in a conservative county could feel sympathy for a man—even a black man—they felt was repelling a gay sexual advance.

"Was it important for him," I ask Michael, "that he didn't want things to be flushed out in the trial, in the public view?"

"You know," says Michael with a smile, "I would say that that was probably a factor that went into his consideration—based on all of the circumstances surrounding this."

I rattle that around my head. Did Vincent McGee just take sixty-five years rather than have it revealed in court that something gay went on between him and Richard? I've been focused on whether Richard might have made an advance. But not what that advance, if it happened, would have meant to Vincent.

I walk out the front of the courthouse. Looking back, I watch the door to Courtroom Two. After Vincent was sentenced, the press left the room, but no one else. Everyone in those pews was there for some other case. No one had turned up for Vincent. No one had turned up for Richard.

Plan B

So much for the big set piece. I was counting on the trial to settle the questions of what Richard Barrett was thinking that night, and what Vincent was thinking.

Calm down, Safran. Earnest didn't mope off when the president of the Confederacy, Jefferson Davis, slipped from his fingers. He ran up the staircase and got him.

So. Plan B.

The district attorney's office has already done a lot of the work. Subpoenas had already been sent to witnesses, and if they're not going to give their evidence in the courtroom, maybe they'll give it to me. The subpoenas were filed at the Rankin County clerk's office. The name *Wayne Humphreys* was on the first subpoena. He's one of the investigators. *Adele Lewis* was on another. She did the autopsy. And I've got my own list of people I want to talk to. I want to know why Vincent was "in the heat of passion"? What had Richard done? Why didn't Vincent want to go to trial?

The Letter

I lick the Cheetos dust off my fingers. I flap my hands to dry them. I don't want Cheetos dust on my keyboard.

Tonight, a white Mississippian preacher crackles from the clock radio in the room.

"The Nazis were formed in a gay bar in Munich!" he says. "This is mainstream history!"

He says Hitler's inner circle was gay. He says his family hosted a German exchange student a few years back. The student told him, "We learn in school that the top Nazis were gay, because we want to learn from history so the Third Reich and the Holocaust never happen again!"

I've been in Mississippi so long, this is the second time I'm hearing him babble this story out. Although last time it was *he* who told the exchange student that the top Nazis were gay and she collapsed, crying, "Why didn't our teachers tell us?"

My hands are now dry. I begin to type.

Vincent McGee
MDOC#: 122412
Current Housing Unit: CMCF R & C TRANSIENT
Institution: CMCF

Post Office Box 88550
3794 Hwy 468
Pearl, MS 39208

Dear Vincent,

I am an Australian writer, writing a book about your case.

Would you be able to place me on your visitors list, so I could meet you?

I've been told you are allowed to fill out a visitors list with ten visitors' names. I've also been told you create this list at Receiving & Classifications.

Please write back to tell me if you have placed me on your visitors list. I have included an envelope, stamp, and paper.

All the best,
John Safran

7.

EVERYBODY TALKS

The Sheriff's Office

nod to the stone Confederate and curve down behind the courthouse to the sheriff's office. It's tucked in the same building as Rankin County Jail. Above me is the walkway in the sky where the prisoners clomp from jail to court.

Vincent is no longer here. After his plea, the van drove him to the enormous Central Mississippi Correctional Facility in Pearl. Not far from Vincent's home, as it happens.

Fourteen sheriffs eyeball me from the wall of the sheriff's office. From sepia Sheriff Harrison (1920–1924) to black-and-white Sheriff Laird (1944–1948) to today's full-color Sheriff Pennington. The air is sticky and the day is nearly over. Everyone here is a little sloppy and giggly, like schoolkids at three o'clock before Christmas break.

Investigators Tim Lawless and Wayne Humphreys are old men with cherub cheeks. When you're this Caucasian, there's nowhere for the burst capillaries to hide. Tim Lawless is a third-generation Mississippi policeman. His father and his grandfather both served in Jackson. Wayne Humphreys is a detective and the local polygraph examiner.

Both were on the McGee case and subpoenaed for the trial that never happened. I don't know why I've ended up with these two men and not some other combination of investigators involved. And I don't know what I'm allowed to ask them.

We sit in the plainest of boardrooms with a polystyrene cup of water each. Tim Lawless pats a pile of folders, then points through the wall.

"That's where we interviewed Vincent. The interview room there."

I say *wow* even though it's just a wall and I can't see the room on the other side.

"Have you checked with him?" Tim chuckles to Wayne.

"Him" is Sheriff Pennington.

"No." Wayne chuckles back.

Tim gets up and returns with the sheriff. He is in his sixties, tall, fit, broad shoulders. In Mississippi the old men have better bodies than the young men, who have succumbed to Xbox and Goldfish crackers and sandwich bread that tastes like cake.

"I'm writing a book on Richard Barrett and Vincent McGee . . ." I fumble out, like a guilty Jew.

The sheriff stares at me blankly.

With my history, with his history, it's like a penguin meeting a giraffe.

". . . and Rankin County and Mississippi," I fumble further.

I tell him about *Race Relations* and Michael Guest and Australia and the book, but it all comes out like a blind man stumbling over rearranged furniture. The sheriff interrupts me.

"Well, you send us three copies," he says, and leaves.

Excellent. I press record on the Dictaphone and point the mic at Tim and Wayne.

"So, what happened?"

What Happened, According to Investigators Tim Lawless and Wayne Humphreys

When they arrived at the scene of the house fire, Tim Lawless, investigator Trip Bayles, and patrol captain Doug Holloway saw a body on the grass, flat on its back. It was basically smoking. The three men rolled the body over and saw what appeared to be numerous stab wounds around the neck and the back area.

"So he was stabbed in the back?" I ask.

"If I remember right, it was in the back." Tim turns to Wayne. "Wasn't it, Wayne? In the neck?"

"It was sixteen times," Wayne says. "Starting at the shoulder and going all the way around his head."

"Oh, gee!" I say. "For some reason, just because I had incomplete information, I assumed it was going to be in the front."

"And Mr. Barrett," Tim continues, "didn't have any clothes on."

"Not even underwear?" I ask.

"He had his underwear. That's all he had on. Just his underwear. It is something we call . . ." Tim stops and herds up his thoughts. "With that many stab wounds and, it appeared to us, someone had intentionally set the body on fire . . . And myself and Captain Holloway—he looked at me and I looked at him—and we basically said, at about the same time, 'That's what I call overkill.' And Captain Holloway said, and I was thinking the same thing, 'This is consistent with a homosexual murder.'"

That's quite the quote. I double-, triple-, quadruple-check the Dictaphone is running.

"I mean, we've seen many murders like this before," Tim says, squaring up the folders in front of him. "Where there's multiple, multiple stab wounds or overkill."

"And mutilation," Wayne says.

"And mutilation," Tim agrees. "And that's consistent sometimes with homosexual murders."

"What does that mean? 'A homosexual murder'? Why would that be different from a non-homosexual murder?"

"I can't explain it," Tim says. "I don't have an answer for that."

"I think they get excited." Wayne takes over. "Or maybe a rage. They get overemotional. You know, there's been lots of times where appendages have been cut off and placed in other parts of the body. And once the person's killed—let's say they shot him—then they shoot them twenty more times, or something like that."

"Could it also be the case," I ask, "where the killer is not the partner or is not a homosexual themselves, but they're in a rage?"

"It could be," says Tim. "It could be a homophobic-type thing. It doesn't mean both parties were homosexual."

I'm a bit confused as to why a first look at a stabbed, burned body would have all this homosexual subtext.

Richard's Body

Tim Lawless opens a cream folder and fans out black-and-white photos of Richard's body.

Richard is lying on a sheet outside his home in his underpants. His arms are stretched above his head. One charred arm and one charred leg. In some photos he's on his back, with a little curve of a belly visible; in others he's on his front. The skin on his back is hard and crispy, like roast chicken skin. Every smear of blood, every drop of water on his body twinkles. Richard is cooling down from the fire, but the sun is heating him up again. My arms and neck goosebump. I met this guy.

A cloth covers his face in some shots, but not in others. His face isn't burned.

"His head was in good shape," Wayne says.

"Except for the hair," says Tim.

When Vincent lit him on fire, he was facedown.

Richard smelled of gasoline.

Wayne says there wasn't much blood on his body. Most of the blood was inside the house, in the kitchen, in the laundry, all the way to the back door. By the time the fire department pulled him out of the house and washed him off with the fire hose, most of the blood had gone.

"How long do you reckon he was burning for?" I ask.

Wayne says no longer than twenty minutes.

"And how did you identify it was Richard?" I say. "Just by his face?"

"Well, we knew he lived there," Tim says. "It was common knowledge that he was a resident in that area. But, you know, we've never really had any complaints, believe it or not, from anybody there. With him being white and living in a predominantly African American neighborhood, he got along with everybody in the neighborhood. Everybody liked him, believe it or not. He was well received there. Kind of felt he lived a double life."

"One final question about the neck," I say. "It's not like his head was falling off or anything?"

"It was not," Tim tells me. "The head was not severed."

"I think that was his intention," Wayne adds. "But he just wasn't good enough to do it. He didn't know how."

"Also, Michael Guest talked about a belt," I say, "around one of his hands?"

"I think he was bound or taped," says Tim, "and had been tied up with that belt."

"Either that," says Wayne, "or he used it to drag him from one spot to the other in the house."

"Why would Vincent want to drag him?" I ask. "Maybe closer to the fire?"

"Vincent moved him from the kitchen to the bedroom," Wayne says.

"And why do you think he did that?"

"I don't know."

If Vincent did drag Richard to the bedroom, he must have later dragged him back to the kitchen, because that's where everyone's telling me—Wayne and Tim included—the body was found. Is it possible they're confusing the bedroom and the kitchen because that might be what would happen in a homosexual murder?

The Welcome Mat

A welcome mat lay at the back doorway. The welcome mat was soaked in blood.

The firemen told Tim, Wayne, and the other investigators it was safe to enter.

Inside the back door was a little laundry area containing a paint tin, a glass bottle of methylated spirits, and on the wall, a framed picture of a unicorn. The laundry floor was glazed in blood.

Blood glazed the kitchen floor, too. A patch in the floor was deeper red, where Richard Barrett had lain for at least ten hours, blood seeping out and blotting into the floorboards. Fireman shoe prints patterned the blood. Tim could make out a streak from this patch to the back door, like one giant paintbrush stroke, where the firemen had dragged Richard out.

Wayne peered down the kitchen, deeper into the home. Vincent had screwed up burning down the house. He'd left the doors and windows shut so there wasn't enough oxygen.

"If he had done it correctly," Wayne says, "he would have opened all the doors, opened some windows, so you'd get a cross blow of air, so it would help with the fire."

Vincent McGee, failed head-severer. Failed evidence-destroyer.

The house was still smoldering. Gray flakes were still alive in the air, most white spaces were grayed by soot, and everywhere smelled of gasoline. Furnishings not burned were waterlogged by the firemen's hose.

"The house was well kept," Wayne says. "If you had walked into it not burned, you wouldn't have known anybody like Richard Barrett, and the views he had, lived there."

"What do you mean?" I ask.

"You know," Wayne says, "you would've expected literature and pictures of people hanging or something in there."

"Or things against black people," Tim says, "or Jewish people."

The kitchen led to a small dining room. A TV tray rested on a coffee table—an unwashed dish and some crumbs of food. Two rooms ran off the dining room, dedicated to a video camera and other recording equipment.

Tim and Wayne brushed past an antique cabinet in the dining room, stocked with china and candelabras, and reached the master bedroom.

"I remember looking in," Tim says. "We looked in the master bedroom and there was a closet. And we opened the door, and the only thing I remember in the closet, hanging on a coat hanger, was a Nazi uniform."

I squeak.

Tim points to his arm.

"With a swastika on there."

"Was it a brown uniform?" I ask.

"If I remember," Tim says, "it was dark Nazi black. Like the Gestapo or the SS."

"If you're going to play," says Wayne, "why not be the king, you know?"

Vincent's Story, According to Tim and Wayne

Vincent slumped in a gray chair, on the other side of the wall, not four meters from where I sit.

To sit in that interview room was to be sealed inside a white cube. A video camera stared down at Vincent from the ceiling as he picked yellow threads from his yellow prison jumpsuit.

"We just talked to him," Tim says. "And told him we pretty much knew what he had done. And probably just after a few minutes, we gave him something to drink. We gave him a soft drink, a soda."

Vincent drank and began to tell his story.

Vincent was not two months out of the state penitentiary and living at his mother's house. "He told us he knew Mr. Barrett when he got out of prison," Tim says. Mr. Barrett had a property, his Nationalist Movement headquarters, an hour's drive away. He and Vincent would go over and keep the lawn cut, and Richard would pay him cash. Apparently this happened several times. On the day of the killing, Vincent had worked all day. Yet, Vincent told Tim bitterly, that day Mr. Barrett had only paid him twenty dollars.

I scribble on my notepad. There's already something different in this version: a much more sustained relationship between Vincent and Richard.

That day, Mr. Barrett dropped off the bitter Vincent at his mother's home.

"If you like," Richard said as Vincent slid out of the big black pickup truck, "tonight you can come back down and get on the computer. You can get on your Facebook account."

At around ten thirty that night, Vincent jumped his mum's back fence and skulked through the moonlight and black woods that linked the McGees' back door to Richard's back door. This wasn't faster than walking out the front door, down the road, to Richard's front door. The woods wasn't a shortcut. It was the secret way.

The back door creaked open. Richard's little moonface poked out. Vincent stepped over the not-yet-blood-soaked doormat, passed the unicorn painting, and headed up into the kitchen. Pushed against the wall in the dining room, on a cane table, a computer glowed. Vincent punched into Facebook and profile-picture Vincent sneered back at real Vincent. He typed his first message, and Richard approached.

"Mr. Barrett basically made a sexual gesture toward him," Tim says. "And Vincent said, 'That's when I just snapped. Here it was, he worked me all day for twenty dollars, and then he wants to turn around and have sex with me to boot.'"

Wayne says Vincent had brought knives from his mum's. "So I guess," Tim says, "in his mind he intended . . . he maybe was going to kill him anyway. But he said basically he went into a rage and that he murdered him."

No one has mentioned before that Vincent was pre-armed.

Vincent darted out the back door, through the secret woods, throwing a knife to the moon on the way.

"You said Richard made a sexual gesture," I say, trying not to sound tabloid. "What does that mean?"

"Well, I asked him about that," Tim says. "I said, 'Well, what do you mean, a sexual gesture?' And he said basically, Mr. Barrett said, you know, 'Do you want to have sex?' So I said, 'Were you ever engaged in any sexual conduct with Mr. Barrett previously?' And he said he had been. He said that he and Mr. Barrett had been involved in sexual conduct. And I said, 'Well, what do you mean? What do you mean, sexual conduct?' And Vincent went on to tell the story.

"He said that Mr. Barrett was attracted to black men. He said Mr. Barrett told him this. And he said that Mr. Barrett had had an older black man that worked for him years before, and they were working partners. And this older black man and him were intimate in a homosexual relationship. But the older man had passed away. The older black man had died. So Mr. Barrett was trying to get into an intimate homosexual relationship with Vincent. And Vincent had had actual sexual contact with Mr. Barrett a few times prior to this.

"And I said to him, 'So what you're trying to tell me is, you're trying to say that you and Mr. Barrett engaged in homosexual activities?' He said, 'Yes. Several times.' You know, previous dates. And I'm just getting the details, and I said, 'Well, what do you mean? Explain.' And he said that Mr. Barrett normally would pay him around two hundred dollars for Vincent to have sex with him. And I said, 'What do you mean? Oral sex? What are you talking about?' He described that Mr. Barrett liked to be taken from behind. Sodomized, basically. And Vincent would say, 'I would sodomize him and that's what Mr. Barrett liked.'

"And I said, 'You expect me to believe this?' And Vincent said, 'I'm telling you, I'm just telling you the truth.' He said, 'I wouldn't just sit here and make this up. I'm confessing to murder and I'm not just going to add this.'

"And I said, 'Well, did Mr. Barrett ever sodomize you?' He said, 'No.' He said, 'Mr. Barrett always wanted me to sodomize him.' So he said he would sodomize Mr. Barrett for money. And that's what happened."

I've stopped taking notes. I quadruple-, quintuple-check the Dictaphone is recording. Tim and Wayne have just described the money shot of my whole "race" career: a white supremacist paying to be sodomized by a black man.

We all pause and swig down water from our polystyrene cups. Tim, Wayne, and I are so white that in our hands and running up our arms you can see the blue veins glow.

"Now, I don't know why anybody in their right mind would confess to murder and admit they're having homosexual relations with somebody when they're not a homosexual, do you understand?" Tim continues. "You know, I love women. I'm married." His gold wedding band attests to this. It glistens in a boardroom that is otherwise plain white (polystyrene cups), off-white (walls), or cream (manila folders). "I'm sure not going to make up a story that I'm having sex with a man. That would demean me—ruin my reputation, as it would any man's."

I can see that Vincent might have had trouble saying this in court. I can see that he would have had trouble with fellow inmates knowing this. That potential trouble could well have led him to disagree with the legal advice to use the sex element in this crime as his defense.

A career of wanting this to be true makes me get greedy again, and I ask if Richard wore the Nazi uniform while being sodomized by a black man.

Wayne tells me Vincent never said anything about a Nazi uniform.

Richard's Head

"I can't explain, you know, the psychological, in Mr. Barrett's head," Tim says. "I can't explain what was going on. Why he openly hated black people or Jew people, but then he was having homosexual relationships with black people. I don't know.

"Now, speculation, okay? You know Vincent went to extremes to burn that computer, and we tried to retrieve that data. It was beyond obtainable. We don't know what was on that computer because it was burned up. We don't know if there were pictures, images. We don't know, but we know that Vincent went to extreme effort to destroy that computer. More than anything else."

"Poured more gas on it," adds Wayne.

"And the bed also," Tim says. "That was the only bed that was destroyed. The other beds were neatly made up in the house. But he made it a point to burn Mr. Barrett's bed. He went to extremes. Why? I mean, if you want me to play psychologist, I could only guess—maybe that's where they would have their relationships. I do not know that. I don't know that firsthand. It could be that there may have been a better reason why he went to extremes to destroy the computer and the bed. I do not know."

Rifles

"We had trouble figuring out why the rifles were on his chest," Wayne volleys in.

Rifles?

When the firemen splashed through the blood pooled up in the kitchen and dragged Richard out, three guns rolled off his chest: a semiautomatic rifle, a semiautomatic shotgun, and a lever-action rifle. They were Richard's. Vincent had scooped them up from somewhere in the house and rested them on Richard's chest. He hoped the heat from the fire would set off the guns and somehow that would make the whole scene look like a suicide.

"He wasn't thinking rationally," Tim says.

"He asked me, 'Did the rifles go off?'" Wayne says. "I said, 'No, the rifles didn't go off.' I said, 'If you wanted to make it look like a suicide, then you use one rifle, not three.'"

"Yeah. So he wasn't thinking right," Tim says.

However, Tim thinks Vincent was thinking right in the interview room on the other side of the wall. He didn't appear drunk or drugged or anything like that.

"He was very coherent," Tim says. "He's a very flashy guy. I said, 'Do you realize that the man you murdered was a very well-known self-proclaimed racist against black people?' He looked at me like, *What?* And when we told him that he'd killed pretty much a famous person, that really kind of made him excited."

"What he thought," says Wayne, "was that he was going to be famous in prison because this happened, and then when he went back to prison he'd be a celebrity. And he told us that he'd go ahead and plead guilty to it that day if we'd buy him a pimp suit with a hat with a feather in it."

"It sounds like he had a sense of humor," I say.

"Oh, he was funny. He was funny," says Wayne. "I could say that it was a conversation like me and you are having a conversation and we're making jokes about this. But he's talking about a guy that he's just killed—and he killed him with a passion, because I sat through the autopsy, and there were holes in Mr. Barrett's shoulders that were about eight or nine inches long and deep, and it was about an eight-inch knife. So that means he plunged it all the way to the handle, several times, in the top of his shoulder."

Knives

Vincent skipped over the welcome mat, into the black woods, two knives in his waistband, one knife in his hand. The one in his hand, Vincent later claimed, was the knife Richard came at him with. Vincent slung it deep into the darkness as he pelted to his mum's back door.

Vincent burst into the living room, sweating, breathing hard, holding his stomach. His stepfather, Alfred, eyed the two butcher knives. One seemed clean, at least to Alfred's eyes, the only light in the living room a glowing TV. The other knife was smeared with blood from tip to handle.

Alfred's black Ford pickup sped toward a town called Piney Woods. He curved into Highway 49, the road gently rising to become a bridge. Vincent rolled down the window as if about to light a cigarette. But he didn't light a cigarette. He flung the two knives out the window. The knives nose-dived over the side of the bridge and landed in thigh-high grass lining a creek.

Wayne remembers a later interview with Vincent in the white cube on the other side of the wall.

"Vincent said, 'Well, I'm going to change my mind here. I'm going to say I didn't do it.' And I said, 'Well, you already confessed to it one hundred times.' He said, 'Yeah, but you don't have the murder weapons.' He said, 'You don't know what happened.' I said, 'Yeah. Yeah, we do.' I said, 'We don't need the murder weapon.' He said, 'Yeah, you do. I watch TV. I know you need the murder weapon.' I said, 'All right, Vincent. I'm going to tell you the truth. We have the murder weapon.' He said, 'No, you don't.' I said, 'Yeah, we do.' He said, 'No, you don't.' I said, 'We found them beside the creek.' He said, 'That creek just up from Florence?' I said, 'Yeah. That creek just up from Florence.' He said, 'What did it look like?' I said, 'Well, it looked like a knife. It got a silver blade and a black handle.' He said, 'Way to go, man!'"

The Oriental Girlfriend

I ask Wayne and Tim if they were familiar with Vincent before the killing. They'd never heard of him. But when the other investigator, Trip Bayles, drove into the McGee driveway, he thought, *I've been down here before.*

"Vincent had a girlfriend," Wayne says. "An Oriental girlfriend that he had assaulted with a knife."

Trip told them Vincent had beaten her like a dog.

"And Trip couldn't remember her name because a couple of years had passed, but he said, 'I do remember that he had assaulted her and tried to cut her with a knife or something, and I believe I wound up putting him in jail or something, on a misdemeanor battery charge, or something like that.'"

"Could that have been when Vincent was underage?" I ask, trying to make it sound like a throwaway question.

"He was underage," Tim says. "He was, like, seventeen at the time or something, and he would've taken him to what we call a juvenile detention center."

I shouldn't know this. This is what the lawyer Vicky Williams had refused to tell me—the reason Vincent was in juvenile detention when he assaulted the police officers.

Having pickpocketed this secret, I quickly change the topic. I ask about race.

Race

Tim and Wayne tell me this case has nothing to do with race.

"You've got to realize," Tim says of Vincent, "that this is a twenty-year-old young man who's been in prison most of his teenage life."

"Richard Barrett had kind of faded out of the picture over the years," says Wayne.

"He didn't know who Richard Barrett was," Tim says. "And that was another thing. When we got to talking to the neighbors, all of the neighbors, the black neighbors, you know, they had heard of Richard Barrett, but they said—one man in particular told me, an older black man, a senior citizen—he said, 'There's no way in this world you can convince me that that man was a racist.' He said, 'He was the nicest man in this neighborhood.' He said, 'If you needed to go down to the barn for some tools,' he said, 'Richard Barrett was there to help. He would loan you his tools. He was there to help.' He said, 'He visited with people, you know, he rode a bicycle there for exercise, Richard Barrett, and he would ride his bicycle up and down the road.' He would stop and visit everybody. Not a single neighbor in that neighborhood who was black said anything negative about him. One man pulled up—an older man, I don't know who he was, a black man who lived in the neighborhood—and when we told him, he said, 'Is Mr. Barrett okay?' I said, 'Well, no sir. He's passed away.' He said, 'What happened?' I said, 'Well, right now, we're not at liberty . . . but he passed away.' That man started crying because he loved him."

Tim drains the last of his water from his polystyrene cup.

The War

"I can't explain it," Tim says. "And then there he is, hating black people, but yet he's wanting black men to sodomize him. Figure that—I don't know. I have no idea. Was he . . . I mean, was there something wrong with Mr. Barrett? Was he suffering from something? I mean, was he suffering from some kind of dysfunction? I don't know, I mean, I can't tell you. I don't know."

"I think he was a Vietnam veteran," Wayne says. "And there was a lot of people who returned from Vietnam that saw battle. And I think he saw battle in Vietnam."

"He may have," Tim says. "Now, did he suffer from post-traumatic stress? I don't know. I'm not saying . . . by no means are we saying that all Vietnam veterans act like this. No. By no means. But we don't know. We can't explain what was going on in his brain."

"In his old newsletter," I tell them, "he'd say Vietnam changed him because the black soldiers weren't as efficient. And didn't back him up as much as the white men would."

"I don't know what you found out," says Tim. "And you've probably got a lot more to go, but you'll probably find out that Richard Barrett was a very, obviously, mysterious person. Very mysterious."

James Drew

I tell Wayne and Tim the Ballad of James Drew. That he was in a holding cell in Rankin County Jail six years ago, with cotton taped on his head to stop the bleeding. And he looked across the cell and there was Mr. Barrett.

That wakes up the room. Tim's bright eyes dart to Wayne's bright eyes.

I tell them Rankin County Justice Court has a record of James's arrest, but not Richard's.

"There you go," says Tim. "But I will tell you this—and I don't know where you need to look—I was told—and I don't know what year this was—but somewhere in Hinds County, whether it was the City of Jackson or one of the local jurisdictions, but some man had filed an affidavit against Richard Barrett. And had him arrested for sexually assaulting him at that time."

Is this corroboration of James's story? James said a boy complained. In Tim's story it's a man. Also, James was certain he was in Rankin County, not Hinds County. Maybe it's another sexual assault or the same one, with the details morphed through the grapevine.

I fold the news about the affidavit away for later and try a shortcut.

"If Richard *was* in a Rankin County holding cell and got out within hours," I ask, "would there be records at all?"

"Let me look to see if he's ever been here." Tim levers himself up with his hairy hands and leaves the boardroom.

There's a venetian blind behind Wayne not quite fully shut. I can make out smudges of the outside world, but nothing more. Now and then lollipop colors from prisoner jumpsuits roll by.

The Return of Tim Lawless

"I couldn't find anything on Richard Barrett being in our jail," Tim says. "If I was you, I would research Hinds County court records real well, because somebody filed an affidavit against him, somewhere."

My two front teeth pull off my pen lid. I ask for the names of the courts in Hinds.

"Oh, gosh," says Tim. "You've got the justice court, misdemeanor courts, you got the circuit court. And then you got the City of Jackson Court, over there with their police department. And then you got Clinton Municipal Court, the little City of Clinton. So there's a lot of places."

Tim twangs the other towns in Hinds: Raymond, Byram, Terry, Utica, Bolton, Edwards. They all have their own courts, too.

"I imagine once he was killed, everyone started talking," I say. "And that's how you found out about this affidavit in Hinds County. Do you think there are other ones?"

"That's all I know," says Tim. "And actually, Vincent's attorney, Mr. Scott, he's the one that leaked that to me about someone filing that against Mr. Barrett years ago. So he knows where it was. Now, I don't know if he's going to tell you. I didn't tell you that. If you want to hit him back up for it, he'll know."

Tim escorts me out, through the jail. A two-minute drift through gray corridors and antiseptic smells. Dozens of young men in lollipop jumpsuits roll past me. The young black men look relaxed: *Hey, this is just a part of life.* The young white men look broken.

Mike Scott Squeaks

I pluck a gum ball from the gum ball machine next to the metal detector at the jail's entrance. I call Mike Scott and tell him I've been told someone filed an affidavit against Richard in a Hinds County court for predatory behavior. Could he point me in the right direction?

Mike squeaks a very brief squeak, which tells me I'm onto something, because Mike isn't a squeaker. He tries to tease out of me who told me. That might help him understand where to point me, he says. I fumble out, "Just someone."

He tells me I might like to try the Hinds Justice Court office in Jackson. Third floor. All I'd need to give is Richard's name.

I bolt to my car and head for Jackson. The only reason I can think of that Mike Scott would tell the police where evidence against Richard Barrett could be found, but not use it in defense of his client, is if Vincent refused to let him.

The Hinds County Justice Court Office, Third Floor

The clerk sealed behind the glass is one of the few white people here. As instructed by Mike Scott, I give her Richard Barrett's name.

She pounds her keyboard and sucks in her face.

"Oh boy, he has a few!" she says. "Ten citations!"

I want to kiss her like you kiss the newsagent guy who sold you the winning ticket.

"Will you need them printed?" she twangs.

"Yes, please!"

To my ears, the hum of her dot matrix printer sounds sweeter than gospel music. She slides ten sheets of paper under the glass, and I dart to a chair in the nearby waiting area.

Okay, the first one is just a traffic offense: "Improper passing, August 13, 1990, $21 fine."

Okay, the second one is also just a traffic offense: "Speeding, January 7, 1991, $200 fine."

Okay, the third is just another traffic offense: "Speeding, January 18, 1995, $100 fine."

My fingers whisk through the rest: three more speeding tickets, two more improper passings, one "No driver's license (expired)," and one "Driving while license suspended."

Where's my goddamn unwanted sexual advance?

Amish Romance

At Walmart, I'm thumbing through *Sisters of the Quilt* in the Amish romance section of the Christian book department when my phone trembles on my thigh. I press the vibrating rat to my ear. It's Mike Scott returning my call. I tell him Hinds County just coughed up Richard Barrett's speeding tickets. He makes the sound of a man shrugging his shoulders. The McGee case may have rolled to a stop, he says, but he's still bound by confidentiality. He says the only way he can talk is if Vincent signs a letter of consent. And I haven't heard back from Vincent.

The Autopsy

After the investigators, the next subpoena the DA's office had prepared for the trial that never happened was for Adele Lewis. She cut open Richard Barrett at the autopsy.

"I use a large ten-inch chef's knife, that you would get from the kitchen store," she tells me over the phone from Tennessee.

She flew in from Tennessee for the autopsy, because Mississippi has too many suspicious deaths and not enough forensic pathologists.

"There is a scale," she continues, "like you see in a grocery store."

These are the bits of Richard she weighed on that scale: heart, lungs, liver, spleen, intestines, adrenal gland, internal genitalia, and kidneys.

I think about Richard's last will and testament. He requested no public or private viewing of his dead body or his remains. There has been no shortage of people denying him that wish in the course of their jobs. *I* leered over his corpse in the investigators' boardroom.

Adele says the official cause of Richard's death is "multiple sharp and blunt force injuries."

"And the investigators told me there were no defensive wounds. Is that true?"

"He did have some scrapes and bruises on his left arm and on the back of his left hand that could be consistent with defense injuries."

"Sorry to be tacky," I say, "but there were suggestions at the start it was a sex crime, and so did you do things like any tests on whether he'd had sex, or whether there was semen on him, or anything like that?"

"No, I wasn't made aware of that until after the autopsy had been completed and the body had been cleaned."

She doesn't sound happy about this.

"Do you think that was a misjudgment by them to not clue you in on that?"

"Well, let me just say, the more information that I have going into the autopsy, the better job I can do."

Adele says had she been made aware of a sex angle she would have examined Richard with that in mind. For instance, she would have examined his anus.

Here's a weird thing: Investigator Wayne Humphreys took me through the autopsy process. He said he was in the room when they cut open Richard. This is what Wayne told me he said to the autopsy person, presumably Adele:

"I said, 'I'm sorry I have to get you to do this, but could you please do a visual look at his rectum to see if there's any foreign objects?' Then they spread him and then made an incision—with, like, hedgers you use to prune—to cut up his anus so she could really get inside. She had a look and couldn't see anything."

Could one of them be misremembering, or confusing Richard with another corpse? Would you be more likely to remember accurately if you were the one using the hedgers or the one watching? Which one is more likely to get carried away with the story?

I'm being punished for being here too long. The longer you stay, the more stories you get. What am I meant to do now? Burst into the sheriff's office: *Wayne, did you lie about the rectum?*

The Murble

"He sucks in his top soup cooler!" cackles the black radio host, a man named Rip. "Ha-ha!"

Rip is sermonizing from the little clock radio on the bedside table in my apartment. The evening air whistles outside my window. Rip says he watched the Republican debate on television. He thinks black candidate Herman Cain intentionally sucks in his top lip to look less African American.

"Stop sucking in your soup cooler, Mr. Cain! We know you're black!"

My phone buzzes. I pluck it from my pocket and press it to my ear.

"Hello," I say.

"Murble aiiiiiii," murbles The Murble.

"Hello?" I say. "Who's this?"

"Murble ya murble yo lettar murble murble," says The Murble.

"Murble," he continues.

This last *murble* bolts into my ear, down my body, and punches my heart.

"Vincent?" I say, more a breath than a word.

"Aiiiii . . . this is Vincent."

My eyes dart east, south, north, west. Where's the Dictaphone? I need to tape this. I'll need to play it back ten times to decode the murble.

"Thank you so much for ringing me," I say.

"Aiii," says Vincent. "Murble murble birfdate murble soshell secureety nomba."

Social security number?

"Because. I'm. Australian . . ." I say. Enunciating. Each. Word. "I. Only. Have. A. Passport. Number."

I skid to my suitcase like it's home base. I make it rain with pens and shirts and socks and peel the passport from the bottom of my suitcase.

I read out my passport number.

"Ya be in penitentry?" Vincent says.

Christ! He must be filling in the visitation form.

"No," I say. "I haven't been in a penitentiary."

"Murble aiiiii dat ell da infomaton a need," he says.

"How will I know when I can visit?" I say. "Can I call you?"

"No."

"Is this your cell phone?" I say.

"No."

"Well, how will I know when it'll be okay to visit?"

"Ya gave a en'vlope," he says.

"Oh," I say, "so you'll send me the information in the envelope?"

"Aiiiiiiii."

Vincent McGee hangs up.

8.

VINCENT

The Roads

've been in Mississippi so long, I can feel the difference between the white roads and the black roads. I can feel the difference vibrate up my spine. The white areas are furnished with smoother roads. The black areas are pockmarked with potholes. The whole story of how the world works could be localized to these roads. Earnest would say, "See, this is how the system works. The whites sort it out so they have better roads." Jim Giles would say, "See, this is what happens. You leave counties in the hands of black officials and they won't take care of their roads." I could drive Earnest and Jim around the lumpy and smooth streets of Mississippi all day and night. There they'd be, in the backseat, screaming, using exactly the same facts to explain how the world works in two opposite ways.

Green Dot Without the Dictaphone

Vincent just rang again. Didn't have the Dictaphone. I was driving. Now I've pulled over. He rang from a different number. It was all slurry. Like, "Aaaiiiiiii." So he asked me about getting paid for my book. And I said, "Oh, listen, I really want to tell your side of the story, but it's against the law," and I told him about the "Son of Sam law" that says a criminal can't profit from his crime. And he didn't argue over it. He just assumed it must be the truth. Because it is. And then he was like, "Oh well, I could write the story." And I said, "You can write some other story. You can write a novel or you can write about something else, but you won't be able to get paid for this particular story." So he said, "Oh, okay." And he started talking about Walmart "Green Dot cards" or something. About whether I could put some money in that. So I just straightaway kind of cracked under the pressure. I said, "Well, you know, I don't know about that." Then he started talking about, well, how much could I put in a Walmart Green Dot card? So I said to him, "Well, listen, I don't even know if I can, but if I can . . . Listen, before, I looked into how much money family and friends can put on a prisoner's account, and the most you can put into that is three hundred dollars." And he said, "Well, what?" Like he's waiting for me to tell him something. He said, "You're going to make a lot out of this book." And I said, "Listen, I don't know about that, but you know that's what it says on the MDOC page—you can only put in three hundred dollars." So then he said, "Well, how much can you put in a Walmart Green Dot account?" So I said, "Oh, I don't know." He goes, "Well, how much are you willing?" And I said, "Well, I don't know, I guess three hundred dollars." And he said, "Well, you know . . ." And then I said, "Well, how much were you thinking?" And so then, for some reason, then he goes, "Oh, listen, put in two hundred dollars in the Walmart Green Dot card." And then he says there's some number on the card and then I can ring him up with that number. So I kind of don't quite know why he haggled me down to two hundred dollars. Maybe that's something he knows about in prison, or something like that. Maybe he made a mistake.

And then I said, "Oh yeah, what about visitation?" And then he said, "Oh listen, the form is still going through." And he sounded pretty genuine, I guess. I mean, maybe he wasn't.

Anyway, so then that was that. So then I hung up. Then he rang back five minutes later and said, "Oh, don't put it all on one card. Put a hundred and fifty on one card and fifty on another." So I was like, "Oh, okay." And then he goes, "Oh, and I think I can get . . ." and he said something about visitation on Thursday or Friday.

It's so delicate, this communication. Vincent has my number, I don't have his. This is just going to happen as God and/or Fate and/or Vincent wants it to happen. Is Tina talking to him? What's she saying to him about me? How perfect if I meet him in prison. That's better than a trial. I'm kind of bummed that money has come into it. Not the money as such, but what it says about Vincent, about the role money has played in this crime perhaps. Wouldn't this be better if he just wanted to tell his story and have the truth out there?

The Reyeses

Two doors up from the address I have for the Reyeses' home, a skinhead is bashing a nail into a post on his white veranda. The house is white, the skinhead is pink, and the sky is overblown blue. I guess I don't actually know he's a skinhead. He could just have a shaved head. But his T-shirt is tight and white and my race antennas are going off.

I reread the file propped up on my steering wheel:

> **Vincent McGee did willfully, unlawfully, and feloniously** . . . **take, steal, and carry away $300 in Mexican Pesos, $200 in Mexican Paper Dollars, and one silver ring with a value of $300, property of Jamie Reyes.**

This was where the "white girl in there somewhere" comes into it, and, according to Vallena Greer, where Vincent got caught up in the race war.

A car pulls into the Reyeses' driveway as I walk to the front door. I immediately regret clomping across the grass rather than sticking to the cement path. A girl—Latin American? late teens? early twenties?—steps from the car. I tell her I'm looking for a Jamie Reyes. To talk about a Vincent McGee.

"Come in," she says warmly, like she's been waiting for me. "I'm Daisy, Jamie's my mom."

There's a lot of neon punching through in the living room. The cushions on the couch, the straws in our iced tea, Jamie's cardigan, Daisy's T-shirt. The Reyeses, mother and daughter, sit opposite me on the couch. Daisy's stepfather, a relatively new addition, I gather, kicks around in the kitchen space. He's not neon, he's dull blue, and the dog slopping at his feet is dull brown.

I don't yet have my bearings as to how everyone here intersects with Vincent McGee.

"I got the impression," Jamie begins, "that the Aborigine people are kind of like the Native Americans? Just kind of tucked away?"

Good Lord! This is pretty much the first time I've heard a Mississippian express curiosity about something going on outside Mississippi.

"I've been to Australia," she continues.

Good Lord!

"When I was in Sydney for just one day, I was walking around the harbor, wanting to do a whale-watching tour," she says. "And there was this Aborigine man and he was sitting playing didgeridoo. And he had paint on and he was near naked, like a tribesman. And I stopped and took a picture of him and bought one of his CDs. I went on the cruise and then I came back and that Aborigine that had been sitting there now had jeans and a T-shirt on, and there was another Aborigine in his place. I guess it was shift change. And I just thought, *Oh!* You know, it was a little disappointing, just seeing him in his jeans and T-shirt."

"Very selfish of him," I say.

"I know—how dare you put clothes on!" she says, and we laugh like kookaburras.

Already I can't understand how the Reyes family got mixed up with someone who stabbed someone else sixteen times. I open up my manila folder marked *Rankin County Circuit Court.*

"Something I came across in Vincent's history was that he'd been charged for grand larceny and there was the name Jamie Reyes on the paperwork."

"Yeah, Daisy kind of dated him," Jamie says. Daisy looks rueful.

So there she is, sitting on the green couch: the so-called white girl-friend whose existence, according to Vallena, Earnest McBride, and Tina McGee, caused the Klan to seek revenge on Vincent.

"Leave that one out," says Daisy's stepfather. I think he's having a go at me, but he's just telling Jamie to leave the iced tea pitcher out.

I start reading aloud from my well-smudged *Jackson Advocate*: "Vincent McGee. Sent to prison at seventeen for dating a white girl."

Jamie and Daisy laugh.

"That's so funny," says Jamie, "because Daisy's not even white. Her dad's Mexican."

For Vallena and Tina, though—black women who grew up in Mississippi, without many in-between people—that's still white, just like Richard's still Klan. I continue with Tina McGee's telling of events: *Vincent had a white girlfriend. And he and his friends had gone to her parents' house for the weekend. I don't know if the parents were gone or what, but some of the other people at the house said that Vincent stole some Mexican money or something. There were other people in the house, but they said Vincent took it, and they charged him with grand larceny and he got five years. They didn't prove that he did nothin'.*

This is not how Daisy and Jamie remember it.

"I have a little journal I wrote everything down in," Daisy says.

She leaves and returns with an exercise book.

This is pretty much the exact scene in *Capote* where the friend of the dead girl retrieves the diary for Truman.

The pages are covered front and back with big-loop, schoolgirl handwriting. The journal is headed: *WEEK FROM HELL*.

Daisy's First Circle of Hell—Meeting Vincent

Daisy's "week from hell" really spanned two to three weeks, or six months I suppose, or continues now, if you want to look at it that way. Regardless, the time between meeting Vincent for the first time and him landing in Rankin County Jail was under three weeks. This is three years ago, when Daisy was sixteen.

Daisy had been hanging out with a black girl from school called Jasmine. They had gone to Battlefield Park.

"A horrible part of town," Daisy tells me. "Part of Jackson. It used to be just a big park, ball fields. But the area around it, I mean, it's horrible. It's just drug- and crime-ridden." There had been several murders in that park, just in broad daylight.

"So is 'Battlefield' a bit of a joke name for it?"

"No, that's what it's really called." A Civil War thing, apparently. (Of course.)

Vincent was with a black kid called Patrick. The two boys slid up to Daisy and Jasmine.

"Vincent had a beautiful smile," Daisy says. "And that's one thing that I notice about people when I first meet them, is their smile. I mean, if they keep their mouths clean. That's the easiest thing to do."

I gently tighten my lips lest my smile be judged.

Her *WEEK FROM HELL* catalogs other things she spotted on Vincent's face.

Star tattoo between eyebrows
2 stars below right eye
Playboy bunny on right side of mouth
Teardrop & butterfly below left eye
Do-rag and black bandanna tied in back

"We are two young girls in a little white car, you know, with chrome rims," Daisy says. "We just got to talking and exchanged numbers, and I think he called me later that night, and he was like, 'I want to hang out with you.'"

"He probably thought: *Okay, this girl, she's driving a really nice car, maybe she's got a little money*," Jamie says.

The next few times Daisy saw Vincent, each time he had a different vehicle. And there was always one window bumped out.

Soon, as *WEEK FROM HELL* catalogs, Daisy got to see under Vincent McGee's T-shirt:

2 bullet scars on shoulder & back of neck

Scar on spine in middle of back, going west to east, maybe 2 inches

That's the first I've heard of Vincent having been shot. I wonder if he really has?

"I guess he had a lot of women, or whatever you want to say, you know, in his life," Daisy says. "So I think that's what drew me to him, was the confidence just in himself. In the sense that, *I can get whoever I want to get, no matter, with no issues.*"

Just as Daisy met Vincent, her family left town for a vacation: her mum, Mexican Dad, and a cousin of Mexican Dad. Daisy had a holiday job, so it sounded normal, responsible even, when she told her parents, "Well, I'm going to stay here and work."

Back then the Reyeses lived on the county line, down Highway 49, part of Rankin County. It was the middle of nowhere, surrounded by woods.

Hours after the Reyeses left for their vacation, Vincent, Jasmine, and Patrick moved into the house in the woods.

The Second Circle of Hell—China

Maybe a week after they had started going out (if that was what was happening), Vincent called Daisy from a hotel in Jackson and said he wanted her to come over.

The hotel was run-down. Might not even get one star. Daisy pushed through the doors of the soiled lobby, where an actual flea jumped on her leg, and then pushed through the doors of the indoor pool area. In the fog and moist air, about to splash in, were Patrick and Jasmine. Cuddling up in the corner of the pool were Vincent and some girl.

"Why did you call me out here?! What are you doing?!" Daisy's questions echoed off the walls.

"He pulled me aside," Daisy says. "And he was like, 'This is my girlfriend, but she's not really my girlfriend—she goes out and makes money for me.' And I was like, 'What do you mean by that, I don't understand what you mean.' And he said, 'Well, I send her to do things and she does them and I get money.' And I thought that was a little strange, so we kind of argued a little bit and then I was ready to leave."

But Vincent grabbed her phone so she couldn't leave. The mysterious girl pulled herself out of the pool. She had scratches and scabs, like road burn, all over her elbows and knees.

Daisy realized she'd seen a picture of this girl in Vincent's room. He had said her name was China.

"Was China her nickname because she was Chinese?" I ask.

Daisy nods.

I tell her what the investigators told me. Vincent's first time in juvenile detention was because he'd beaten an Asian girlfriend to a pulp and threatened to cut her with a knife.

Daisy tells me that Vincent had said China had thrown herself out of a moving car in an attempt to abort a baby. Daisy didn't ask whether it was Vincent's baby.

"Are Asian people common in Jackson?" I ask, entertaining the possibility Vincent had two Asian girlfriends.

"Not common at all," Daisy tells me.

Back at the pool, screams ricocheted from wall to wall: Daisy screaming at Vincent to give her phone back, Jasmine screaming at Vincent, China screaming at Jasmine to stop screaming at Vincent. Then China moved on to Daisy.

"You need to quit calling Vincent," screamed China. "I don't know what you're doing!"

"He's calling me!" yelled Daisy. "You know I'm never making a phone call. I don't know which number to call. He calls me from a different number each time."

"I was scared," Daisy says. "You know, I'd never been in a fight, I didn't know what to do. I mean, do you push her? So she kept getting in my face and yelling at me and threatening me. At one point she did tell me she'd kill me, and I just thought, you know, *Yeah right, you're twenty-five pounds and you know I'm bigger than you—I'll just step on you.*"

The Third Circle of Hell—The White Car

WEEK FROM HELL catalogs another tattoo of Vincent's: *Mama's name on right hand.*

And just one week and a half from their meeting at Battlefield Park, that right hand with Mama's name was around Daisy's throat. The two were at the house in the woods.

"He wanted to take my car," Daisy says. "And I told him no. And he ended up choking me and telling me, 'I'm taking your car.' I had red marks on my neck. It made me think, *God—take my car and please leave.* And he took my keys and left. From somebody who had never been in any kind of abuse in her life, to have somebody right in your face choking you . . . I mean, it scared me."

Daisy stares down at the *WEEK FROM HELL* in my lap.

"Vincent did not like the word *no*," she says. I picture Vincent demanding from Richard the rest of his wages, and Richard refusing.

One hour later, Vincent came back with Daisy's little white car. He had kicked in one of the doors.

"When he came back, it was that, 'Oh, I'm so sorry. I never meant to hurt you.' You know, that kind of manipulation. Making me feel like I was the one who was wrong for getting mad or getting upset."

The Fourth Circle of Hell—The Truck

A couple of nights after the strangulation, Vincent and Patrick took Mexican Dad's truck and burst a tire. The boys had no phone and walked back to the house in the woods.

Daisy told them, "No problem." The three of them plus Jasmine piled into the other truck on hand, belonging to cousin of Mexican Dad.

They drove off to Mexican Dad's truck, changed the tire, and split in two for the trip back home: Jasmine and Patrick in Mexican Dad's truck, Vincent and Daisy in the other.

The two drivers, Vincent and Jasmine, pushed it on the highway.

They started speeding.

Then racing.

Other cars were beeping and flashing their lights.

Vincent didn't stop in time to turn down Daisy's road. He just kept going. Jasmine swerved into Daisy's road at the last moment, but there were lots of loose rocks on the turnoff. She skidded straight into an electrical pole. The transformer on the top of the pole fell off and crushed the truck.

Jasmine and Patrick were okay, but Mexican Dad's truck was totaled.

The Fifth Circle of Hell—Arrest

Daisy looks miserable for a cherry-cheeked girl in a bright lime top, sipping iced tea from a neon straw.

"I don't know why at that point I didn't wake up and think, *What are you doing? You just totaled your dad's . . . What's he going to think when he gets back from vacation and his truck is totaled?* But, you know, things happened."

What happened was that Daisy, Vincent, Patrick, and Jasmine went to a party. Daisy took her first ecstasy pill. Patrick and Vincent went into

Was I a naive fan when I reenacted Billy Idol's photoshoot or did I already sense I was playing with fire? By the time I met Richard Barrett, in the last US state to fly the Confederate flag, I was an unambiguous Race Trekkie. As was Richard, in his own way. He showed off his bona fides in pamphlets like this one, grinning with Klansman Edgar Ray Killen, the subject of *Mississippi Burning*.

The coonhounds of white separatist Jim
Giles seemed to be able to sniff out that
I wasn't of pure Aryan stock, despite my
blending in with a baby-blue sweater.
Below, journalist Earnest McBride. He
had the leads, but I had the car. What
a match.

Snooping around the Murder House. (Are you even allowed to snoop around the Murder House? "Easier to get forgiveness than permission" is something I learned early in my snooping career.)

JOHN SAFRAN
WRITER

Hello,

I'm an Australian writer, looking to find someone I believe lived at this address, or nearby.

If you could ring me it would be much appreciated.

Yours Sincerely
JOHN SAFRAN
601 - 209 - 1728
johnsafran@gmail.com

Poking my nose where it arguably didn't belong didn't always get results. No smoking gun (or literal one) in the garbage behind Richard's Nationalist Movement headquarters. But in a drawer in a trailer in a forest there were photos of him in his army days and as a child with his sister. A *sister*! Could I find her?

The Confederate soldier that greets every black person on his or her way to Rankin County courthouse, presumably including Chokwe Lumumba (above right), one of the killer's elusive lawyers, who I finally caught at the Martin Luther King Day festivities. Plenty of Secret Society black folk at the festival, too, much to the annoyance of Earnest McBride.

Mississippi portraits. Eddie Sandifer (top left), the gay civil rights activist who saw Richard in action in the 1960s. James Drew (top right), who says he watched from his cell as Richard slipped jail with suspicious ease. Investigators Tim Lawless and Wayne Humphreys (middle), who first questioned Vincent McGee. And Curtis Rumfelt (below), who grew up on Richard's street and found him to be a creepy houseguest as a boy.

Facing a back street, Mississippi's State Capitol building is petulantly turned away from Washington, in a sulk after losing the Civil War. Inside (above right), Representative John Moore distanced himself from Richard, despite having been named in the dead man's will.

Exhibit A: The knife Vincent says Richard threatened him with, in the woods where he threw it the night of the killing. Exhibit B: The photo of Vincent his defense lawyer Mike Scott told me was taken by Richard.

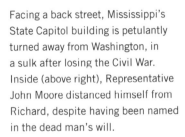

Vincent McGee
MDOC#: 122412
EMCF
10641 HIGHWAY 80 WEST
MERIDIAN, MS 39307

Michael L. Scott PLLC
213 South Lamar Street
Jackson MS, 39201

Dear Michael,

I have ~~talked~~ to writer John Safran. I give you permission to talk to him too about my case too.

Yours Sincerely

Vincent McGee

Vincent McGee

Micheal L. Scott
I give my full permission
For you to tALK to John Safran
about my case
x Vincent McGee

My encounters with Vincent
started with a glimpse of him
in court as he delivered his plea.
It got stranger from there.

a room—she didn't know what they were doing in there, but they came out with red eyes. She was also smoking pot, falling down the back of the couch like a dollar coin.

Time to go. Vincent got behind the wheel of cousin of Mexican Dad's truck (not Daisy's white car with the door kicked in, or the truck wrapped around the pole at the end of Daisy's street). Vincent swerved off. Patrick was with them, but Daisy realized Jasmine had been left behind. Daisy's eyes were pumping like little hearts. Now red was rolling in and out. Now a siren. Vincent was zigzagging on the road. Now she was pushed against a cop car, being frisked. They were squeezing her legs like they were trying to get toothpaste.

Out from Daisy's pocket the cops pulled a little pinch of pot.

Out of Patrick's pocket they pulled Mexican coins and Mexican bills.

"Hey, that's not his!" Daisy slurred. "They've taken that from my home!"

The cops said, "Shut up," and frisked Vincent.

Out from Vincent's pocket they pulled a knife.

Vincent started spinning tales. He told them his name was Dave. He then told them his brother's name and information.

They soon figured out who he was. And that he was out on probation with a knife in his pocket. Vincent was arrested and charged with careless driving, public drunkenness, giving false information to police, no driver's license, no insurance.

And he was charged with one more thing: grand larceny, for the stolen Mexican money. The cops carted Vincent to Rankin County Jail.

Daisy was charged with possession. Just shy of seventeen, she was sent to a different location, Rankin County Juvenile Detention Center in Pearl.

The Sixth Circle of Hell—Juvie

Daisy spent four days and nights in juvenile detention. She met girls who had to sleep with men for food. *I'm not supposed to be here,* she thought. *Where are my parents?*

"Your parents could have gotten you out," the jail officer told her, "but they didn't."

What, are they just gonna leave me? she thought, distressed and furious.

She had come in Friday morning, and on Tuesday morning, the judge decided to release her without a record but *with* an ankle bracelet. It was her seventeenth birthday.

Jamie was, to say the least, furious. It was now summer holidays, and these would be the rules: no friends, no cell phone, no Internet. Each morning, Jamie would wrap up the computer modem and cords in her handbag so Daisy could meditate like a disgraced monk without distraction over what she'd done. Daisy and her ankle bracelet wallowed all by themselves in the house for months.

Meanwhile, mother was having her own adventures with Daisy's confiscated cell phone. A male called and left a voice message: "I'm gonna come to your house and I'm gonna shoot your family. You got my brah arrested. It's your fault."

Jamie took the cell phone to the police and played the message. The policeman said, "Be careful." That was it.

Back home, Jamie called the number back.

"If you come to my house, there's only one person that's gonna get shot, and it's not gonna be me," said Jamie.

"Oh, I . . . I . . . I was just joking, I was just joking," said the gangsta at the other end.

Jamie was terrified.

The Seventh Circle of Hell—The Trial

Even that wasn't completely the end. Daisy and Jamie were called to court to appear as witnesses in the first trial of Vincent McGee.

Mum and daughter Reyes pulled up at the perfectly neat square in the center of Brandon. They walked past the Confederate soldier statue and into the Rankin County Courthouse. Daisy was terrified. This would be the first time she'd seen him, the car-kicker, the throat-choker, since the arrest. Two men had volunteered to go with her, to "be a presence," keeping Daisy at ease, and perhaps warning Vincent not to try anything: an uncle who was a highway patrolman and a cousin who was a constable.

Daisy and her two policemen sat down in the front pew.

Vincent entered the courtroom.

Jamie saw Vincent, her daughter's beau, for the first time.

"The sad thing was, when he walked in, he smiled," Jamie says. "This big, bright, beautiful smile. I mean, he's a handsome kid. And none of his family were there, and I just thought that was so sad."

"Well, his family continued not to be there when he was sentenced to sixty-five years," I tell her.

Jamie looks glum. "Really? Even though, you know, I'm sure they're so sick of him and all that he's done in his life, it was just sad that nobody showed up."

Vincent did have a beautiful smile. But the meaning of that smile was up for debate.

"He felt very entitled, and when he walked into that courtroom, I mean, I saw it," Jamie says. "It just, like, oozed out of him that he was this wonderful person that everyone should want to be like, when really he's . . . I mean, he's a murderer, you know? And who would want to be like that?"

Fantastically, Vincent had declined a lawyer. It was announced he'd represent himself. To keep things simple, the prosecution focused on one charge, which happened to be the grand larceny: $300 in Mexican pesos, $200 in Mexican paper dollars, and Jamie Reyes's three-hundred-dollar silver ring.

Vincent had sat still through the mention of his other transgressions. But he snapped at the words *grand larceny*.

"No! I didn't do that!" said Vincent.

The judge told Vincent to shut his mouth.

Daisy took the stand. Vincent McGee, attorney-at-law, paced back and forth before her.

"You really gonna say I did this?" Vincent said. "Are you really gonna try and blame me for all this that you did?"

"Yes," Daisy said.

Vincent snapped.

"Are you stupid?" he said. He started calling Daisy all sorts of names.

The floorboards creaked where Daisy's two policemen sat, as they prepared for *something*.

"Get off the stand! This is done!" said the judge. He found Vincent guilty and gave him ten years for grand larceny, suspending nine of them. But that meant the four years suspended for assaulting the law enforcement officers came down on him, and so that morning Vincent was sentenced to five years in state prison. His ankles were shackled. His hands were cuffed to his belt. And then he was gone.

Minutes later a court official walked over to the front pew. He crouched a little. He told Jamie and Daisy to stay put.

"Don't leave the building," the man said, "because we don't have him."

Vincent had escaped.

"They ended up getting him," Daisy tells me. "I mean, he couldn't go far with the shackles."

Outside the Reyeses'

I sit in the car with a dozen knots either tied or untied in my brain.

Tina, Vallena, and Earnest said Vincent was charged with and convicted of grand larceny "primarily" as punishment for dating a white girl. Vallena thought Richard attacked Vincent years later for the same reason, as a warning from the Klan.

Daisy is Mexican. That distinction mightn't make any difference to Vallena, but would the Klan really get so worked up about a black man dating a Mexican? Tina, Vallena, and Earnest also said officers connected to Daisy's family bashed Vincent in his cell. But the chronology's all wrong: Vincent doesn't meet Daisy until a year and a half after he gets out of jail for the fight with the two officers. The two police officers by Daisy's side in the courtroom have, through a game of telephone, traveled backward in time and become the two officers in the cell in the minds of Earnest, Vallena, and Tina.

Yet.

Vincent was arrested for grand larceny, giving false information to police, careless driving, public drunkenness, no driver's license, no insurance. The district attorney chose to pursue only one charge—the grand larceny for the stolen Mexican money.

But weren't the pesos in fact in Patrick's pocket, not Vincent's?

In Daisy's *WEEK FROM HELL*, recording events as they happened, she wrote: *Patrick took dad's Mexican pesos & gold clip & some coins.*

I had brought this up back in the house. That Patrick swiped the pesos, not Vincent. This distinction didn't seem to strike Daisy as important. Why should it? Here was this psycho who choked her, kicked in her door, pimped a prostitute, and was driving drunk without a license. What's one little extra thing on the list, even if that thing is not necessarily true? He was the one who brought Patrick into her life, so he was responsible.

To Vincent and his family, however, this distinction is the main event. It's the *only* event. Never mind choking a girl, kicking in a car, stealing vehicles, bashing China and selling her for sex, and drunk driving—these didn't happen, or at the very least didn't matter (and perhaps they didn't know about most of them): He didn't take the pesos.

And I can't get past it, either. Vincent might have deserved to be in jail for what he did, but still, he was put in jail for something he *didn't* do.

In its own messy, clunky way, this was the archetypal Deep South tale: a black man thrown in prison for a crime he didn't commit.

It should be remembered that Vincent ended up serving a little under three years, rather than five, and less than two months after he was released he stabbed Richard in the neck so many times, Richard's head nearly fell off. Some might argue this vindicated locking him up in the first place. But that's not how justice is meant to work.

There's one other knot that revealed itself on the Reyeses' couch with the neon cushions. A knot that was either untied or tied up twice as tightly, I don't know anymore. Daisy said that when she was at the juvenile detention center, "the jail officers told me my parents could have got me out but they didn't." This sent Daisy into a flux of fury and distress. And there was a follow-up: "But then when I got out, my parents told me they *weren't* able to get me out."

Her parents had tried and were denied. Someone had lied to Daisy, telling one of the cruelest lies of all: that she had been abandoned by her parents.

This is uncannily similar to what happened to Vincent before the fight with the officers. *McGee understood that he was to be released on this day and no one had come to pick him up. Upon being told that his mother had been notified to pick him up but had failed to do so, McGee became very unruly.* Had Vincent been lied to as well? Had Tina been denied?

I've been dark on Tina McGee for abandoning him that day. I've framed her choice as the tipping point, the action that set in motion another action that set in motion another, all rolling down a hill to that night in the crummy little house and the killing of Richard Barrett. But what if she *did* want to get Vincent out but was told she couldn't, as happened with Jamie and Daisy? What if she couldn't get in to see Vincent, just like she had claimed to me she wasn't allowed to see him before the trial?

What if this is the way that power asserts itself over the helpless in Mississippi?

What if Tina is a better mother than I first thought?

Lord it's hard to work out what's going on. Although I feel like I'm plodding in a concentric circle toward *something*. If I keep plodding, I'll eventually get to the center, won't I?

Vincent's Call

The skin on my left wrist hurts. It hurts because I'm biting it. I'm biting it because I'm seething and I hate myself. For five minutes I thought my Dictaphone, with the lapel microphone sticky-taped to my cell phone, was recording.

My eyes just caught the counter flashing *00:00:00:00*. My finger torpedoes to the red record button.

Vincent McGee is the man I haven't been recording for five minutes. He's sealed in his little cell. I'm hunched over my coffee table.

Two Walmart Green Dot cards—one for a hundred and fifty dollars and one for fifty—sit on the table before me. He asked for the numbers right away. I said, "Hello," and he said, "You got the numbers?" My fingernail scratched the silver panels on the cards—like on instant lottery cards—and I read them out.

"Sorry, I didn't get that," I say, the Dictaphone recording now, and my teeth released from biting my flesh. "So they wouldn't let you use the phone to get home, so then the fight escalated from there?"

I'm asking Vincent about the fight with the policemen, the incident that rolled him out of juvenile detention into the adult prison system.

"Right," Vincent says, his voice tiny and crackly, traveling through his cell phone, across the Mississippi sky, and into my ear. Even tiny and crackly, his words echo off his prison cell walls. "'Cause I was in court and the judge released me. So I was trying to call somebody to come pick me up, but they wouldn't give me access to a phone."

"It says in the report," I tell him, "it's because your mother didn't come to pick you up and that's why you got angry."

"No!" Vincent says. "That wasn't the case—they didn't want me to leave."

"Oh yeah, I understand," I say. "They wanted to punish you for being in the Vice Lords gang?"

"Say what?"

"They wanted to keep you incarcerated for being in the Vice Lords."

"Something like that, you know what I'm sayin'?" he says. "They didn't like what I was. They didn't respect me. They thought they had more authority on me and all types of stuff like this."

Not quite the same lie as to Daisy, then, but certainly close.

"I heard," I say, "that sometimes the officers in juvenile detention centers, they tease and pick on the prisoners until they get angry and upset."

"Right," says Vincent. "They do that all the time here. That's what caused most of the fights, you hear? You see, I was behind my door. They had to open my cell in order for the confrontation to take place, you see?"

"Yeah," I say, "I found that strange. Because they were saying you were being angry, but even if that was the case, you were already locked up, so there was no need for them to open up the door."

"Correct," he says.

I ask Vincent how old he was when he first met Richard Barrett.

"I think I was around about fifteen, sixteen."

"And what happened? Where did you meet him?"

"Me and my little brother, we were walking up the street. He called us to his yard and he was telling us about a job, you know what I'm sayin'? Paint his deck. So that's how it went."

"And what happened with that job? Did both you and your brother do it, or only you?"

"Just me," he says. "You know what I'm sayin', I went and did it. But I ain't finished it because he tried to pay me in slave wages, you hear?"

The vernacular "slave wages" sounds more heated when muttered in Mississippi.

"He tried to give me a dollar for painting the whole building, you hear? I did the front part, and then I told him, 'I don't think I'm being paid fair. It's too hard.' So I was like, 'No, I'm through.' But he took me to the house to pay me for what I did, and he gave me a dollar."

He did that to other people. I've spoken to other workmen who he ripped off. And they were all very angry at him. One young man (white) I tracked down had started legal action against him and was still seething years later. "Is that the only time you worked with him? Or did you work with him a few times?"

"A few times. I worked with him when I was twenty-two."

That was the time Richard ended up with a knife in his neck.

"Why did you work with him again," I say, "when you knew he hadn't paid you money last time?"

"I really don't know myself, you hear? I really don't understand, but, you know, one day he came to my yard. He sounded like he needed some help, so I was gonna go give him some help, you hear? He tried to pull the same stunt on me again, you hear? I wasn't gonna have it—God knows, I had grew up."

To Vincent, growing up was stabbing a man. This was his lesson learned.

"And so, how did the fight break out in his house?"

"But look, we're moving fast right now, you hear? That's another topic for another day, you hear?"

"Sure, no, I understand."

"Yo. You're gonna write exactly what I'm saying and don't twist my words."

Vincent says if I twist his words, it could mess up his future chances in the courtroom.

"One charge they gave me—I got manslaughter, arson, burglary—the burglary charge, they had no evidence. I just went along with it for the plea so I could get the time that I got. I got to go to the court and try to get the time back."

That burglary charge was twenty-five years. Why would you go along with another twenty-five years?

"Send a letter with the questions on it, you know what I'm sayin'? I'll take my time to think my thoughts."

"Sure," I say. "You're still at MDOC in Pearl?"

"Yes," he says. "I need those Green Dot numbers one more time."

I pluck the cards off the coffee table and hold them under the lamp next to the couch and read out the numbers.

"A'right."

I tell him I also need a letter so I can talk to his lawyer, Mike Scott. We haggle and hit on a hundred and fifty Green Dot.

I'd be lying if I said paying Vincent was weighing heavily on my conscience. I suspect he's using his Green Dot money for little luxuries like cigarettes. I can't help but think, *So what?* I used cash to hustle my way into the crucifixion ceremony in the Philippines in *Race Relations*. And the sperm bank in Palestine. Maybe I've just been greasing palms for too long.

The Ballad of James Rankin

When I first got to Mississippi, Jim Giles mentioned that one of Richard Barrett's young men had been involved with a bomb crime.

It's taken me a while, but I've found him.

The headline in the old newspaper reads: MAN HELD ON WEAPONS COUNT: 19-YEAR-OLD ALLEGEDLY SOLD SUITCASE BOMB TO UNDERCOVER AGENT FOR $130.

The journalist describes James Rankin shackled in a courtroom and his mother trying to pass him a Bible. The photograph with the article isn't of them, though; it's of Richard Barrett.

Two years earlier, in her home in Pennsylvania, James Rankin's mother was flitting around the Internet when she stumbled onto the Nationalist Movement website. She began to chat with Richard online, and then on the phone. Richard told her he would help out her and her son. Soon she packed up her life and squeezed it in a car and drove to Mississippi. James and his mother moved into Richard's crummy little house in Pearl.

Richard tells the journalist he tried his best to assist, but he could tell after several weeks it wasn't going to work. He kicked them out of his home and canceled James's Nationalist Movement membership. There seem to be missing pieces to the story. Who invites a seventeen-year-old boy and his mother to come halfway across the country and move in?

The article tells me James and his mother's old address—3175 US Highway 80—but cruelly does not attach a town name. There are "3175 US Highway 80s" dotted all over Mississippi, from Jackson to Pelahatchie. For two days my knuckles rap on doors across the state, until a man in one of the 3175s tells me he remembers the incident. But James didn't live at his house, he lived across the road.

Across the road, a kind-faced old man opens the door. I hand him my business card.

"I'm writing a book about Richard Barrett," I say.

"All right!" he wheezes. "I don't even want . . . You've mentioned the wrong name there. So, get your ass off my place!"

"Okay, sorry," I say, and back away. As I slide in my car I look back toward his doorway. The old man's face has turned red. He's ripped up my business card and is throwing it to the sky like confetti.

But I reddened the old man's face for no reason. A Rankin County bail bondsman, who offered to help me out, found James Rankin. He's boxed in a federal prison in Pennsylvania.

So now I'm sitting out on the balcony at my apartment, in the sun, scratching my whiskers with my non-cell-phone hand. A couple of black residents strolling to the pool are ruining my chance to paint the apartments as a quasi-gated white community.

"Did you hear about Richard being killed?" I ask James Rankin.

"Yes, I was in Z block in prison here in Lewisburg and it said that he got stabbed—it was in the *USA Today*. And, like, a week later, I got stabbed!" James laughs in an *ain't life funny* way.

"Oh my God! Why did you get stabbed?"

"I just went in the wrong cage and I got stabbed by two people forty-five times and that was it."

"Are you okay?"

"Yeah, I'm fine."

"Why did they stab you?"

"Don't know, no idea. I thought that was funny that . . . what a co-incidence, you know? He died and I almost died!" James chuckles again at the serendipity of their mutual stabbings.

James has to squeeze his six-foot-four body into his cell. "It is really small. It's as small as they get—the smallest I've ever seen. You can't really even, like, pace. They got two beds and they got a hot pipe that heats up for winter. They got a window that you open with a stick."

Although two beds are squashed into the cell, James is alone, locked down for twenty-three hours a day. He passes his time reading German philosopher Oswald Spengler.

James tells me his dad darted out of his life early, leaving him and his mum alone.

"I have a sister named Lulu," James says. "She's in Peru prison right now on a cocaine conspiracy."

Richard offered James an internship at the Nationalist Movement.

"What did the internship involve?" I ask.

"I was mowing his lawn," James says. And James would also follow Richard about his Nationalist Movement headquarters as Richard dictated notes for the week's telephone lecture. "You could call 601-FREE-TIP," James says, "and he'd give this little dictum about what he believed and what was in the news."

Richard would lecture James about the history of his Nationalist Movement while James mowed the lawn.

I tell James, "He said that he had a bad experience in the war fighting, 'cause he felt the black soldiers weren't as loyal as the white soldiers."

"He mentioned that one time he stayed back for something," James says, "and the whole platoon got murdered. Had he not been off that day, he would have been killed also. He felt bad that he wasn't there getting murdered with them, more than *Woo-hoo, I won!* He was more like, *I wish*, or *I'm saddened that I wasn't there with them*. And he said that in such a subtle way that you know he didn't say it to get an effect, like he had a heart of bravery. That was not, like, a key part of his talks or anything."

"And do you know where he went off to when his . . . Where was he when his platoon was getting killed?"

"I can't even remember," James says.

That sounds like Richard. When the shit's going down, he's snuck off somewhere. If the story's even true in the first place.

One afternoon, Richard summoned James to the backyard of his crummy little house and introduced James to a man in a khaki uniform. "He was about thirty or something. I think he was in the Ku Klux Klan more than anything."

James does not want to name him. The two became close, "hunting and doing all that stuff—outdoor shit," which included blowing things up. But the man turned informant for the law enforcement agency, the Bureau of Alcohol, Tobacco, Firearms and Explosives (ATF). Or perhaps he was an informant the whole time. According to James, the man set him up. The man told the ATF James had manufactured some grenade bodies he hadn't in fact manufactured. In the ATF's version, after this tip-off, they had a female undercover agent buy a briefcase bomb from James Rankin, which she said was to kill her ex-husband. According to the report, "Rankin assured her that the bomb would kill him. If the bomb for some reason did not work, Rankin said he would give her the next one free." After Rankin was arrested, explosives experts confirmed the bomb would indeed have worked.

James Rankin was sentenced to ten years in a federal penitentiary. Richard claimed to have no idea what they'd been up to.

"Do you think Richard actually did know you were involved in bomb-making?" I ask.

"I think . . . I think he did know," James says. After all, Richard had made the introductions.

James doesn't remember being booted out of the Nationalist Movement.

"It's possible he said that for legal purposes," James says. "He was always about the book and the law and that's it. Everything was . . . That was his whole leverage that he took pride in, was the legalities and all that. It was . . . like, it would put a smile on his face if he found out that something was legal. That was his whole thing—was legal, legal, legal, the law, and that was it."

"But he introduced you to somebody who taught you how to make explosives. It sounds like maybe he didn't mind if other people did things *not* by the book."

"Correct, yeah," says James. "I think you're right about that."

I ease into the awkward main game. Did Richard sleaze on James? Why did Richard invite a then seventeen-year-old stranger and his mother to move in? And why did he kick them out soon after?

"The guy who killed Richard," I tell James, "said Richard made sexual advances on him."

"Wow!" James says. "That's weird. That's really strange."

"Does that add up in your head based on your experiences?"

"No, not at all," he says. "That's wild. I mean . . . it doesn't sound right at all."

James says Richard didn't even stay in the same house as him and his mum. Richard put James and his mother up in his home in Pearl and he stayed in a house in Jackson.

Even without the sexual aspect, there's a lot that's familiar here. Another young man without a father, lost in the world, doing yard work for Richard, ending up in jail. But in this story, the young man is white.

Accessory

I phone the number Vincent last called me from. I haven't been cleared to visit him or received the letter for Mike Scott yet, either.

"You want to talk to Vincent McGee, huh?" says a man without a murble.

His cousin, Michael Dent, has picked up. Vincent's stepfather, Alfred, drove Vincent to Michael's house the night of the killing. Michael was arrested as an accessory along with Alfred, Tina, and Michael's mother, Vicky. Michael is the only other one who ended up locked in prison.

"Do you want me to tell you all the story, man?" Michael says.

"Yeah," I say, "I don't mind."

"Tell you the story for real?"

"Yep."

"No, man," Michael says suddenly, backing away. "I'm gonna let you and Vincent get on that shit."

Vincent snaps the phone off Michael.

"Yeah, what's up, man?" murbles Vincent. "Got the numbers?"

"Yeah, I got the Green Dot numbers," I say. "But I need the Mike Scott letter."

He swears he'll pop the letter in the Monday post, but he needs the numbers now.

I cough up the numbers.

"You just spoke to Michael Dent, too, yeah?" says Vincent.

"Yeah, yeah," I say. "So it seems like you're friends again?"

"I wouldn't say that, you hear? But listen, if anyone calls you and asks you for anything, don't give it to them."

"Oh, yeah," I say, "sure."

Six Hours Later

Vincent is murbling down the crackly line. He's almost inaudible. The fridge hum is louder than Vincent. I walk to the kitchen and unplug the fridge. I can hear him a little better now. Something about a fight.

"So, how many inmates did you get in a fight with?" I say.

"I guess twenty murblestatic Michael," he says.

"Wow, so your cousin Michael was also in the fight?"

"No! I said me and him were murble. Murble Meridian murble crumbly ensane."

"Crumbly?" I say.

"CRI-MAN-LEE," he spits.

Syllable by syllable, spit by spit, Vincent tells the story. He roused a fight with twenty inmates. After the brawl, he was pulled into a van and driven to another prison, the East Mississippi Correctional Facility in Meridian. This is a prison for the criminally insane.

He needs three hundred dollars on Green Dot cards to buy another phone. He's speaking from another prisoner's, and he needs his own if I want to talk. He'll ring tomorrow night for the Green Dot numbers.

"A'right?" he asks.

"Sure."

Vincent Calls the Next Night

"How long do you have on the phone now?" I ask Vincent. "Can you talk now?"

"Murble," says Vincent.

"Okay, cool. So tell us why—I'm taping this—tell us why you got let go from the other prison and moved into this prison?"

"I got caught with a cell phone, then I busted six windows out, then got into a fight with another inmate, all this type of shit. You hear?"

"Sure."

"But look," he says, "I need those numbers real quick. I gotta go. I got some business."

I walk under the fluorescent light in the kitchen and read him the numbers.

"A'right."

"So when will you be able to ring me back for a proper interview?"

"I gotta get somebody to give me a cell phone, you know what I'm sayin'? Check this out, how much is this one?"

"That's two hundred and fifty."

"What's the other one?"

"The other one is fifty. Before you go, tell me, why did you plead guilty when it was going to be sixty-five years?"

"I'm gonna tell you the truth why I pled guilty," he says. "One simple thing—that when I called my people, they weren't ready to give me the help that I need, you know what I'm sayin'? I had all of those white officers at the county jail that were jumping on me and they were playing with my food, putting stuff in my food. So I was like, you know what I'm sayin', so I was thinking I had to leave Rankin County Jail or they were gonna kill me, or they were gonna fuck me up by feeding me other shit."

Somehow, almost uncannily, the story's already echoing the Reyeses' story—let down by his family, taunted by the petty power of the authorities.

"Why did you think they were trying to kill you in Rankin County Jail?"

"You see, every day we were fighting. The officers, they were making racist comments to me, you know what I'm sayin'? They cuff my legs and my arms and leave me like that for hours, and I'm being attacked and shit like that. So I had to get myself out of that situation quickly. So you know what I'm sayin', they were taking my canteen and they were taking me downstairs in maximum isolation. And when I ordered my canteen, they won't bring it to me. Shit, I had to do what I had to do, you know what I'm sayin'?"

"Why did you think it was going to be safer in MDOC?" I say. "Wouldn't another prison also be dangerous for you?"

"Listen, I gotta go. A dude's coming for the phone."

Vincent tells me he'll call tomorrow.

The Next Day

When I speak to Vincent the next day, I ask him why he split with Precious Martin.

"I really don't feel like talking that shit to no tape right now, you know what I'm sayin'? You might burn a hole in my shit. I don't know what's gonna happen you might take my voice and make it say something else." That's what Jim Giles was suspicious I'd do, too. "What day of the week is it?" He doesn't know the day of the week?

"It's Sunday night."

"I'm gonna need three hundred dollars from you, you hear? Fo' Friday."

"What's happening Friday?"

"I got something I need to do, you know what I'm sayin'? To help me in here, you hear?"

"I can't just give you three hundred dollars. I'm going to need to interview you, you know? I've already given you six hundred dollars."

"That ain't shit. I ain't trying to sound, you know what I'm sayin', ungrateful, but that ain't nothing."

"Yeah, well, you haven't given me much, either. Everything I want to talk about, you say, 'That's for another day.' You haven't gotten me visitation, you haven't sent me the Mike Scott letter."

"I'm saying, at the same time, you ain't in my situation. I can't just walk out and do what I wanna do. I got some kind of business tied up here, you know what I'm sayin'? I'm trying to get in, you hear? So I'm gonna need a hundred and twenty dollars. You know what I'm sayin'?"

We haggle. Instead of him flicking me a scrap here and there, I get to the heart of what I want. If he tells me what happened the night he killed Richard *plus* sends me the Mike Scott letter, I'll give him fifteen hundred dollars.

A man bellows "VINCENT!" in the East Mississippi prison for the criminally insane. Vincent says he has to go. He says he'll call back soon.

Do No Harm

Janet Malcolm wrote a book *about* a true crime book and its author, Joe McGinniss. Joe buddied up to the killer. Told him he thought he was innocent, that his book would argue he should be a free man. So the killer opened up to him. The book came out. It did *not* argue anything of the sort. Rather, it painted the killer as a guilty, narcissistic monster. The killer sued Joe for breaking their agreement. Five out of six jurors sided with the killer. They found a man jailed for murdering his wife and children a more sympathetic character than the deceptive true crime writer.

Janet Malcolm, in *her* book, slowly tortures Joe McGinniss for his deception. Janet says most writers do harm.

I've imagined Janet reading everything I write.

The Second Man in the Will

Vincent Thornton, Richard's Nationalist Movement sidekick, was bequeathed Richard's earthly possessions. Third in line was the government of Iran. Which for a while made me forget about the second man in the will: John Moore.

But tonight as I gobbled a catfish at a Jackson bar, my greasy fingers flicked through old Spirit of America Day booklets. Beneath a tiny photo in one booklet was the name *John Moore*. The man wore a business suit, a gold medallion pinned to his lapel.

I skidded to the apartment, leaving half my catfish in the basket, creaked open my silver laptop, and started to snoop.

It turns out searching for a John Moore in Mississippi is like searching for a Mohammad in Tehran. But with the photo in the booklet, I whittle down the John Moores to one: a Republican politician. He sits in the Mississippi House of Representatives. He represents District 60, which takes in Rankin County.

I pluck Richard's will from my folder. Unlike the government of Iran, John Moore has signed off on it, as executor.

Mississippians tell me Richard was an impotent outsider, that modern Mississippians rejected him and his views. So why is the most powerful politician in Rankin County in Richard's last will and testament?

John Moore

In the marble-and-stained-glass Mississippi State Capitol, the original 1903 golden elevator cranks me to the third floor. This is where the state legislature sits when it sits. It's not sitting today. John Moore told me to meet him here. He's the first Mississippian I've lured in under vague pretenses. I told everyone else I want to talk about Richard Barrett. I told John Moore I want to talk about Mississippi "and stuff."

One hundred and twenty-two leather chairs, big as thrones, circle the House of Representatives. All are empty bar two, taken by the Johns Moore and Safran.

"Make yourself comfortable," John Moore says, pointing at my throne. "That's actually my seat there I sit in."

"Oh, okay," I say. "Am I allowed to?"

"Oh, absolutely. Yep, put your feet on the desk, I don't care."

John Moore scoops up a *John Moore* pen from a bowl of *John Moore* pens on the desk and tells me I can have a second one, too, if I'd like.

"I was actually raised on a farm," he says, "and had the experience that every young person should have. It's just a different lifestyle. You know, much slower."

I aim my *John Moore* pen at my yellow notepad.

"How old are you?" I ask.

"None of your business. I'm fifty-seven."

I ask him what he thinks about Mississippi's reputation.

"The view from the outside, a lot of it has been a big lie. The news media, for some reason, wants to keep Mississippi looking like the old slave state."

John Moore tells me Mississippi isn't split between black and white anymore. He then tells me it is.

"It's still segregated because it's not forced," John Moore says. "You know, blacks like to go hang out with blacks, that's their family. And, see, whites are the same way. There's not something sinister or some conspiracy behind it all. It's just the way communities behave. It's just a natural thing. But that also is mutating over time, as the areas become more integrated."

A rattlesnake pokes its tongue at me on a little yellow flag on John Moore's desk. DON'T TREAD ON ME read the words beneath the snake.

"Just don't try to force it!" John hisses. "That's what has created a lot of animosity down through the years. The stinking federal government trying to force people to do things that if you leave them alone they're going to do anyway. It's kind of like setting the speed limit on the highway. You know, lots of people are gonna speed just because it's the speed limit." John Moore laughs. "You get the logic there? The speed limit's seventy, so that means I'm s'posed to drive seventy-five!"

John leans back in his throne, crossing his arms over his maroon polo shirt with JOHN MOORE DISTRICT 60 on the pocket. I suppose I get the logic, but I'm here for something else.

"A few years back," I say, "I came to Mississippi and did a documentary on this man I think you know, called Richard Barrett."

"Oh, yeah, yeah. Yeah, Richard was tragically murdered, what, a couple of years ago or something like that?" John Moore says, not sounding like he knows the guy well enough to be number two in his will.

"And I saw," I say, "that you've gone to one of his Spirit of America Days."

John Moore pinks a little.

"Well, no, I . . . I never . . . You know, that was kind of a . . . I never spoke at any of his things. I . . . I never went to one of them."

John Moore glances over at the rattlesnake for support.

"Now, there's a whole bunch of House and Senate members and governors and lieutenant governors that *have* spoken at it. At its . . . Which is actually . . . That's one of those things. Richard Barrett was branded as a racist, and I'm telling you he was, but he didn't hate blacks. Matter of fact, the guy that killed him, Richard had been taking care of him. The guy had been in prison, got out, couldn't get a job. Richard paid him to do whatever he was doing—I don't know and don't care."

That "I don't know and don't care" is delivered as a knowing aside. I try to think of a reason that John Moore has said those words in that way that doesn't involve sexual innuendo, but can't.

"The only association I ever had with Barrett was back, gosh, ten or eleven years ago."

John Moore tells me that each March, for years, a member of the House, a lady, would stand up from her throne and call for a resolution to recognize the Spirit of America Day. One day, ten years ago, the lady woke up sick. She rang John Moore and asked him to do it. "For sure, yeah, I don't care," he told her.

That year, John Moore stood up from his throne and called for the resolution. He glanced up at the public gallery and caught the eyes of the young athletes. He didn't see Richard, though.

"He knew that he was branded a racist," John Moore tells me. "He wouldn't even get in the balcony, he would stay back. He knew it would cause strife on the floor, even though what he was doing was a good thing. They were good kids, you know. It wasn't like they were skinheads or anything."

From then on, once a year, the phone rang in his office and Richard's voice came through the crackle.

"Look, my kids are coming on March the first. Will you do it again?" Richard would say.

"Sure will," said John Moore each year.

"But that would be the only time we'd communicate," John Moore tells me.

"That was it?" I ask.

"Yep," says John Moore, not sounding like a man who's number two on Richard Barrett's will. "You know, admittedly, Barrett said and did some stupid things. I'm not going to sit here and tell you he was a wonderful, great guy. He was aware he had a lot of folks offended. And there was a lot of . . . There was even the . . . a family situation that he actually had . . . He actually had a sister and stuff that I . . ."

John Moore's mouth clunks and rattles to a halt. Did he see my blue eyes ping when he said *sister*? He reaches for a crystal bowl on the desk, between the *John Moore* pens and the rattlesnake flag.

"Would you care for a piece of candy?"

"Thank you," I say, and pluck a red striped candy.

"Compliments of the City of Jackson."

"I don't know if I want to eat it or keep it," I say, my mouth actually watering for more *sister* news.

He plucks two more candies, one for me, one for himself.

"Well here, have one to eat, one for home. Get as many as you want. They've been sitting there for a while."

John Moore peels the cellophane from his candy and sucks it up.

"After he had been dead for, gosh, two or three weeks," he says through sucks, "I get this strange call from Florida. And it's his sister."

A puff of joy poofs in my heart as *Florida* leaves his lips and is scribbled down on my yellow notepad. I feel like I've caught a rare butterfly.

"Geraldine?" I say.

John Moore dodges confirming the name.

"Well, he kept all of that very secretive," he says, "because he was afraid they would be hurt. See, he knew his reputation. And he loved his family very much—just like all of us do—and he was afraid for anybody to know where his family lived."

With a gulp that waters his eyes, he sucks his candy down his throat.

"I connected his sister with our chancery clerk in Rankin County. A gentleman by the name of Larry Swales. He's the one who kind of keeps up with all the wills. Richard's sister and me, we probably had a thirty-minute conversation. Richard was always going down there."

"To Florida to meet her?"

John Moore now dodges confirming Florida like he dodged her name.

"She was trying to find out everything I knew. Which was nothing. Because you've just heard all the communication Richard and I had all these years, which was nothing," John Moore says, like he's not number two in Richard Barrett's will.

"On that point," I say, "I've got here, and this is public record . . ."

I pull Richard Barrett's last will and testament from a manila folder on my lap.

John Moore starts scratching his arm.

"Oh yeah, the will . . ." he says.

"Have you heard about this already?"

"Oh yeah, yeah, I've seen it."

"What does it mean?"

"Okay, what . . . He called me and said, 'Look, can I come over to your house and talk to you?' I said, 'Yeah, I guess so.' So he came to the house. I didn't even have a clue he knew where I lived, you know. And he said, 'Look, you know, I'm . . . I'm not going to leave my estate to anybody, and I'd love to name you as one of the executors of my estate.' I thought, *Sure.* Well I'm . . . I'm sitting there thinking, *Okay, I'm as old as he is, I'm going to die before he does, so this is a nonissue.*"

My antennas flit.

"And I'm telling you, when he left I folded the paperwork up and threw it in the garbage. 'Cause I'll never have any use for it. And then lo and behold, it wasn't a year or so after that he actually was murdered."

Hearing the news of Richard's death, John Moore rang Larry Swales, the man who handles the wills.

"See, I was named as the second guy," John Moore tells me. "I said to Larry Swales, 'So if this other guy'—and I couldn't even remember the guy's name 'cause I'd thrown the will away, I threw it in the garbage—I said, 'If the guy doesn't come forward, let me know.' Well, the other guy came forward, so I never really thought about it again."

I ask him why he and this other guy—Vince Thornton—were in the will, but not Richard's sister.

He says he has no idea. "I mean, all you do as an executor is you read the will and you do what it says and that's it."

"But don't you also get everything if the other guy doesn't?"

"Well, not necessarily."

Perhaps not necessarily, but in the case of Richard's will, *yes.*

If, for any reason, the aforesaid VINCE THORNTON predeceases me or is unwilling, unable, or disqualified to receive the bequest, hereunder, then I give, devise, and bequeath all my worldly
possessions to JOHN MOORE of Brandon, Mississippi.

"I hadn't read the thing before entirely," John Moore says of the will
he says he threw in the garbage bin. "But I think it actually says that the
money was s'posed to be given to somebody or to something."

Having been given the world's vaguest explanation, I move to the
will's number three—the government of Iran.

John Moore looks like a pained man trying hard not to look like a
pained man. A bead of sweat has grown underneath his nose. He wipes
it off with a knuckle.

"I knew it was there," he says. "But, you know, it's his money, he
can give it to whoever he wants. Don't tell me who I can give my money
to, you know? Just as long as he wasn't giving it to the Taliban or
something."

I refrain from saying that many would think the government of Iran
is the "something" in "or something."

Another knuckle to the nose brushes another drop of sweat.

"You know, I think Barrett, from a reputation standpoint, got what
he asked for. I can't defend his reputation and I'm surely not going to
defend his words," John Moore says, after a fair while of defending his
reputation and defending his words.

"The connection—the will and stuff—I don't know why. I guess because I had done this favor for him for ten years and that he might not
have had any other friends. I don't know if the only friends in the world
he had might've been his few neighbors out there, that were all black.
That's what you need to do. Hunt down his neighbors."

I stand from my throne, thread my *John Moore* pen in my collar, and
pocket my City of Jackson candy.

John Moore eyes my Dictaphone.

"Ever heard of Peavey Electronics?" John Moore says.

I tell him I have not.

"They build a lot of big sound systems. You know where they're made?"

"I think the answer's going to be Mississippi."

"Meridian, Mississippi," he says. "The founder started building sound systems under his garage. Now it's a $250 million corporation."

I wonder where this is all heading.

"It's a slow culture. We're the hospitality state," John Moore tells me with his eyes locked on mine, "but don't associate us being that way with us being dumb."

I feel a salty bead of sweat underneath my nose.

Larry Swales

So I go to see Larry Swales, the man in charge of the wills in Rankin County, to see whether he's still got Richard's sister's phone number.

Larry is silver-haired and in a particularly good mood. He was reelected chancery clerk last week. He calls his secretary into his office. "She knows how to use the computer better than me," he chirps.

"Barrett," I tell her, and she punches the name into his computer.

"Do you have a first name?" she asks.

"Richard."

"Oh," Larry says, "the man lit on fire?"

"Yes."

This changes everything. Larry turns "Barrett Pink"—the color a lot of white people turn when you mention his name.

"Well, I didn't know him," Larry says.

(I never said you did.)

"Always alone," he flusters. "Didn't have anyone."

Larry's secretary interjects: "He wore knickers."

"Knickers?" I ask.

She says he wore long socks up to his knees and shorts so wide, they looked like a skirt.

Larry pulls out a nail file and starts filing his nails.

"He had one close friend," Larry says, "and I can't remember his name . . . John? John Moore?"

In the same way I can't figure out why he's filing his nails, I can't work out why he's clearly faking stumbling over John Moore's name.

Larry's secretary tells me Richard's sister isn't in the database. I get up to leave.

"John Moore," Larry says. "He called up because he thought he was going to get all the money. That it was all going to go to him. And he was real mad when I said that it wasn't."

These men in power who get nervous when Richard's name comes up—I wonder what they know about the time Richard was quietly released from Rankin County Jail.

Bearing Witness

Janet Malcolm, I know what you think of us true crime writers.

Being outsiders to these communities, poking our noses where they're not wanted, looks bad on paper.

But I caught up with the district attorney again and asked him why he took the death penalty off the table. He said because those cases are expensive and time-consuming, and with an execution in play, juries can be more reluctant to return a guilty verdict. But he also added: "We wanted to try to simplify this as much as we could. We didn't want to add any more excitement to the case. I mean, with your being here—you know, there's already kind of a following about the case."

Janet, to the district attorney, I was bearing witness, a little stone in his shoe, when everyone else had gone home.

Black Man's Chest

Ten twenty p.m. It's pitch-black in my bedroom. My cell phone hums on my bedside table, and I flip it open to a text.

A black man has sent me a photo of his chest. No face. I squint. Is that a tattoo or just wiry springs of hair?

The phone hums in my hand. Another text:

> **Wrong person delete that pic.**

Three minutes later, another text from the same fellow:

> **This michael dent so how I get a book I got a story to tell the real one**

I type back:

> **Hi Michael you can be in the book im writing if you want**

He shoots back a text straightaway:

> **Im gone tell u the whole story just be ready to record.**

Michael wants three hundred dollars in Green Dot cards.

Michael Dent

"Hey, Michael Dent?" I say. "It's John Safran."

"How you doing?" Michael says. Not a question I've ever heard leave the lips of Vincent McGee.

Michael owns a deep voice, fuzzed up by phone reception. I drift to the kitchen and unplug the fridge. I flick off the ceiling fan.

"Can you put me on your visitation list," I say, "so I can come and meet you, please?"

I called Vincent's new prison. They said no media ever, and no visitors for Vincent anyway, because of the horrific fight that landed him in there in the first place. Vincent is still promising he can get me in, however.

"See, I can't get visitors because I'm in the hole," Michael says. "In lockdown."

"Why are you in lockdown?"

"Because it was a high-profile murder case."

"You're still in lockdown all these months later because of Richard Barrett?" I say, surprised. "What, are they worried that some white prisoner is going to kill you?"

"That's what I believe it is."

"Richard didn't have many friends," I tell him, "so I don't think you have to worry about that."

"I know. But once you're in the Klan, they always stick together, so I don't know."

Like James Rankin, Michael is in lockdown, alone, twenty-three hours a day.

"You just have to sit in your cell?"

"That's it."

"Wow! And how big is your cell?"

"Like a damn sandbox."

I tell him I heard Vincent's been moved to another prison.

"Yes, he got moved. He was busting out windows."

"He was trying to break out?"

"No, but he busted five windows and he fought with the police."

Vincent sparked the riot in the one non-lockdown hour.

"Have you got the story?" Michael says. "I mean, do you know what even happened?"

I tell him I don't really know what happened from Vincent's side.

"This is all I know of what happened, right? Vincent went and worked for the man. From what I know, the only reason Vincent went back down to the house was to get—well, to ask for—more money, so he could pay his ERS, because you know he was out on ERS."

"What does that mean?"

"ERS is 'Early Release System.' It's something they do in the prison system. That means that you get out early, and if you don't pay fifty-two dollars on time a month, they'll lock you back up."

"Wow," I say. So that's why Vincent took up Richard's offer of work, despite having been ripped off before. And Richard almost certainly knew denying him the measly amount *he'd earned* could push him back in prison. I thought I'd been desensitized to Richard's scumbaggery, but there's an anger rising in me. "And it's just because Vincent's quite extreme, so if he gets into a fight it can get pretty aggressive?"

"Yes," Michael says. "The whole thing of Vincent getting moved to another prison . . . I was telling him I feel like I'm locked up for nothing. That's how I feel. You know, I ain't really a part of the damn Richard Barrett thing. I ain't killed anyone and I'm locked up. And I told him that and he got mad. He busted the windows out."

Vincent might feel guilty about what happened to Michael. Doesn't this mean he's capable of empathy?

"What about the night he came to meet you? Just after he killed Richard Barrett. Did he threaten you or force you to help him out?"

"When Vincent came to my house, I didn't know he killed the man until the next day, and that's when I seen him on the news. I thought something was funny, because when his stepdad, Alfred, dropped him off, he left automatically. He didn't say *Hey*. He just left. I was outside, and Vincent talked and talked and talked about females and stuff; he really didn't go into killing a man."

"One of the stories the investigators told me was that Vincent burned Richard Barrett's wallet in your backyard."

"I didn't ever see no wallet!" Michael protests. "My momma had called me back to the house and she was like, 'What is Vincent doing there?' I said, 'I don't know.' My momma don't really like Vincent being around me because he always get in trouble, and I told my momma, I said, 'I don't know.'"

"The investigators said he brought an old-fashioned gun with him."

"He did have a gun," Michael says. "But he didn't tell me where the damn gun came from. He pointed the gun at me, putting it in my face. He pointed the gun at me, and I said, 'Whoa, man. Get the gun down.' I was scared to death. I ain't ever had a gun pointed at my face, you know what I'm sayin'?"

Vincent spent the night under a blanket on the Dents' couch. The next morning Michael's mother, Vicky, sped the young men back toward the McGee home. She wanted him far away, and quickly.

Vincent told Vicky to pull over at a gas station. Vincent said he wanted gas for the mower, to cut the lawn for a party. In three days' time, Michael's sister was to host her twentieth birthday at the McGees' home.

"He told me to get some gas, to buy him a shirt, and get some cigarettes," Michael says.

Michael walked into the store and handed over money for a red gas can. Michael walked to a pump and filled the can. He twisted on the lid.

Michael, Vicky, Vincent, and the red gas can pulled into the driveway at the McGees'.

"Now, who was there?" Michael says. "My momma was in the house talking to Tina. And I was talking to my uncle Stanley in the yard out back about a job, because he was doing details on eighteen-wheeler trucks."

Uncle Stanley noticed Vincent jump the wire back fence and drift into the woods.

"I asked my uncle, 'What the hell did he go to the woods for?' The first thing that came to mind is his brother, Justin, has some dogs in the woods. I thought, *Okay, maybe he's going out there to see the dogs.*"

Not long afterward, an alarm started wailing somewhere in the distance. The wail shot up through the woods into the McGees' yard.

"Vincent came out of the woods screaming," Michael says. "It wasn't even screaming, it was more like a hysterical thing. It was more like panic and breathing hard. He called my name from the woods. He goes, 'Oh, take me away! Take me away from here!' My momma came rushing outside and said, 'What the hell's going on?' I said, 'I don't know!' He jumped in the truck with his stepdad, Alfred, and took off." Vincent hid at his sister Daphne's mobile home, where he was arrested.

"The investigators said that you were a good person. They said that you were different from Vincent. So why do you think they locked you up?"

"Man, I don't know why. To this day I really don't know how the hell I got locked up. I told them what they wanted to know. I told them I bought the gas, and that's what got me locked up. I didn't know what the gas was being used for at that time. I see Alfred as a bitch-ass dude, man, because of a simple thing. He knew what the hell happened before and he still brought that Vincent to my house. And then he told the police that when Vincent got out the truck, I said, 'Vincent, did you kill that white man?' I didn't say anything like that. I didn't say any goddamn thing like that. I don't want anybody locked up. But hell, if anybody should be locked up, I feel like it should have been Alfred and Vincent."

Michael Dent's teddy-bear face was already in a file at the Rankin County sheriff's department. He had served two years and two months in Pearl MDOC for grand larceny (not connected to Vincent McGee's grand larceny case). Michael was released forty-five days before Alfred dropped Vincent (who himself had been out of jail only two months) on his doorstep.

The investigators pulled Michael into the interrogation room. Did Vincent kill Richard because he was in the Klan? Did Vincent kill Richard because they were lovers? Michael wept and said he didn't know anything.

"In the Rankin County Jail, I asked Vincent, 'Now, what the hell happened? Why did you do it? The investigators are saying the Klan.' But what he told me was the only reason that he went back down to the man's house was because to get some money, to pay his ERS lady. I asked Vincent, 'Was he gay?' and he said no, and I left it alone because I knew where the conversation was going to lead to."

An inmate or guard screams in the background at Pearl MDOC.

"I'm trying to think what else I've heard," I say. "One thing that Peter Holmes told me when I spoke to him—you know, Vincent's brother-in-law—was when Vincent was in jail he was on medication to keep him calm."

"Yes, that's true."

"Do you know what kind of medication?"

"Risperdal. They give it to the inmates up here. It calms you down and really puts you to sleep; you won't be so hyper, so energetic, or anything like that."

"Peter Holmes said that maybe when he came out of prison, and straightaway he had those drugs cut off, that might have been why he was so angry. It must be hard when they release someone from prison. Because how can they monitor the person to make sure they're still taking the drugs?"

"Right," says Michael. "That's a good question. You'll have to ask Christopher Epps."

"Who?"

"Christopher Epps. He's the commissioner of the prisons," Michael says.

My head fumbles about for what to say next.

"I'll tell you a little secret, you hear?" Michael says. "You know when Vincent was in Walnut?" Vincent served his grand larceny term in a prison in Walnut Grove, Mississippi. "There was a rumor going around that he raped his roommate. I asked him about it, and he said he didn't do it."

My chest stings.

"What do you mean? His roommate in prison?"

"Right."

"But who told you that?"

"Inmates. It was all over the prison."

"Wow!" I say. "Everything is really strange, isn't it?"

"Yeah, it is," says Michael.

For months I've been burrowing, trying to find a story that reveals Richard as a gay sexual aggressor. Now Michael drops in my lap a story where Vincent is one. How does this impact on what went on in the crummy little house that night?

"I noticed his mother and his family didn't turn up to the court when he was being sentenced to sixty-five years' jail," I try. "No one from his family was there."

"Like I said, man, when you grow up living with poverty all your life, attacked by the system, the legal system, and when you're scared of the police, you really don't want to be around the police. So I really don't know what to say about that. I really don't know."

"What do you think is going to happen to Vincent now? Because he's talking about trying to get another trial."

"I don't know. The crime happened in Rankin County, and everybody knows Rankin County to be racist. When I was in the back of the police car coming to Rankin County Jail when I got picked up in the morning, the police told me, 'I ought to kill you now.' He actually stopped the car. He said, 'I ought to kill your nigger ass right now.' The exact words. Everybody knows Rankin County is racist. Everybody knows that. They shouldn't have taken our pleas or anything else in Rankin County. Everything should have been moved to a different court."

"I guess the killing happened in Rankin County so it had to be there?"

"Not really. You can have a change of venue when you've got a case with a white supremacist."

Something clangs in the background at Pearl MDOC.

"Hey listen, I call you right back," Michael says, and hangs up.

I write *Rape* on my yellow notepad on the coffee table. I collapse into the couch.

One Hour Later

One hour later, my laptop is opened on my belly, showing the Wikipedia page covering Risperdal:

"Risperidone (trade name Risperdal, and generics) is a potent anti-psychotic drug which is mainly used to treat schizophrenia (including adolescent schizophrenia), schizoaffective disorder, the mixed and manic states associated with bipolar disorder, and irritability in people with autism."

There is an insect buzz in my pocket. I pull out my phone. Michael has sent a text:

> Is Vincent gay? Yes. Did he hurt that man over some gay shit? Maybe. But I know the truth and I will tell you if you help me today.
>
> Me: How did you know that he was gay?
>
> Michael: Help me and I'll give you a story everyone would want to read.
>
> Me: How do you know he was gay? Do you know if he slept with Richard Barrett?
>
> Michael: Listen for the last time I will give you the whole story. You should name the book "Sex, lies and murder." Today the truth will come out.

I leave it a few minutes. The insect buzzes again.

> Michael: Did you know Vincent got raped by a relative when he was a kid? You help me this last time and you won't need to again

because I'm tell you the whole story. Did Tina tell you she had trouble taking care of her kids and that's the reason Vincent got so much built up madness?

Me: How much needed?

Michael: $300

I claw the car keys off the floor and head out to Walmart.

Soon After

"Tell me about the relative," I say to Michael, unplugging the fridge, snapping closed the window, and flicking off the fan.

"Okay. Well, since he were little, like I said, it seemed to me like his momma couldn't really take care of him. I remember Vincent used to break into people's houses stealing food. She used to go to parties and drink and stay away from the house. So when Vincent was little, he got sexually assaulted by this relative. And, um, the whole family knows this. They know. They kept it secret. I think he was about eight or nine at the time. And, um, that relative, he is definitely gay. I mean he's a homosexual. So I guess that probably had a big effect on Vincent to this day, and what he did when he was locked up at Walnut, when he raped his roommate."

"Okay, wow. So he must have been a bit upset with his mother because his mother didn't stand up for him."

"Yeah, I would have been upset with my momma, too. I'm pretty sure you would have been upset, too, right?"

"Yeah, definitely—absolutely."

"Listen, my phone is going dead. I can call you back later, but my phone is going dead."

What was the drug they gave Vincent? If I were some other writer, this story could be about pharmaceutical multinationals and drugs they sell to the prison-industrial complex. But I've already forgotten the name of the drug they fed Vincent. Instead, my head's returned to where it always returns. Family is everything. And, boy, what meat I have to support that proposition after hearing out Michael Dent.

The Mother Lode

I snap on the lights and squint. For months, while in bed, I've been churning through the thousands of pages of Richard's files, from the FBI, local law enforcement, and Mississippi's spy agency, the Sovereignty Commission. I've struck the mother lode. In a bad photocopy of a Sovereignty Commission report, a woman purports to tell the story of Richard's childhood.

That woman is Richard Barrett's mother.

The Ballad of Young Richard Barrett, as Told by Richard's Mother to Mississippi's Spy Agency

Report of Conversation with Mrs. A. J. (Eleanor) Barrett
June 22, 1968

Richard Barrett grew up in Orange, New Jersey. At age six he was taken to a psychiatrist for examination and treatment, and again at age twelve.

The psychiatrist concluded that there was nothing further that could be done, that Barrett was a borderline violence case. The psychiatrist told the Barretts that Richard hated them both intensely.

In the few months before he left home, at age seventeen, never to return, Mrs. Barrett said she became afraid that Richard "may do bodily harm to her."

He had been expelled from high school several times for distributing hate literature, but the precipitating event for him leaving home was his father's refusal to let him hang a Nazi flag on the house.

Richard then resided with his maternal aunt while attending Rutgers University. He "stole money" from the aunt, according to Mrs. Barrett, and was asked to leave.

Mrs. Barrett reports she had heard of similar incidents of theft from people all over the country, especially the South.

Richard claims he is an orphan. On the contrary, his mother says she and his father love him very much and have tried to help him. His father went to Mississippi about six months ago to see Richard and was ordered by him to leave or he would call the police. Mrs. Barrett says that her husband returned from Jackson "with tears in his eyes." They have repeatedly written to him and the only reply from him was a letter saying he hated them and wanted nothing to do with them.

His parents have received numerous calls from ministers, members and officers of various organizations complaining of embarrassing incidents including theft, lying, fraud, and exhibitionism. Mrs. Barrett reports that they can do nothing about this, but she is willing to go anywhere at any time to see him if it would help him, but says he would refuse to see her. In fact, she says that she fears if Richard had a suspicion that anyone had talked to her about him, he "might do anything!"

Mrs. Barrett says that "the boy is mentally sick," "continues to lie," and has "caused great heartsick." "Any time he is crossed he will go over the edge!"

Another Sovereignty Commission file repeats some of this information, with a little extra color.

His father and mother were contacted by phone and said Richard had left home to live with an aunt in New Jersey. He reportedly had

an argument with this aunt and beat her up, leaving her for dead,
and stole her car.

So here is the woman Richard beat up—his own aunt. And stole her
car. This paragraph from the Sovereignty Commission could just as
easily have been written about Vincent.

Richard may have been a klutz and a fantasist, but that doesn't mean
he couldn't have been dangerous.

Money

Cornelius is a black bail bondsman. I see him at the Rankin County
clerk's office sometimes, pecking on the database computer. He's like a
lizard trying to blend into the tree trunk. Hat pulled down, no sudden
moves. Cornelius has been able to get me information that I can't find
elsewhere. That James Rankin is in prison in Pennsylvania, for instance.
Addresses mainly, although not even he can find Richard's sister or
Vincent's father. I'm in his big white truck in the parking lot of the
courthouse, facing out to the street.

"Vincent McGee, he's not the sharpest tool in the woodshed," Cornelius softly creaks. "But he probably didn't have enough money for a private attorney. A lot of the times, these public attorneys, they're not really
going to do a lot of work for you. They will get you a plea, but . . . they
work with the district attorney, Michael Guest's office, every day."

"What does that mean?"

"You've got to realize these public defenders have grown up with
Michael Guest. When they were younger, they went to law school with
him and all of that. They take an oath to have their clients' interests at
hand, but I don't think, when you get down to the real nuts and bolts of
it, they do."

Cornelius points out of the parking lot, past the Confederate soldier
statue, and across the street to a small office.

"Like that lawyer over there. I know him. He does public defender work for Rankin County. The thing is, once he disposes of your case, he's going to have to do work in the future with Michael Guest's office."

Cornelius repoints his finger.

"So it's not like hiring Ed Rainer, a private attorney down the street here. The police don't like him, and he doesn't like them. He goes to war with them in the courtroom, but he costs a lot of money."

"What do you reckon happened with Precious?" I ask.

"Precious Martin, he's one of a set of triplets. They've been on *The Oprah Winfrey Show*, and all of that."

I picture three otters in vests whooshing about the Martin family rumpus room, bumping into one another. It occurs to me now I'm never going to see that Precious *isn't* an otter.

"I think that, in my personal opinion, that Precious Martin was look-ing for the fame," Cornelius says. "But see, once the story fizzled down, then it was time for him to go."

As I climb out of his truck I ask Cornelius if he thinks it's true Rich-ard slept with Vincent.

"A lot of these guys that have been to prison, they have sex with men, and what they will do, they will let another man perform oral sex on them. If they're the receiver of oral sex or if they're penetrating another man, but the man is not penetrating them, in their mind they're not gay—which is as stupid as you can get. I think that if anything was going on, that could have been going on."

Vincent's "Story," Finally

"You've got some numbers, right?" Vincent says to my *Hello*.

"Listen," I say, "I'm telling you, we're going to have to talk first. I want the story, or if you don't want to give me the story, then that's fine, but I'm not doing it anymore where I just keep on giving you numbers and you don't tell me anything."

"You've got the numbers, though?"

"Yes! Listen! If you tell me the story, I can give you some of the money now, and then if you send me the letter for Mike Scott, then I can give you the rest then."

"But look. I'm gonna send the letter, but I'm going to need all the money tonight before I give the story, you hear?"

"No! If you tell me the story, I can give you about two-thirds of it tonight."

"What's two-thirds?"

"It's a thousand dollars."

"A thousand?" Vincent scoffs, like I've offered him a buck. "A'right, c'mon. What's the numbers?"

"No, no, no!" I'm plodding about the room, my non-phone hand flailing about. "You're going to tell me the story. I'm sick of this, Vincent. Tell me the story now, and then I'll give you the numbers afterward."

"A'right," he says. "You got the tape recorder on?"

"Yep."

"Okay, what you wanna know?"

"Well, let's start with your Richard thing."

"Okay, well, look," he says, "but by the time I tell you about the Richard thing, I'll need the whole thousand."

"I'm just sick of this game!"

"Listen, this ain't no game, ain't no game, okay? Let's do it. You've got this recorded? What do you want to know, man?"

"What happened between you and Richard, on the night?" I ask.

"A'right. Shit, you know what I'm sayin'? He came to my house on the Thursday, right, you know what I'm sayin'. He came up standing there, yo, and he wanted to talk to me. So you know what I'm sayin', we talked for a few minutes, and then he asked me, did I want to help him do something? And I was like, you know what I'm sayin', 'Not really.' He came back the next day.

"The next day I was just sitting around the house bored and he asked me to go back to his house with him, you know what I'm sayin', to help him cut some trees down, you know what I'm sayin', do the landscape around, you know what I'm sayin', so it look good. Right? And so the next day, when I went down there and he brought me home, you know what I'm sayin', he told me about some government plan. He's like, 'Come back to the house,' and he was going to get, like, on the computer and show me this thing called . . . it's some kind of government plan for convicted felons, you know what I'm sayin', who are looking for a job. You know, I was tryin'a do right that time in my life. And so, you know, I went back to his house. I was down there on the computer on Facebook; he was in there on the other computer trying to look up, you know what I'm sayin', the shit I was telling you about, the government program."

My ears are acclimatizing to Vincent, I think to myself. His murble sounds less of a murble.

"Yeah, yeah," I say. "So there were two computers and he was looking up one and you were looking up the other?"

"Yeah. This is where everything went the way it did, you know. We got into an altercation, you know what I'm sayin'. What he did, he pulled a brown kind of butcher knife right on me, you know what I'm sayin', he was threatening my life, right? And so . . . you know what I'm sayin'?"

"Why did he pull a knife on you?"

"I don't know. You know what I'm sayin', when I was down at his house he was making all racist comments, just like he was saying stuff like . . . He was making racist comments, but I just can't remember every word he said. But it was R-rated. He was getting on my bad side, you know. We got into the altercation, and I got the best of him and I stabbed him. Is that all you want to know?"

"Yeah, maybe. Some people are saying that he tried to rape you or molest you?"

"No!" Vincent says, frustrated and squeaky. "That's what my momma says. She wrote this thing and said he tried to do that, but he didn't try to do that, you know what I'm sayin'? But he did, you know what I'm sayin', get a grip on me, and I was, you know what I'm sayin', defending my life. Like I said, he pulled a butcher knife out on me so I had really . . . just went into survival mode, and it's a me-or-him situation. So I felt like if I didn't kill him, he was gonna kill me."

"So why did you have to stab him sixteen times, though? Because you would have been able to have stopped him without that."

"You know what I'm sayin', like, I blacked out, but I remember everything. He kept tryin'a get the best of me, so when I grabbed his knife and started stabbing him, when he was down, I tried to restrain him, but he kept on. I did try to restrain him, though, by tying his arms up. When I settled down, by that time he was already dead, you know, he was dying, you hear? You could feel it. I had to cover this crime up. The crime to say that I went to the house. The next day I came back and burned the house down, and it was just because, you know, like I had said, I was a convicted felon and I knew I couldn't go to the police and tell the police, 'Okay, this dude tried to kill me.' They would be like, 'Okay, what you doing going down his house?' You know what I'm sayin'. I didn't know he was involved in all this white supremacist bullshit, you hear?"

"So you didn't know any of that beforehand?"

"Not really. I heard murble Ku Klux Klan bull, but I thought that was just the talk and rumors and shit. I don't believe nothing until I see it. I thought he was just really trying to help me. I thought he was a nice person, but he wasn't."

"It sounds a bit strange that he just suddenly had a knife," I say. "Like, what led up to that? Sounds like there must have been something that led up to the knife."

"No," he says. "I was on Facebook and he was telling me, he thinks it's time for me to get off Facebook, right? So I was like, 'Shit, hold on, I'm comin',' you hear? And so, like, he just started talking real aggressive, you know what I'm sayin', so I got aggressive back. And so, goddamn it, one thing led to another—he grabbed the knife. I had two knives on me because I walked around with knives on me, you hear? And so, shit, that's how it happened."

Hmmm. All the pieces aren't quite there.

"So why did your mother say that he tried to molest you or sexually assault you?"

"Because the police came to my house and they told my momma that if they catch me they were going to kill me. I guess her being my momma, she tried to make the situation less stressful for me 'cause she feel like I was just defending myself. But she knew she couldn't just tell them, okay, he tried to kill me, because it wouldn't look right, it wouldn't sound right. People wouldn't believe that. So she tried to do what she could to make it better for me, you hear?"

"The investigator said that you said to them that Richard had paid you for sex."

Vincent pauses. I can hear inmates or guards clinking and plonking in the background at the East Mississippi prison for the criminally insane.

"He said that I said that?"

"Yes. That's what the investigator said."

"Who was the investigator who told you this?"

"Wayne Humphreys and Tim Lawless."

"No! I never told them that. They were telling me shit, like, 'Okay you're going to be a hero to a lot of people' and this shit, but I didn't really care about that. Like I said, the police told my momma that the Klan were going to kill my brother, my sister. It's all the truth. They said they were going to kill my people if they couldn't catch me, and so, shit, that's why my momma ended up telling the police that I was at my sister's house. Because they threatened all my people's lives. My momma had to move from her house to my aunt's. She moved from her house just because the Klan members, they were murble, you hear?"

"Wow."

"I don't understand why they make those lies up, but no, that's not true," he says.

I peer down at the next question squiggled on my yellow pad on the coffee table. I suck in the air.

"The other thing I heard was that one of the reasons you've grown up to be so angry is that when you were young, one of your relatives molested you and you went and told your mother and your mother didn't stand up for you."

Matter-of-factly, he tells me the name of the relative. It's a name I haven't heard before.

"Yeah. I don't know who told you that, right? But it wasn't what you think. It ain't nothing that happened. He didn't fuck me or no shit like that, you hear? When I was little I had this relative who used to try to get on me when I was about eight, nine, ten, you hear? He had to be, like, twenty. My momma took me down to my uncle's house and this other relative would come around. Shit, I used to tell my momma, 'Don't take me down there.' Shit like that. And you know . . . I don't know who told you this shit, but I would like to know the name of the person who told you, you hear?"

"Did your family not believe you?"

"They knew, they knew, the motherfuckers, they knew."

"Did they do anything about it? Like, scream at the guy?"

"No, they didn't do shit, you know what I'm sayin'? But at the same time, that just made me more the man that I am today. He gave me a low example of a man, you hear?"

Another life lesson from Vincent that is so twisted I can't figure out if it makes sense or not.

"But your family didn't, like, stand up for you?"

"No. They didn't do shit."

"That's awful."

"That's what I say, you know what I'm sayin'? But shit. I don't know how you found that out, though, man, but like I said, I'm going to tell you the truth. I'm going to tell you the truth about everything to help, you hear?"

I ask Vincent if Richard ever told him about his life.

"No," Vincent says. "I didn't get in no conversation about his life. All I knew was he was a lawyer and he stayed down the street. That's all I knew about him."

"Because the investigator said that Richard told you that he used to have a black boyfriend."

"No. He told me he had a black friend. This is what I heard. He said he had a black friend that used to work for him and he had got cut, he cut his knee off or some shit like that, with a chain saw."

"So Richard tried to hurt him?" I ask, led by something in Vincent's tone.

"That's how I took it." One morning Vincent was over at Richard's house and Richard was on the phone, telling someone the story of the black man and the chain-saw accident. Vincent thought Richard was telling the story so he could overhear it. "Like he was telling me he could get me killed, you hear?"

I look down at my yellow notepad and suck in the air again.

"The other thing that I heard was last time you were in prison you were in a cell with a white guy and you got into a fight with him and you may have raped him."

"Who told you that?" Vincent says, baffled.

"Someone from the prison."

"This is what really happened, you hear? I was in the cell just writing. He owed me a hundred dollars, all right? He didn't pay me my money, so the first day I took his tray and everything so he doesn't eat no food and I tied him to the railing. And I took a plastic cup with a handle on it and beat his ass for, like, three days. He was so hungry. I beat his ass and stick a bottle up his ass."

"You stuck a bottle up his ass?"

"A bottle, yo," he says. "That's it."

"That's it" is an unusual way to look at it, it strikes me.

"But then he tried to get out of my cell, and the day he tried to run out of my cell I beat his head with a tray. I beat him up with a lunch tray in the face and shit, and that's all that happened. I didn't take none of my body parts and touch him, you know what I mean?"

"Yeah. Sure. You just stuck a bottle up his ass."

"Right."

"Because he owed you a hundred dollars?"

"Right. It was all about money. That's what I'm about—money. Now that other shit, that shit is just to scandalize my name. It ain't shit to me. I don't understand why my own people are saying this shit. They the ones saying this shit—I don't know why they're the ones saying this shit, you hear?"

"What about your last fight you just had, that got you moved to this prison?"

"I took a do-rag from a dude, and he tried to come back to my cell late at night to get it back. And so when he opened the door, I hit him in the face with a tray. I had a hard tray left in my cell. I always keep a tray just in case I've got to hit them off in the mouth or something. So I had a tray and, goddamn it, we got into a fight. I hit him about twenty times. He folded up on the ground and he grabbed me, and when he grabbed me he hit me two or three times, and I spilled his ass on the floor. Hit his ass some more. And goddamn, when he left he was bleeding everywhere."

"But why did you hit him? What did he do to you?"

"He tried to take the do-rag that I took from him back."

"A do-rag is like a head wrap?"

"Yeah."

"Why did that make you so angry, seeing as it was *his* do-rag?"

"Because like I said, he came in my cell. I felt already threatened. I was in a one-man cell. I'm the only person supposed to be in the cell, and this older dude, he comes to my cell. And so when he come to my cell and he come inside my cell, he already was eager to do something to me or I was going to do something to him. So I went ahead and did something to him first."

I tell him what Michael Guest told me. That he had pleaded guilty to avoid homosexual details rolling out in the court case.

"No!" Vincent bleats. "I didn't want a trial because while I was in Rankin County Jail all the white officers putting stuff in my food, putting stuff in my Kool-Aid, and all the white officers were jumping on me, threatening me. The only way I could get the lieutenant or captain to come down and talk to me is to flood my cell. Like block the toilet up and make it overflow or stick my arm out the door so a tray would hit somebody, or do something and make somebody come down, and that's why I didn't go to trial. I wanted to go to trial. I tried to get a speedy trial. But they wouldn't even let me do that. When I talked to my lawyer Precious Martin, he was like the DA. He wasn't ready to go to trial. He wanted to charge me twenty-four thousand dollars. At the same time I thought he didn't really want to help me. Seemed to me like he was almost working for the Rankin County DA's. Every time I would say something, he was like, 'The DA ain't ready for that.' My sixth sense told me to fire him."

"So Mike Scott was a lot better, was he?"

"Yeah," Vincent says. "He was the real thing. He really didn't have to do much because I just told him, 'I'm ready to take a plea and get out of Rankin County Jail, no matter what, and I'll come back later to fight in court.'"

A male bellows, "Vincent!" Vincent tells me his phone time is over. He says he'll mail the Mike Scott letter in Monday's postal round.

Vincent couldn't be ticking more prosecution boxes if he tried. Doing something to someone before they do something to him; attacking people who owe him money and an older dude who came into his space; blaming his own people for "saying shit" in his defense. It doesn't sound like Richard would necessarily have had to have made a move on Vincent to provoke him.

The call is over. I glance at my hands. The silver from the Green Dot cards is trapped under my nails.

9.

ROAD TRIP

The Cemetery

The clock radio glows 1:07 a.m. I think I've found her. I tumbled into her while not looking.

I was poking around cemetery records websites, snooping for Richard's mother's grave. Attached to a record as an "associate" is Gerry Krafft. I thought he must be Richard's mother's executor or something.

Then my brain thawed out: Gerry. Geraldine.

I punched *Gerry Krafft* into the WhitePages. Eighty-nine listed across America. One listed in a city in Florida.

Now I'm looking over Google Maps for airports. I could drive, but it's thirteen hours and I reckon I'll need a clear head to get in the front door.

Okay, it's now about three in the morning. I've booked a flight to Miami, Florida.

On Google Maps they've got a street view—outside what I think is Richard's sister's house is an aqua-blue flag with a peace sign on it. So: The siblings have different tastes in flags.

Miami Airport Parking Lot

"What's that noise?" snaps Vincent.

"It's just the air conditioner." I'm slouched in my red rental at Miami International Airport dictating Green Dot digits.

"5-1-2-3-7-6-7-2-3-6," I say. "Hey, I might be seeing Richard Barrett's sister today. So do you want me to pass on any message to her?"

"What kind of message do you think I should say?" Vincent sounds thrown. "Like, I should apologize or something?"

"I don't know."

"How can I apologize?" he whines. "I can't apologize when my life was in jeopardy, right? You know what I'm sayin'? I can feel her loss, but at the same time, I had to do what I had to do, d'you hear? Have you got the other two cards for me?"

I begin to scratch the silver.

"Where the sister stayin' at?"

"What?" I say, having heard him perfectly clearly.

"I said, where she stay at?"

"Oh yeah, no, she's in another state. She lives in . . . She doesn't live in Mississippi or anything. She lives far away."

I nicely dodge coughing up her location.

"I thought you said you was gonna go and see her?"

"Yeah, yeah. I'm not in Mississippi at the moment. I'm in Florida." Christ!

"Oh, you're in Florida?"

"Yeah, yeah," I mope.

"What do the hos look like out there, yo?"

"Oh, the females here—I haven't seen any yet 'cause it's just a Sunday so there's not many women."

I recite the Green Dot numbers and tell Vincent I have to go.

"Yo," Vincent says as I'm about to hang up. "Tell Richard's sister I say, hey, how's she doin'?" He chuckles. "No, I'm fucking with you," he says.

I twist the key in the red rental. The map says two hours to Richard's sister.

Gerry Krafft

The sun is overexposing every color in the street. The road surface is white, and the palm trees bend. The orange and white homes have plenty of breathing room on their big green lawns. Cement dolphins poke up where there are usually garden gnomes.

American flags flap on poles in front yards. To Mississippian home-owners, that flag represents defeat in the Civil War, so the flag they hoist instead is the Confederate. Florida, it should be noted, is also in the South and also fought with the Confederacy in the Civil War. But here they are, and there Mississippi is.

I park with an angry crank of the brake. I'm sulking because I cut myself shaving in the Shell gas station toilet. My neck is still leaking blood into toilet paper.

Out my windshield, two black kids shoot hoops with a white kid and an Asian kid. The first thought that rolls into my head is, *Oh, that's unusual.*

I've been in Mississippi too long.

A translucent curtain runs along the window next to Gerry's front door (or at least, what I hope is Gerry's front door). I squint and see a kitchen and a blond head bopping.

A chesty tanned man creaks open the door.

"G'day," I say. "I'm looking for a Gerry Krafft."

"Hold on, man," he says, turning to the kitchen. "Gerry!"

Gerry can see me flailing as I grab for folders from my bag and fumble out the backstory, twirling from *Race Relations* to true crime books to Joe McNamee to DA Michael Guest to cemetery websites to her front door. Gerry understands I'm pitching to her to not slam the door in my face.

"It's okay," she says gently. "I'm interested."

The Florida sun has tanned Gerry, without shriveling her. She doesn't look sixty four.

"I can show you what I've dug up. I've spoken to the district attorney; I've spoken to the killer."

"Well, the guy got the death penalty."

She can't have been following the case recently if that is what she thinks.

"His reasoning," she asks, "was because it was a dispute over what he paid him for the yard work?"

"It depends who you want to listen to," I say. "The investigators don't think it was just over money."

"Well, I've had many conversations with . . . He was friends with a lot of high-end politicians," she says proudly. "They said something about sexual advances, and I said, 'You know what? Being a white supremacist, he would have never made a sexual advance on a black guy. Never!'" Gerry says she knows he wasn't gay. "I knew his girlfriend in high school. They dated a long time, nine years, as a matter of fact. I put a fly in her soup when she came over for dinner."

I open my folder, hoping to show her a photo of Vincent. It opens on a photo of one of Vincent's knives.

"Oh hang on, don't look at that!" I say, my face heating up.

"The knife." She giggles.

Gerry says she's surprised I found her.

"The one thing he tried to do was to protect me," she says, proud again, "because of his political involvement, so nobody even knew that I existed. He didn't want them to."

Gerry tells me she had worked for the government in Washington, DC. She decoded messages from Vietnam during the war and had top security clearance. In *The Commission* Richard said his father worked with the foreign service. Secrets seem to have been the family trade.

"He really left an impression everywhere," I tell Gerry, trying to smooth my way into the awkward stuff.

"Well, everybody that I've talked to said they had great respect for him," she says.

I hand the Sovereignty Commission report through the doorway. She lowers her eyes and scans the page. *At age six . . . at age twelve . . . nothing further that could be done . . . borderline violence case. The psychiatrist told the Barretts that Richard hated them both intensely.*

She lifts her eyes. They've moistened, but she's not crying.

"He went to many, many, many psychiatrists and was an A-plus student, and he decided he couldn't have restrictions so he went to live with my aunt."

"But why did he have to go to a psychiatrist?"

"Because he was so smart," she says defiantly. "You're talking Einstein-level. Anyone who's a musician and an artist and doesn't accept anything less than an A is weird. Nobody understood him. I had to follow behind him in school, and the teachers said to me, 'Why aren't you like him?' The teachers, they had never experienced anybody that had that deep level of intelligence. He was a chess expert. We played chess."

She stares into the street. Her face turns a little sour.

"I think he cheated with me," she says.

She has been defending her brother to this point. This is the first fracture.

I point my nose toward my open blue folder.

"He reportedly had an argument with his aunt in New Jersey," I read, "and beat her up, leaving her for dead, and stole her car, but she never tried to get it back."

"Well, that's pretty true," she says. "Because the car was still there in his house."

"What?" I say, surprised. "That's true that he beat her up?"

"I don't know. She never disclosed that to me. Could have been. I don't know that for sure."

The awestruck little sister seems to have vanished.

I tug one more document from the folder.

"I assume you've read his interesting last will and testament?"

"No, I haven't. Did he leave his money to Iran?"

That's a detail you can't just guess out of thin air.

"The government of Iran was on the will," I say. "What was going on there?"

"He was not generous in life. So whoever gets it, so be it."

"And he seems to be quite angry. I don't know how wills usually are, but he says, *I expressly decline to include any individual*—"

"No family members," she interrupts.

"Why do you reckon he was like that?"

"He was not generous in life. For my wedding he gave me a teddy bear." Her voice sharpens. "He was at my wedding. As a matter of fact, he caught the garter."

"He caught the garter?"

"I have pictures—he's putting it on, and just laughing and laughing."

She tells me the man who catches the garter marries next.

"So why do you think he never got married, then?"

"Because," she says, "he would not part with one dollar. If you get married, you have to share your money."

"And why do you think he was so cheap?"

"I have no idea. As a matter of fact, we went to breakfast and there were, like, twelve of us, and everybody threw a tip on the table, and he took the tip. See, and those kind of things stick in my mind. That's how cheap he was. And he had plenty of money. And he'd steal the tip off the table. So my father went back and, you know, put another tip. But yeah, I mean he's the cheapest person I ever met in my life."

"Were your parents upset with his infamy?"

"They never really talked about it. I think they were more hurt."

Gerry looks hurt, too.

"When my mother died he left a message on my father's answering machine: 'Sorry for your loss.'" He didn't attend the funeral. "I never hated him. I just never understood him."

"So why do you think he ended up with his racist views?"

"My father wasn't even born in this country. Where that came from I have no idea."

Richard's grandparents were Christian missionaries from England who traveled to Venezuela, where Richard's father was born.

"As a matter of fact, one of Richard's first friends was a black guy," she continues. "He came over for lunch. So I don't know what happened. You never know. I put it on the same level as what makes people serial killers, you know? You never know what happens in your brain to make you change. You never know."

I tell Gerry about Richard and his obsession with athletes and the Spirit of America Day.

"He was not athletic," she says. "I mean, I did all kinds of acrobatics, football, baseball . . ."

"And he didn't do anything?"

"No."

I unconsciously brush my finger on my fresh shaving cut. The Florida sun has already baked it to a scab.

"Just so you know," Gerry says, "and I don't know if this will help you or not—but as a very young person our rooms were across from each other. And we'd go to bed and he would be emperor of the universe. And we would talk back and forth. And he was going to rule the whole nebula of the planets. And I was like—if it was in today's world—the Klingon. He was the grand emperor of the entire universe."

"You were the Klingon?"

"Uh-huh. I was the enemy. But we would do this, you know, at night, talk back and forth—but he was always the ruler of the entire world."

She tells me Vince Thornton wants to give her Richard's ashes.

"I talked to a cemetery in Mississippi," Gerry says. "I can sprinkle them over there. And whenever I get back to Mississippi, that's probably what I'm going to do."

John and Vincent's Road Trip

I'm squeezing tight on the steering wheel, eyeing the green road signs as they roll over, looking out for the airplane symbol. In the passenger seat, Vincent slouches back. He's in his yellow jumpsuit with one sandal on the dashboard. Fine! In fact, it's my cell flipped open, thrown on the passenger seat. Vincent *is* chatting, though. I've put him on speakerphone. The road unwinds for two hours before I hit Miami International Airport, so I appreciate the company.

"I went to speak to Richard's sister just before," I tell him.

"What'd she say?" says road-trip-buddy Vincent.

"She said he definitely wasn't gay."

"That's what I said!" Vincent complains.

I turn to the passenger seat.

"Hey, I heard about your girlfriend China. Is she still your girlfriend?" The question wobbles Vincent.

"No," he says, full of suspicion. "How'd you hear about that?"

"I've been asking a lot of people things."

"I see. Oh, nigger, I see you know a lot. Who told you about her?"

I won't tell him. He's pleading. I tell him I have to concentrate on the road, not have some screaming match.

"She wasn't my girlfriend in the first place. She was something like . . . like one of my hos, you hear?"

"You pimped her out or something?"

"You could say that. Ha! Whatever way it was, you hear?"

"Was she in love with you?"

"Ah, all women in love with me, you hear?"

I can't tell if he's joking.

"Someone says she once jumped out of your car."

"Yeah, she did!"

I squint out the window, lower my eyes to the asphalt darting by, and imagine leaping from a moving car. My arms and legs feel the burn.

"Because," I continue, "she was pregnant and didn't want to have the baby."

This wobbles Vincent, too.

"Oh, for real?" he says softly, fascinated. "I ain't know nothing about it, you hear? I didn't know she was pregnant till she got to the hospital and she told me that she had a miscarriage, but she said she wanted the baby, you hear?"

"Do you have a girlfriend on the outside now?"

"Something like that."

"So how are you going to keep that relationship going, seeing you've got a jail in between you?"

"Shit, you know, they're gonna do what they're gonna do. If she gonna ride, she's gonna ride—if she ain't gonna ride, she ain't. Right now, everything's one hundred, though."

"But do you reckon she'll wait sixty-five years for you?"

"Ha-ha! Who said anything about doing sixty-five years?"

Vincent says a day is knocked off for every day served, if he behaves.

"I can get out in thirty!"

"Thirty years is still a lot of time."

"Yeah," he mutters sadly, "it's a lot of time, dude. A lot of time."

The purple sky is dimming. I twist the headlights to full.

"Do you know a lot about when your family first came to Mississippi?" I ask. "Like, your grandparents and your great-grandparents. How long have they been in Mississippi?"

"I wouldn't even know, you know what I'm sayin'? I know I've got some people staying in Las Vegas, Chicago, you know, I've got some people spread out, but I ain't never heard . . . Nobody never did sit me down and talk to me about shit like that, you hear?"

Vincent sounds as glum as "it's a lot of time, dude." Before I left Australia, my dad was telling me a story about his dad I'd never heard before, that he built planes in Germany. Then he immigrated before World War II and started building warplanes for Australia. He told the plant owners about the superior clutches they built in his factory in Germany. So the Australian plant changed designs, and the warplanes flew with the Safran clutch.

"I ain't never had no role models and shit. When I come around, my people, they tell me to just get out the house, you hear?"

Vincent chuckles sadly. I ask him about his father, JD. "I met my dad really about three times in my whole life, right? The last time I met him, I stayed with him about a year. And that was the last time I've seen him, though."

"Oh really, how old were you when you stayed with him for a year?"

"About twelve, going on thirteen. I would have liked to know him, you hear? I never had somebody, you know what I'm sayin', just show me right from wrong. 'Cause I really didn't know what right from wrong was till I got older and learned, you know what I'm sayin'? Like, you can say, 'The Bible guides' and all this. You can tell somebody something, but if you don't give them the meaning and all that, and show them the example, then all they know is the words, you hear? I just knew the words— I ain't know what they do, you hear?"

"Where does JD live? Does he live in Jackson?"

"I don't know where he stay."

I don't feel so bad that Cornelius and I haven't been able to track him down, either.

"When you got sentenced, sixty-five years, none of your family was there in the court."

"Nobody went—there wasn't nobody there, you hear? There was nobody there but strangers. Even those strangers, you know what I'm sayin', showing me more support than my own people, you hear?"

I turn to phone-Vincent.

"I was there," I tell him. "I saw it."

"You were there?" Vincent sparks up.

"Yeah, I was there. I saw it. You were wearing a yellow jumpsuit."

"Yeah, yeah, yeah." He giggles. "I didn't see you out there, motherfucker!"

"I was trying to be, you know, just inconspicuous."

"Oh, that's what's up." He chuckles.

I catch my face in the car mirror. A bedraggled near-Afro springs atop my head. The shaving cut scab runs down my throat.

"Someone told me that the last time you were in jail you had some medication to keep you calm. And then when you left you stopped having the medication and that might have been why you got so violent."

"I was taking medication for seeing things, you know what I'm sayin', because there was a voice in my head telling me to kill people dead."

My arms tighten up.

"I had depression," he says. "I was taking a lot of shit."

"So, even last time you were in jail there was a voice in your head saying to kill people?"

"Yeah, it's still in here, it comes around sometimes."

"Wow, that's pretty scary. So what, you just suddenly start hearing a voice? What does it sound like? Is it you? Or is it like an angel?"

"It'll be a whisper and it'll be calling my name, like, in a whisper, and I'd be looking there, and nothing'd be there. It'd be saying shit like *Kill* and shit like that. It'd be whispering to me, you hear?"

"No way! Are you telling the truth?"

"I'm dead serious. Then I'd be seeing the grim reaper and all that shit."

"Really? I wish I could see your face now to see whether you're telling the truth or joking."

"I'm dead serious. I ain't here laughing."

"How old were you when you first saw things?"

"I was old. I was about nineteen, twenty. Something like that. But ever since I was little I used to see, I used to see all types of strange things, you know what I'm sayin'? Like, to this day I feel if I'm in the room with the lights off, I can see red—every color—and it be little balls, like drops of water, floating around the room. I can see anytime in the room with the light off. When it's on I don't see it, when the light goes off I can just see all these colors floatin' around, and they look like raindrops."

"What . . . what do you reckon it is?"

"I don't know."

"Do you reckon it's 'cause you took drugs or do you reckon it's, like, angels or something?"

"I believe it's something like—I don't know about no angels—I'd say it's energy or something, you hear?"

"Yeah, sure."

"Like, like, energy. I could see it anytime with the lights down low."

"And is it scary or is it good?"

"It ain't scary, you know what I'm sayin'? It's like looking at a rainbow, but broke down into little drops, you hear?"

"And what . . . what about the voices? The voices must be scary, though?"

"Hell, yeah. Those motherfuckers keep me up many nights. I hear . . . I hear stuff callin' my name. I wake up in my sleep, sweatin'. You know what I mean? I remember this one night I woke up and I was just laughing, you hear, and I just couldn't stop laughing, and that just scared the hell out of me."

"You were laughing when you were still asleep and you didn't know?"

"Yeah, and I woke up laughing, though. Still laughing. I couldn't stop."

"Oh, no!"

"I believe I'm possessed, man, like *The Exorcist* or something."

"Really?! No way, you really reckon you are?"

"Oh, nigga, I tell ya, like, I'm wide awake, you hear? I'm layin' on my back and the grim reaper reached into my chest and he was pulling, like, he was pulling all the energy up out my back, and I resisted and everything went back to normal."

"How did you resist it?"

"I just, like . . . I couldn't move my hands and stuff, it was, like, my will, you know what I'm sayin', like I had the will. I feel he was gonna snap my soul up. And in my mind I was, like, pullin' back, but I wasn't movin' my body, you hear?"

My foot pushes down and the streetlights speed by like balls of flame.

"Is Richard the only person you've killed?"

"I ain't gonna get into that."

"Oh, you're not going to get into that? Oh, okay, that's ominous, but fair enough. Of course."

"What you talkin' about?" he whines. "You're talking about stuff that could get me more time. Yeah, we're talking about shit that's already happened."

"Yep, no, I understand. Your cousin, Michael Dent, he sort of feels that you got him in a lot of trouble that he didn't need to get into."

"Man, fuck Michael Dent!" he spits. "You hear? I don't need fuck with Michael Dent!"

"That's fair enough."

"I hate, you know what I'm sayin', that he got into this trouble an' all. And that's why I gotta say *shit* happen, you know what I'm sayin'? And I can't change the fact."

Vincent's voice cracks on *fact*, like he's crying or he's high just for that one word.

"The investigators said that Michael is a criminal, but he's not really as violent and as dangerous as you."

"I'm a human being, man," Vincent says earnestly, "you know what I'm sayin'?"

"Sure."

"Shit, Michael Dent, he'd probably, you know what I'm sayin', kill a motherfucker or whatever he do—he gonna do his thing. Shit, if *you* get in a wrong situation, *you* would kill, right?"

"Yeah," I say, uncertain.

"In the Bible, it say there's a time for everything. There's a time to kill and there's a time for peace and there's a time for war, you hear?"

"And do you think when you've killed it's been the time for war?"

"It was the time to kill, you hear? You know, just think, if you was a young man, you hear, and you only twenty-two, you've got your whole life ahead of you. I was startin' up my little rap career and everything. And then shit. And you're faced with this life-or-death situation, you know what I'm sayin'? You ain't seen no more bad things and all of a sudden you got a obstacle in your way—somebody's trying to kill you, so what you gonna do? You gonna defend yourself the best you can. You know what I'm sayin'? That's what I did, you hear?"

"But people say that because he was a sixty-five-year-old man he wasn't strong enough to kill you. That's why they're suspicious about your story. Because they're saying, because you're young and strong, that you would have been able to . . . even if Richard had attacked you, that you would have been able to stop him without having to kill him."

"That's where they lying," he objects. "The man was strong to me. I've seen the man take an ax and chop a motherfuckin' tree down, you hear? You know it's all about how you keep your body in shape, you hear?"

"Oh, so you think Richard was strong enough to kill you?"

"No, I ain't gonna say all that, know what I'm sayin'? I don't feel like no one's strong enough to kill me."

"You were saying that you blacked out when you stabbed Richard, but is that true? Did you really black out or are you just saying that so you don't have to take responsibility?"

"I was sayin' that because it was some, like, outta-body experience, you hear? It was like I see everything that happened but I really couldn't control it, it was like I couldn't control it, you know what I'm sayin'? Like, once I got in that mode, I all the way in that mode. It's like, just say you step out of your body and you just sit there watchin' yourself do this, and you know you need to stop it, but your mind and your heart won't let you stop it."

"And were you scared when you were doing it? Or were you . . . were you thrilled?"

"I was thrilled. I ain't gonna lie, you know what I'm sayin'? It's like an adrenaline rush. But, you know, I'm sane. I'm a sane human being, know what I'm sayin'? I don't walk around causin' people problems for no reason."

"Yeah. But once you kind of got into it, you just couldn't stop, and it was, like, exhilarating?"

"Right. Like a high or something, you hear?"

"Yeah. Wow."

"It was like I gained strength from it, you hear? Just to tell you the truth about the situation, I gained strength."

"You gained strength from it?"

"Yeah. Like I got his power. Like I got his power, man, like real tough, you know, man? It's like I had pumped all the way up—felt like I could jump through the roof!"

"And do you reckon he was dead when you left him the first night? Or do you reckon he was still a bit alive?"

"Oh, I wouldn't know. I ain't checkin' his pulse, you hear?"

I cough out a laugh. "The woman who did the autopsy, she told me that she didn't know when he died; he could have been, like, alive all night, but she didn't know."

"I doubt that, though."

"And when you went in the next morning, was he just . . . He must have not been moving?"

"He was just laying up."

"And he was definitely dead then?"

"Yessir."

"Wow. And so did you try to move his body about some, or did you just leave it there?"

"When it first happened, the first night, I tried to move him, know what I'm sayin'? That's why I tied the belt on, around the arm, tried to move him, know what I'm sayin', 'cause, like, I knew they was going to try to pin something on me. 'Cause I was a black man and I had been institutionalized two times already. And I knew, know what I'm sayin'? Once they catch up and find out what happened, they won't take my side of the story. Just look at the whole situation, right? So I had, know what I'm sayin', to cover up what I did. Out of fear of going back to jail, know what I'm sayin'? I ain't wanna go back to jail—penitentiary. This ain't no place for a human being to live, you hear?"

"Yeah."

"This right here will make you out an animal, you hear?"

"And so where were you trying to drag him? You stabbed him in the kitchen, but then were you trying to drag him somewhere else?"

"I was gonna put him in a truck, drive him somewhere to bury him, you hear?"

"Oh! I get it. Where were you going to take him?"

"I ain't gonna spill all this tonight, you hear?"

I laugh, maybe out of nerves, but throw back another question.

"And how long did you drag him before you realized it was gonna be too hard?"

"I didn't say it was gonna be too hard, you know what I'm sayin'? I ain't wanna run back up the street and be seen, though. And the truck was locked up in the, uh, garage, so I said fuck him. Left him now, you hear me? And I come back and see him tomorrow, cleaned up."

"Sure."

"But then I got—know what I'm sayin'—I tell everybody what happened. They was like, 'Shit, man, you gonna go to jail for life.' I'm like, 'Man, hell no.' I say, 'Shit, I'm gonna go burn the whole house down.'"

My road trip buddy and me laugh.

"You know," I tell him, "they said you screwed up because you didn't leave the windows open, so it was hard for the fire to start. You should have, like, opened the doors a bit more to let air come through to help the fires go."

"That's what I said!" He laughs ruefully. "I was sittin' down in my cell one day. I thought about it, there was shit I could have did, you hear?"

"Sure."

"Too little, too late, man. You know, learn from your mistakes."

"And um, what was Richard saying when you were stabbing him—was he telling you to stop?"

"Nah, he said one thing, you know, he scream my name, you know, he screamed like, 'Vincent!' He was attacking me, too, you hear?" he adds defensively. "I had scratches on me, you know what I'm sayin'? This, like what I said, nobody want to hear my side of the story. All they want to do is make me out as a murderer, know what I'm sayin'? 'You killed him'; that's all. They don't want to hear 'Okay, he had a knife,' they don't want to hear it. All they wanted to hear was 'We got our man. He's gonna do time.'"

"From my point of view, when I hear you tell your story, your side sounds correct, except I feel like you're leaving out something."

Vincent laughs. "Ha-ha!"

"I feel like something happened that made Richard attack you or something. It just seems like too odd that, like, oh, suddenly Richard—"

"We got into an argument, right?" Vincent interrupts. "He told me to get off his computer—I was using his computer to look up my Facebook, right?"

"Yeah."

"An' we got into an argument about that an' shit, you know what I'm sayin'? He was tryin' to tell me that I don't respect authority an' shit. An' I was like, what authority he has, you hear? For real. He was tryin' to act like a white supremacist, you hear?"

"Mmm," I mmmed, unsatisfied.

"So you have a big white supremacist dude, right?"

"Yeah, sure."

"An' he was like, 'Damn,' and I was like, 'Dude, what you mean?' And he was talking about, like, he, know what I'm sayin', how he, like, just don't like black people. He was tryin' to play me, right? And that's why it escalate."

I put this alongside the other white men who tried to play Vincent, the prison officers who told him his mother didn't come, the prison officers he fought. But is that enough?

"Sure. Okay, fine. I don't know, I feel like . . . I really feel like there's some missing piece."

Vincent laughs. The nighttime and my sleepiness are bonding me to Vincent. But I'm not so out of it to not be frustrated that, out of everything in his life, not leaving the windows open is the mistake he's mulling over while in his prison cell.

"But listen," he says, "one more shit, man. You know I got a new girl-friend, her name's Chywanna?"

I throw my eyes around the car. My pen is lying on the passenger seat floor, vibrating a little with the car.

"Her name's what?" I say, calculating how I can snatch it and not skid into trees.

"Chywanna," Vincent says. "Ain't nobody told you her name yet?"

"No, no, no, what's her name?"

"You wanna call her on a three-way?"

I scoop the pen up. I bite the lid off with my teeth and spit it to my feet.

"I'm gonna talk to her, you hear me?" he says. "You just put her on three-way and listen, you hear?"

"Okay."

"Don't bring no . . . Don't bring up no crazy shit around her, you hear?"

"Okay, so what do you want me to say, then? Or . . . Oh, okay, do you want me to ring her? Now?"

"Yeah, you just ask her what type of dude I am, you know what I'm sayin'? She gonna tell you while I'm on the phone."

"How do we do the three-way?" I squeak. "I don't understand how you do that on the phone."

I ready the pen to scribble on my hand.

"But what's her name?" I say. "I didn't get her name. How do you spell it?"

"Hold up, hold up," Vincent instructs.

He puts me on hold.

Golden light explodes in my eyes. A jerk with switched-on high beams speeds past. I shake my head to reorient myself and rattle the glowing shapes from my vision.

Vincent returns.

"She's asleep, you hear?" Vincent says vulnerably. "Have to be another time, you hear? I'm gonna take my ass to sleep, too."

Vincent says he posted the Mike Scott letter so it should be sitting in my mailbox when I pull in to my apartment.

"We gotta seal the deal, nigga, you hear? So go ahead and get the Green Dot, you hear?"

"Yeah. As soon as the letter comes I'll give it to you. You know I will. How can you not think I will?"

"Nah, I ain't said you won't. I just said you gonna need to go do it tomorrow. I got some business an' you holdin' me up, right? I gotta handle this business."

"I'm so sorry I'm holding you up on business."

"Hey," Vincent says, "don't be writing nothing bad about my people."

"Yeah, sure."

"The only one you can write bad about is Michael Dent."

"Oh, I can write bad about Michael Dent, can I?"

"Me and Michael Dent don't get along, really. Real talk."

"Sure. I think he's just annoyed, to be honest. I think he's just annoyed 'cause he's, like, in jail and he says that if you didn't come over to the house, he wouldn't have ended up in jail."

"Fuck Michael Dent," Vincent says. "Tell him I said fuck him in his ass, you hear?"

The Mailbox

The first thing I do upon my return to my apartment is check the mailbox. Vincent's letter hasn't arrived.

I text him:

Hi Vincent, letter hasn't come yet. Maybe it'll come tomorrow

Vincent: A Bitch better have my money on deck. FlyBoyDahLasDon

Me: What does that mean?

> **Vincent: It means pay up or die slow. FlyBoyDahLasDon**

> **Me: A bitch better have my letter to Mike Scott on deck.**
> **FlyBoyJohn**

I think of Gerry's story of Richard stealing the waitress's tip. I think of Vincent turning furious when I don't cave in to his Green Dot demands. Guy most likely to rip you off, meet guy most likely to snap if you rip him off.

My half day in Florida is bobbing in my head. I spoke to one person, Gerry, so I could write with clarity and confidence about Richard as a boy. But what if I had stayed a week? I would have talked to that man who had answered the door. He might tell me a different version of a story than Gerry had told me. So I'd have two variations on the story. I might then meet a niece of Gerry's who doesn't like her, who tells me Gerry often paints others in the worst light. And I would have asked myself, taking that into account, could I really trust everything Gerry said about Richard? And then I'd meet someone who would diss the niece. And on and on.

In Mississippi, the more layers of the onion I peel, the more I'm standing in a mess of onion.

Tonight, Three Days After Florida, Drunk, Twelve Thirty a.m. in New Orleans, with Dictaphone

It's about twelve thirty at night. I'm walking down the corridor of Le Pavillon in New Orleans. I'm trying to get into my door because I'm drunk. I've gotten in through my door. It's a four-and-a-half-star hotel. It's small, but beautiful.

New Orleans hasn't worked out. I came to hunt down the black people Richard lawyered out of a home. I really wanted to talk to them because they were a solid example of Richard fucking over some black people. I wanted to look into their eyes and get something real and human. But they weren't home and no one knew where they were, so I guess I'm not going to get that.

I've just come from the bars with Ali Winters. She's twenty-five, a writer from Western Australia. She heard I was in Mississippi and hit me up on Twitter. She's here covering the case of a guy on death row called Corey. She thinks he's innocent. The lawyers think he's innocent. The legal aid lawyers, who have thousands of cases and not enough money, think that it's worth dedicating time to him. She's on the outside now because she oversold herself as a social justice journalist who was there just to advocate for Corey. They found out that she had been writing these articles that they felt were self-serving.

It was good to compare Corey's case with Vincent's. I'm not sure that Vincent doesn't deserve life or lots of time. Like Daisy Reyes with the Mexican money, they might have the wrong crime, but they've got the right guy. He raped a guy with a bottle. He beat China. That's putting aside killing Richard. With Richard, it's like, *Oh, he was a white supremacist. Oh, maybe he attacked Vincent. Who knows what happened in that little house?* But Vincent doesn't deny that he beat China and he absolutely doesn't deny that he shoved a bottle in the arse of his white cellmate.

I remember when I was cut off by the McGee family, I thought, *This is so annoying,* because I wanted a book where I would get to be the advocate for this guy. But now that more and more of the story has come out and I've been able to rest on it, I'm glad there's no pressure about being the advocate for him. There's minor pressure from Earnest McBride to be the advocate for Vincent McGee, victim of a racist system. I tried to get across to Earnest that I think that there's more to this than, *Oh, this guy's been set up for dating a white girl.* I really tried to present to him—without being offensive or confrontational—that Vincent's a dangerous man, but he weaved around the topic.

I texted Vincent and phoned him tonight and he hasn't gotten back to me. He texted me and phoned me the night before and I didn't get back to him. Is he trying to get revenge?

I talked to Ali about how Vincent's very impulsive, how he seems to have no forward thinking even in his manipulations. To give you an example: To my mind, it never seems to occur to him that I might be helpful to him next week, or in two days' time, so he should put on his charming act and reveal a little. Like, as soon as it's some instant thing that he needs—a phone card, a Walmart Green Dot card—then suddenly he reveals all to me. He's happy then, in that moment, to be kind of charming or give me a little of what happened, shed a little light on the truth of that night, because he needs that card, that number, that minute, that second. But it doesn't register with him that maybe he should—even as a manipulator, not as a person, but as a manipulator—maybe he should think a bit more ahead. I could be an advocate for him, but now I'm kind of not one. I said to Ali that if I met some guy here in Mississippi who I thought could help me in a year's time with a potential documentary or something, I'd think, *Oh, I should be charming to him now. Because he might help me next year. Or people might help me next week or next month.* But Vincent, he can't seem to think beyond the minute. He can't even seem to think two hours ahead. So he'll be a jerk to me. He'll cut me off, and then when he needs it, that minute, that's when he'll be charming and give me what I need. Yeah, yeah, I suppose I've used my power— Green Dots, the prospect of telling his story—to get what I want from him, but sorry, I don't think telling a story is bad. I'm drunk, by the way.

10.

THE LETTER OF THE LAW

Richard's War Record

A Vietnam veteran who lived near the Nationalist Movement head-quarters told me he didn't buy Richard's war stories.

"I said, 'Where'd you fight?' He said, 'Dankok.' I said, 'Where's that?' He said, 'South of Da Nang.' I said, 'I was at Da Nang, I never heard of Dankok.' If you're going to lie about being a vet, I just walk away."

Another fellow, a white supremacist who knew Richard in the 1960s, told me he'd tease Richard about his war record. To earn a Purple Heart you needed to be killed or wounded. Richard, he told me, couldn't produce a wound.

Richard's war record arrived in the mail today. His severe 1964 face snarls at me from his ID picture. The document tells me he *did* spend eleven months in Vietnam. He *did* receive a Purple Heart with First Oak Leaf Cluster.

In *The Commission* Richard says he received his Purple Heart after he was thrown from a helicopter hovering close to the ground, just before it exploded under enemy fire. I notice a detail on his military record. Everything on the document is typed. The document says he served as a "security guard" in Vietnam. But a hand has crossed that out and scribbled in with pen "door gunner"—that is, a gunman on a helicopter. Why is it that the one detail on the document that is needed to match up with his dramatic story in *The Commission* is scribbled in by hand?

How the World Works, According to John Moore

John Moore told me that if I want to see how Mississippi works, I should come down to the House of Representatives today. They don't usually sit this time of the year, but they're convening to pass a special bill.

The public gallery is closed for plastering, so a cable runs from the House to a crackly speaker in a boardroom. The speaker looks down like a black eye on black and white Mississippians spread around the table. Men from the chamber of commerce and women from the trade union mix in with the journalists.

The House is discussing a bill that will offer $175 million in incentives to two companies to lure them to Mississippi. Eighteen hundred jobs will be created, so no one, Republican or Democrat, is against the bill in general.

John Moore rises. He wants an amendment made before the bill is passed.

Mississippi is the poorest state in America. The poorest of the poor live along the Delta, mostly black and in permanent recession. Ten years ago, the Black Caucus pushed for a $2 million study to work out how to draw business to the Delta, but the study was never funded. With $175 million being found to lure business to other parts of the state, the Black Caucus says now is the time to fund the study.

John Moore clears his throat. He tells the House he wants the $2 million study cut from the bill.

"Oh, this is outrageous," Rufus Straughter, a black Democrat from the Delta, snaps at John. "Why are you making such a fuss over this $2 million?"

John Moore says he has nothing against the study. He just wants the money to come from another kitty.

"There's no other kitty!" yells Rufus Straughter. "You know there's no other kitty!"

Asking to find the money elsewhere will kill off the study.

I glance around the boardroom. One minute ago we were a bunch of people sitting around a table. Now every black face has twisted to sourness and every white one is pretending they're not noticing the mood shift.

Now Rufus is shouting about "sins of the father." He says blacks in the Delta suffered under slavery and segregation and now they are being left behind.

"This is our Mississippi, too!" yells Rufus. "God help me, I'll preach this till the day I die!"

I drift down to a white guy sitting at the end of the boardroom. He turns out to be from the chamber of commerce.

"What just happened?" I ask.

"Oh, look," he says calmly, "John Moore just doesn't want the money coming out of bonds. The governor made a point last year that the government's taking out too many bonds."

"Was there another level to it, where he was trying to be provocative?" I ask.

The man from the chamber of commerce sniffs out what I'm getting at.

"Oh, no, no," he mumbles, and starts staring at his BlackBerry.

I've noticed Mississippians just stop talking until the dead air is so awkward, you just walk away.

The bill is passed with the $2 million study cut out.

Floating out the front of the State Capitol Building are two white Republicans. They tell me the $2 million would have been a waste. It was just the Delta asking for a handout.

"What kind of business could set up in the Delta?" asks one.

"Well, not a call center!" says the other, and they both laugh.

I don't get it.

"Oh, look," the first one says, "he was joking, but in the Delta they're a bit less educated, so they'd have a bit of trouble speaking to people from lots of different areas. You wouldn't really be able to understand them."

The other one tells me there are no ice pops in the Delta. The electricity is down so often, the corner shops can't rely on refrigeration. On the counters of the shops are big jars of Kool-Aid with pickles floating about. He says the kids have to suck on these pickles instead of ice pops.

The two politicians laugh.

I find Rufus Straughter.

He tells me foreign companies have no preconceptions that this bit of Mississippi is better than that bit. They go where the government authorities steer them. And they steer them toward the places politicians like John Moore want them steered.

"When John Moore spoke," I say to Rufus, "you threw around expressions like 'sins of your father' and 'slavery.'"

"Always during the House sessions, situations like this are popping up," Rufus says. "When John Moore and his people get up and oppose a proposal like this, we strongly believe that it's historical. We know exactly where they're coming from. And when one uses a term about their forefathers, you know, we all the time hear them say that 'we're not like our fathers, we are a different age now.' Well, I'm sure you've heard an old saying that an apple don't fall too far away from the tree."

Did John Moore want me to see him get Richard's work done, in a way that is softer, more polite, and bleeds all the way to the Delta? Why else did the number two on Richard's will suggest that I come along today?

The Mailbox Again

It's arrived. Vincent McGee has squiggled his signature at the bottom of the consent letter. I skid out to OfficeMax to fax the page to Mike Scott.

Mike Scott

"Do you enjoy being a lawyer?" I ask.

"Well, it lets me come to work at noon, so yeah," Mike Scott says, blue-eyed and handsome.

Water flows and the occasional bird chirps from the Bang & Olufsen speakers, and I toss up whether to ask him to shut off the goddamn relaxation music so my Dictaphone recording is clean.

"What did Vincent tell you happened?" I ask.

"He said Richard came on to him and that he snapped."

Mike Scott believes this version because of another incident. In 1995, Richard turned up at a police station and told an officer that a young man had stolen jewelry from him. Mike says this was to undermine the young man, who Richard feared was about to file a complaint of his own about a sexual advance. The young man was indicted for theft, although the case never made it to court. The young man told his side of the story in an affidavit. Not secondhand gossip. A sworn and signed first-person story of Richard's predatory nature! That affidavit is presumably in the manila folder marked *McGee* sitting before Mike Scott.

Mike says most documents like this—a fifteen-year-old affidavit for a trial that never happened—essentially disappear into puffs of smoke. They certainly aren't stored in data banks. However, the day Mike was first assigned to Vincent's case, he received a phone call. The voice on the other end of the phone told him about the incident and where to find the affidavit.

My eyes are going numb staring at the manila folder, trying to see through the cardboard. *Calm down, John, it sounds like he's going to give you the document.*

Mike Scott taps the folder.

"And," Mike says, "I thought I had a copy of his affidavit that he gave, but I don't for some reason."

My chest puffs out a tiny squeak of pain.

Mike Scott says it's missing from his file, but I might find it at the Hinds County police department. He has the indictment number.

"The guy's name is Daniel Earl Cox. He was at the time, in '95, he would've been twenty-three. So roughly the same age as Vincent."

"Was he white or black?"

"He was white."

Mike Scott did flap the affidavit in the district attorney's face, showing Richard Barrett had a history of such behavior, but the affidavit lost its value once Vincent switched his story to one without a sexual advance.

A dolphin bleats from the Bang & Olufsen speakers.

I ask Mike why he let Vincent plead to sixty-five years. Nearly everyone else involved in the case is unashamedly conservative. Mike's the only one who feels he has to defend himself on progressive terms. Mike tells me there's no way Vincent will serve that. That he'll get a day knocked off for every day he serves, good behavior, so he'll be out in about thirty. And that there are other prison programs that knock off time, too. He says if he'd allowed Vincent to go to trial and lost, he would have been given life without the chance of "one-for-one."

Mike says the district attorney *knows* Vincent will be out in thirty, and his tough talk is theater for the voters of Rankin County. He says county officials are in a bind. Their conservative constituents have two demands: (1) Lock 'em away and throw away the key, and (2) don't raise taxes. So officials go through the show of being arch-conservative, then, when faced with paying the prison bill, they release prisoners early. In fact, Mike says, this is why Vincent was out of prison early and able to kill Richard.

"I thought I'd show you something," Mike Scott says.

He opens the manila folder, which activates a naughty smirk on his face.

He slides a large glossy photo across the desk.

I stare down at Vincent McGee.

Vincent stands in a narrow hallway. He is topless. It's a posed photograph. He is muscular and gorgeous. He clenches his fists, bulging out his arm and chest muscles further. His eyes, with the long, feminine lashes, are gently shut. Vincent is not smiling.

Mike Scott's finger points to a detail, not at first apparent. A mirror hangs from a door behind Vincent. Reflecting in the mirror is the hand of the cameraman.

"That's Barrett," says Mike Scott.

"No way," I say.

"And that's Barrett's house," says Mike Scott.

Vincent blocks the reflection except for the hand. But what other hand would be in Barrett's crummy little home? And why else would that crummy little home have the room full of photographic equipment that the investigators found?

"Oh! Wow!" I say. "How did you get this?"

"It just got sent."

"That's amazing, 'cause that sort of suggests something's going on."

"Uh-hm," says Mike Scott with a smirk.

He scribbles Daniel Earl Cox's indictment number on a sheet of paper and slides it across the desk.

In Search of Daniel Earl Cox: Plan A

I run down toward the Jackson public library, gripping my topless photo of Vincent McGee. Mike Scott told me a clerk at the Hinds County police department might have the affidavit. But it's kicked me in the face that someone else might, too—Daniel Earl Cox himself.

Squeezed between men with Afros and stained tracksuits in the library's computer room, I punch *Daniel Earl Cox* into PeopleFinder .com. Then, hovering around the Goodwill bin in the library parking lot, I flip out my phone and dial the first of several leads that the computer coughed up.

A man picks up my call. He's baffled by both my accent and my question.

Yes, he knows Daniel Earl Cox. He's dead.

The man breathes an upset breath and hangs up.

A woman soon calls me from the same number. Why am I ringing about Daniel? she asks anxiously. I begin to explain. She says she doesn't want to talk about Daniel and hangs up, too.

Maybe this isn't going to work.

Plan B: Hinds County Police Department

Deputy Sheriff Steve Pickett brings me into the sheriff's office so we can stretch out and pull some drinks from the minibar.

After twenty years of service, the sheriff and deputy sheriff are finishing up. They lost office. What happened?

"Demographics," Steve says.

"What do you mean?"

"They voted the black guy in."

"Where did all these new black people come from?"

"The wrong question," Steve says. "It's not where the black people came *from*, it's where the white people *went*." Rankin County, of course.

Steve remembers Richard.

"He was leprosy," Steve says.

He says he knows the case Mike Scott is talking about. He picks up the phone and asks someone to find Richard's file.

"That's odd," Steve finally says.

Richard's name is in the computer system, but all other information has been wiped. He recommends I try the Hinds County district attorney.

Plan C: Hinds County District Attorney's Office

A black woman at the Hinds County district attorney's office hands me a plump folder. I skip through the pages and hit the document that matches the indictment number provided by Mike Scott.

It's not Daniel Earl Cox's affidavit.

It's a single-page document labeled *Grand larceny*. There's not a word about sexual advances. Nor a word elaborating on grand larceny. It's like a receipt from an electronics store.

It takes a minute to think through. Richard filed a complaint against Daniel for stealing his jewelry—grand larceny—and the affidavit was merely Daniel writing down his side of the tale. And the case never went to trial. That's why I'm staring at a page of numbers and names and nothing more.

The woman touches her red fingernail to one of the names on the page: André de Gruy. He was the lawyer who represented Daniel Earl Cox in 1995.

He works not far from here, she says.

Plan D: André de Gruy

The sixth floor of the Robert E. Lee Building holds the Office of Capital Defense Counsel, the people who'll take care of you if you're broke and the district attorney wants to execute you. Sitting at a wooden table in the corner is André de Gruy, with blue eyes and a Roman nose, gobbling on a chicken sub sandwich.

Yes, he remembers Daniel Earl Cox. Yes, he's dead. No, he doesn't keep copies of affidavits from 1995. No, he says indignantly, he was not the man who tipped off Mike Scott about the incident. He says he's unclear about client-lawyer confidentiality when the client is dead, so he can't say more. He kicks me down the street to the Office of State Public Defender.

Plan E: The Office of State Public Defender

The Office of State Public Defender will take care of you if you're broke and the district attorney *doesn't* want to execute you. It looks like a bed-and-breakfast from the outside, or perhaps a nice, tucked-away Italian restaurant.

The bald public defender, William LaBarre, sits in a big office that's a crack den of manila folders. They tower in piles all over his desk and floor.

I darted out of Mike Scott's office four hours ago, and in some circular serendipity he happens to be in this building, walking past William's door, as I begin to tell William my story. I had dropped Mike's name to William not a minute ago. Am I a wizard?

"Hey, Mike," shouts William, "you know this guy?"

"I do," says Mike. "I did not send John over here, by the way."

"He was asking me about Daniel Cox," William says. "I don't know if he's dead."

I tell William and Mike he is dead.

"I had a copy but I can't find it," says Mike.

William scans the crack den. "I had a copy of it, too."

William remembers this particular document because soon after Richard Barrett was killed, André de Gruy foraged around his office for it so he could tip off Mike Scott about the incident.

William swats his hand on the far end of his desk like he's killing a fly.

"Here it is," says William.

William and Mike shrug back and forth about whether I'm allowed to have it. Usually, probably not, but the fact Daniel is dead may make things different.

William blows out his cheeks and slides the affidavit across the desk.

The Affidavit

In the Circuit Court of Hinds County, Mississippi

First Judicial District

State of Mississippi

VS No. 96-1-64 DANIEL COX, DEFENDANT

STATEMENT OF DEFENDANT

I am Daniel Earl Cox, the defendant in the above numbered case. I have been charged by way of indictment with the offense of grand larceny. I am giving this statement on my own free will and everything contained herein is true and correct to the best of my knowledge.

Sometime in June 1995 I was at a gas station in south Jackson, where I met a man who gave me some money for gas for my motorcycle. We discussed some work the man had for me clearing land. He told me where he lived, and I went to his house the next day.

The man invited me in his house, where he had a lot of photography equipment set up. The man started talking about taking photos of me. I felt he wanted me to pose nude for photos. I became very uncomfortable and let him know. As I started to leave, he became angry. He followed me out of the house and was yelling at me. I have not seen the man since that day, nor did I take anything from his house. The first I heard about his accusations were at the time of my arrest.

This is all I know about the accusations made against me.

A lot of photography equipment set up. But Jesus! Why did it have to say "I felt"? *I felt he wanted me to pose nude for photos.* Why couldn't it just be *He 100 percent, unambiguously, no question, asked me to pose nude and got angry when I refused?* But that's not how this story works. It's not how most things work.

Is it possible the difficulty I had in finding the document says as much about Richard as the document itself? I've never been sure about the high-power connections Richard claimed to have. But could those connections have erased details off the police computer and emptied files from law enforcement filing cabinets?

I slide the affidavit into my folder, under the photo of Vincent McGee, topless in the hallway, with his eyes gently shut.

Southern Hills Baptist Church

I'm running out of time in Mississippi, but not places to burrow for a smoking gun. Why, for instance, was Richard booted out of the Southern Hills Baptist Church in the 1990s? I suppose a book set in Mississippi was always going to end up in church at some point.

"Lord, we come to you with our families and friends who need you to intervene medically for them to live!" the pastor cries, thumping the altar. "Agnes is back in the hospital. She usually tells us everything to pray for. We pray for her knee operation, and hopefully she'll be able to go home the next day!"

I'm squashed between the pastor's wife and a man so sour, he's twitching. Ten minutes ago joy stretched his smile and sparkled in his eyes, before I spoke these words: *I'm writing about Richard Barrett.* The man, Milton, said we could talk later in the back room.

Later, five church members squish around the table in the small back room. Three look like their anger may escalate into spasms. The pastor and his wife, however, are more recent additions to the church and have never met Richard Barrett.

Milton says this all started when Richard had bumbled into church one Sunday morning, walked down the apricot carpet, and asked the previous pastor, Pastor Farris, if he could join.

"I taught him many Sundays at my Sunday School class," snaps another man at the table, Doug. "I had a great conflict with him over the fact that not only did he despise blacks, he despised Jews. My Savior, in the flesh, was born as a Jew!"

Whispers blew back to Pastor Farris and the congregation. Richard had been on the radio, blurting that he and the church were fighting the same fight for segregation.

"This is a place of worship and service to the King of Kings and the Lord of Lords!" cries Doug. He waves his arms about and probably would wave more, but his elbow would smash the walls in this small room. "Well, Richard Barrett, when he came here, the main purpose in coming was because he felt that our ideas coincided with his ideas. And they only did in part."

Pastor Farris called Richard to the church. He told Richard to stop yapping to the media that the church backed his views. Richard did not stop yapping. Pastor Farris summoned Richard again. This time for a meeting with the whole congregation. And despite agreeing not to bring the press, Richard marched up the stony road toward the church with news crews fluttering about.

Pastor Farris screamed, "Hold up!" He told the newspeople they'd have to wait at the tip of the church's driveway. Richard marched into the church.

"We gave him a chance to speak," Milton says. "We did it by bylaws of the church constitution. And a great majority of the church voted against him, you know, to get him excommunicated."

Richard would not leave the church.

"Remember the night?" Milton asks the table. "He got so mad. He went to the piano." Richard pounded away at "God Bless America," over and over, refusing to stop, sweat flying from his face.

Even after that he didn't let things rest, bashing on the door of Pastor Farris's private home, threatening to bash Pastor Farris.

There's a dimension to this story that is being flicked to me in crumbs, and it's taking my brain a while to roll it together.

Did Doug say before that Richard Barrett, when he came here, the main purpose in coming was because he felt that their ideas coincided with his ideas *and they only did in part*? Which part?

Doug leans forward, agitated and defensive, and explains.

"Now, we inherited a school system called the Council school system.

It was given to us because the people who established it, basically, so far as school, so far as gatherings in the church and all that, they were basically for the white race."

"The Council" is short for "the White Citizens' Council." After the US Supreme Court told government schools they must integrate in 1954, pro-white groups set up "segregation academies." Because they were private institutions, they weren't bound by the court ruling. Southern Hills Baptist Church took over several of these academies, although it ran them as separate entities The church was overseeing these academies when Richard bumbled in and asked to join the congregation in the early 1990s.

Doug flaps his finger and his cheeks pink up.

"But the reason this church voted to accept that school system," he cries, "was simply because we saw it as a means of extending the name of God in those young people. Not necessarily to teach racism, but to expand and extend the kingdom of God in their hearts."

Thirty-five segregation academies survive in Mississippi today. That's the figure from a Columbia University report. Richard didn't spin a globe, poke his finger out, and randomly hit Southern Hills Baptist Church. He chose this church because it ran segregation academies.

When Richard blurted to the media that he and the church were fighting the same fight, he was kind of right.

James Rankin said that Richard was never more thrilled than when he discovered something was legal. *His whole leverage that he took pride in, was the legalities and all that.*

Did some Mississippians not like Richard because he drew attention to things—ugly, lawful things—they would prefer remain discreet?

11.

REAL TALK

Chywanna

The Peach Street Café does not sit in a street lined with peach trees; it sits in a megastore parking lot. Each time the door opens, the scent of exhaust fumes dances down the aisle and up my nostrils.

"I'm eighteen years old and in college now," Chywanna tells me over the phone. "I'm studying dental hygiene."

Chywanna is weaving down a corridor to class as we speak. Students bustling in the background is a nice alternative to the primal screams from prisoners in the East Mississippi prison for the criminally insane.

You know I got a new girlfriend, her name's Chywanna? Vincent told me on the road trip. They have since broken up, he updated me yesterday. It's not always easy for me to keep up. Chywanna is different from China, the girl he pimped out, my notes confirm.

"I was in, what, fifth grade," Chywanna says. "It was fifth or sixth grade when I was seeing Vincent around and I kind of had a little crush on him 'cause he's cute, you know?" She giggles. "I mean, there was a lot of girls that had a crush on Vincent 'cause he was cute."

Chywanna tells me she wasn't aware she and Vincent were dating last week. They've only dated for one stretch of time: over a year ago, for a month and a half.

"And why did you break up?"

"Well, it's just that my parents didn't really agree with me talking to him, 'cause they really wanted me to be with somebody who was in school and trying to do something with their life."

"And did he have tattoos on his face when you knew him?"

"Yes. He had, I think, six or five maybe. Yeah, my parents didn't approve of that, either."

"He doesn't like being rejected, but he seems to do things that will make people reject him. Like, you know, getting tattoos on his face, for example."

"Yeah. He really . . . I mean, the tattoos on his face really say that he really didn't wanna do anything with his life. I don't really like the fact that he had tattoos on his face, but he was a nice person toward me."

One evening Chywanna told him it was over and watched him amble away down the street, slowly shrinking from a man to a speck in the distance. Two weeks rolled on before she saw him again. This time he shuffled into her family's living room, through the television, in his yellow prison jumpsuit.

"Had you seen that side of him before?" I ask. "Like, him being angry enough to kill someone?"

"No, not at all," she says. "He didn't act that way toward me at all, so it was really shocking."

"What about his mother?" I ask. "Did you like his mother, Tina?"

"Yeah, she was pretty nice. She was really nice, but I mean, he, he would disrespect her a lot, though. Like, you're supposed to talk to your mom in a respectful way, but he didn't. It's almost like he was a controlling husband over his mom, instead of his mother's son."

Chywanna clucks, then blows a little huff.

"I feel like, if I would never have broken up with him, I feel like I could've at least stopped him from killing the man. You know how somebody makes you mad and you call your friend and you're like, 'Man, guess what happened to me today? This man tried to do this and this. I think I'm going to do this to the man for doing that to me, you know?'

So I thought maybe he would tell me about it, and I would be, 'You know, I don't think that's a good idea.'"

Chywanna says he called her on the morning after he'd lit the house on fire but before the police pointed a gun in his face and cuffed him.

"He told me that he wanted to see me, but I couldn't because I was at school, on my way to class. I was like, 'I can't.'"

"Yeah, it was probably lucky you couldn't catch up with him, because everyone who he rang up that morning and who met him ended up being dragged to the police station."

"Really?"

"Don't tell him I told you this, but I think you're very lucky to get away from him."

"Everybody says that."

"Yeah, yeah." I can't help thinking about Daisy and China. "He's a very nice . . . On one hand he's very . . . I'm just telling you this, you know, just in case . . . Not that, you know, you don't know how to take care of yourself, but I've been talking to him a bit and he's definitely a bit volatile and prone to breaking into violence and stuff. So, yeah, you should be careful. But he's going to be in jail probably for decades, so you should be okay."

"Yeah. And he . . . he calls me all the time and he's talking about he wants to marry me and stuff like that, but I don't want to tell him that I have moved on—but I have."

I think of how a normal family life stopped Chywanna from being drawn into the madness.

Because she was off to school, she couldn't catch up.

Real Talk

"Mike Scott found another man," I tell Vincent, straightening the affidavit on my coffee table. "Another man complained Richard Barrett sexually harassed him."

I slurp a mouthful of black coffee.

"For real?" Vincent says, surprised.

I tell him for real.

"Damn, yeah? I don't know nothin' about it, right? Like I said, the motherfucker ain't did me no kind of way like that, you hear?"

I squint at the topless photo of Vincent next to the affidavit.

"Someone also sent Mike Scott a photograph of you. In the mirror it looks like Richard Barrett is taking the photo of you."

"No! Hell no!" Vincent laughs, then shouts, "Hell no! That's bullshit! The only motherfucker who takes photos of me is me!"

"There's someone's arm." I laugh, too. "He definitely looks white." I roll my finger down Vincent's arm. "I didn't know you had a Satan's star on your shoulder."

"Man, listen, I got a whole lot of tattoos you don't know about. That ain't no satanic star, though. I ain't no satanist, you hear?" he says. "You tryin' to make me out to be a devil worshipper?"

"No, no, no."

Vincent tells me he's still trying to get me a visitation. I tell him I'm leaving in exactly a week.

"Now tell me," he says, "what all you and Chywanna talked about me? You weren't talkin' that sideways shit. You didn't bring up that bullshit that he tried to make sexual advances?"

"It was in the newspapers," I say, weaseling out of the question. "People know about it. They don't know if it's true, but they've heard about it."

A primal "AAAARGGHHH" ricochets off the walls in Meridian's East Mississippi Correctional Facility.

"Hold up!" Vincent says to me. "Hold up!"

Vincent pushes his face to the bars to suss the source of the *AAAARGGHHH*.

"Someone's started a fire or some dumb shit," Vincent tells me.

"Is everybody mentally unstable in Meridian?" I ask.

"Yeah," Vincent says. "I ain't got no mental problems, though."

I laugh. "Well, you know, you do seem to have a propensity for violence."

"Man," he says, exasperated, "everybody's violent, goddamn it."

"But most people don't do all the violent stuff you do. I'm just being honest with you."

"I'm sayin' everybody is violenter than me in prison. I'm the only person that seems like I'm sane. Everybody else is crazy."

"Do you remember being really young and not being violent?"

"I used to, like, find dogs and shit, you hear? We'd take those bitches and hang them in trees."

I put down my coffee. Have I misheard or misunderstood? My arms don't think so. They've prickled up with goose bumps.

"You hung dogs in trees?"

Vincent names a relative. It's a name I haven't heard before.

"He started payin' me to catch them. He used to pay me to go catch everybody else's dogs in the neighborhood, you hear? And shit, I'd bring them back to him, he'd take 'em bitches and tie a rope around their necks and hang 'em bitches from a tree, you know?"

Vincent watched his relative tape shut the mouths of the dogs. Vincent stood back from the tree. His relative drifted to his car, parked nearby, and creaked opened the door. Pit bull puppies scuttled out of the backseat.

His relative was training the pits for fighting.

He led the puppies to the tree. The neighborhood dogs flapped on the branches, wailing through the tape. The pit bulls tore up the dogs.

The pit bulls would eventually calm down, and his relative would herd them back to the car. Vincent would gaze at the carcasses swinging from the tree. It wouldn't take long for the flies to arrive.

"How old were you?" I ask.

"I was about eight," Vincent says with a slurred, pained giggle. "He's the one who put me on to this shit."

"That's a pretty horrific thing for you to have to see."

"That's what I used to do. I used to fight any motherfuckin' thing that would fight—cats, dogs, chicken. Oh man! I used to fight mother-fuckin' little black ants with the little pincer on their mouths!"

Vincent giggles a woozy giggle.

"But when did you move on to people?"

"Why you tryin'a make it seem like I'm so violent, man, when I'm so friendly, I'm so nice and pleasant?"

Vincent's serious. I chuckle.

"I mean, I think there are two sides to you," I say. "I think you're nice, but you're also violent. I'm just trying to understand what happened in your life that made you end up being able to stab people."

"I'm gonna tell you what happened, right? I finally realized either you were doin' it to them or they were gonna do it to you, you know what I'm sayin'? In this world, nigga, you gotta be . . . It's a dog-eat-dog world, you hear? Only the strong survive—that's my motto. Only the strong sur-vive, and the weak die."

Vincent says that aged ten he would shoot dice with his adult cous-ins. They'd jump him if he won and he'd have to fight to keep his winnings.

"So, you know what I'm sayin'? I've been fighting for my life. All my life, man."

A clang echoes down the corridor in the East Mississippi prison.

"Hold up," says Vincent, "hold up."

Cicadas scream outside my apartment, and the sky is turning purple.

A minute later Vincent whispers in my ear.

"Hey, listen," he says, "talk down low 'cause there's lots of police around here, you hear?"

"Yeah, sure."

"But I'm gonna need you to do somethin' for me, you hear? I need some G-Dot cards, you hear? I got some big business coming through, you hear? Gonna need twenty-five hundred. And get it in single one-hundreds, you hear?"

"I can't give you twenty-five hundred dollars. I don't have much money left," I say. "You're going to have to figure out another plan."

"No," he says. "*You* the plan."

I laugh. "You're going to need another plan."

"Uh-uh," he says. "No. Uh-uh."

"No, uh-uh," I mimic back.

"Say, John Safran?" he says.

"Yes?"

"I can get you killed from right behind this door, man. Real talk."

"You can get me killed from behind your door?"

"Real talk," he says. "I can get your motherfuckin' ass killed from behind this door, if you playin'. I've got niggers right now, on my honor, that can come up to your motherfuckin' house and put your brains outside the curb."

"Pardon?"

My "pardon" is me buying time to sort this out in my head, while fear rushes through me.

"I said, by a motherfuckin' player, I can get you killed in your motherfuckin' house tonight. I got the address on the letter: 5201 Lakeland Boulevard, Flowood. Apartment F58. Motherfucker's brains be in the street."

"That's rather scary, you know?" I say. "It's pretty scary to hear that. I don't understand when you say things like that whether you're being serious or you're being funny."

"No, I ain't laughing. I'm serious. Serious as a motherfuckin' heart attack or a stroke."

"Jesus!" I say, then, "Mmmmm," not sure where to take this next.

"Listen, this is real nigga shit," he says. "I'm gonna need you to send some flowers to somebody, too, you hear? I gotta get her address tomorrow and call you back."

Vincent hangs up, ending the strangest turn of conversation I've ever had in my life.

The purple sky turns black, and I fall asleep to cicada screams.

My eyes snap open at two in the morning. I'm sure I can hear a key rattling in the keyhole. I roll my shoulders back and breathe. Everything soft is loud—the refrigerator hum, the tap drip, the breeze on the window.

The Next Day

"I'm leaning toward not sending them flowers to no bitch," Vincent tells me. As usual he's called me. He still holds control as to when we talk. "I ask myself, what has the bitch done for me, you hear?"

"Yeah," I say. "I understand."

I'm stretched out on a lounge chair under the gazebo by the pool.

My non-cell-phone hand is thumbing through Ann Rule's *The Stranger Beside Me: The Shocking Inside Story of Serial Killer Ted Bundy.* I'm hunting down the chunk about Ted witnessing animal cruelty as a child.

Here we go: Ted Bundy watched his grandfather kick family dogs till they cried and swing neighborhood cats by their tails.

"I'm thinking," says the man who watched the dogs sway from the tree in Jackson, "I think it should go to my mom or my grandma."

I plonked this thought in Vincent's mind at the start of this call. That perhaps he would like me to drop flowers to his mother and grandma as well as this mystery girl.

I, of course, have my reason for plonking this in his mind. It would allow me to circumvent the unspoken Tina ban and knock on her door. *Vincent asked me to deliver these flowers.* And Vincent will have to cough up an address for his grandmother, too. Who knows what detail she'll add to the story of Vincent McGee?

"Hey, wait a minute," Vincent says, "actually I might send some to that bitch. At the same time, I don't really know."

"What's the longest," I ask, "you've ever gone out with a girl?"

"Couple of months, like, three months, some shit like that."

"That's not very long."

"At the same time, it's like—this is what I'm saying. I always been in jail, man. I go to jail so much, that's how my relationships end, you know what I mean? No bitch never break up with me while I'm on the street. But when I'm back in the penitentiary and shit, we break then, you see? That's why I say I gotta murblestatic them all over, see the little girl, the honey, before I try to send them some flowers and shit. I don't know murblestatic but she murblestatic gave them back, you hear?"

"You're worried she's going to give the flowers back," I say, "and not accept them?"

"No!" he spits defiantly. "Hey, man—I don't get no flowers back. They gonna keep that shit, you hear? Just so they can tell their friends, 'He sent me some flowers,' you hear?"

An old man waddles through the pool gate. He spots me in prime gazebo position and pulls a disappointed face.

"Send that shit to Momma, you hear?" he says. "And my grandma. But fuck a bitch."

"Okay, not for a bitch, but for your mum and grandma?"

"I don't want to get out there on a limb with this female I'm talking about," he says. "'Cause she's got a motherfuckin' chain saw and could cut the limb, right? You hear?"

Vincent wavers back and forth on whether to send flowers or not. The old man keeps darting eyes at me to try to psychologically drive me out of the gazebo.

Vincent finally locks in. He *will* send flowers to the mystery girl.

"Make sure they're some roses, man," he says. "How are you gonna send them?"

"I'm just going to drive them over."

"Get the fuck out of here!" He laughs.

"Why? What's wrong with driving there with flowers?"

"There ain't nothing wrong with it, I'm just sayin' this is how I want you to show up. Have a little card I wrote. I mean I'll write some playa shit on the card and you read it to her, but it'll be my words."

"Okay. Yeah, sure."

"You should say, 'I work for Vincent McGee and he just told me to deliver these flowers because I'm his secretary.'"

I laugh. "Okay."

"Where are you going to get the flowers from?"

"I can look it up on the Internet."

"I don't want you to go pulling no flowers out of the yard and take them to her, you hear? I want the romantic type—like it popped in my head that I wanna send her some flowers and I'm thinking about her and shit."

Vincent tells me to prepare my pen. This is what he wants jotted on the card. I pull my yellow notepad onto my lap in the lounge chair. I can hear Vincent's feet plod around the prison cell.

"I need a rider . . ." Vincent dictates.

"What's a rider?"

"You just write it!" Vincent says. "And she's gonna know what I'm talking about. *I need a rider. Somebody who understands me. And understands what I'm going through. I need to be with somebody. Together.* You hear?"

I scribble fast.

"Strike that out," Vincent now instructs. "Entirely. Okay, I'm gonna start over. Tell her, *I'm that nigga*—No, put, *I'm the* man *to hold it down. When you need a shoulder to lean on, you hear? I'mma be there when you needed it. I'mma be there. But at the same time, when I need the same thing, I'mma need you to be there.* Read that back."

"I'm the man to hold it down," I say. "When you need a shoulder to lean on, you hear?"

"Hold up!" Vincent snaps. "Why'd you put in 'you hear'? I didn't say no motherfuckin' 'you hear.'"

I strike out *you hear.*

"And," Vincent continues dictating, feet clomping around the cell floor, *"we'll enjoy all the good experiences together on our journey through this world,* you hear? *Behind every strong man is a strong woman. All I ask is for you to put forth effort to make my thoughts and beliefs a reality . . ."*

Vincent's dictating springs along, faster and faster, happier and happier.

"Because when I conquer the earth," he continues, *"I'mma put the sun and the moon around your neck,* you hear? *I'mma put the stars around your wrist. But it still couldn't compare to, you know what I'm sayin'? It still won't outshine your beauty,* you hear?"

Vincent laughs a joyous and satisfied laugh. He's worked out just what a woman wants to hear.

"Yo!" Vincent laughs. "Put 'you hear,' you hear?"

"You hear?" I mimic back.

"You hear?" Vincent spits back in an Australian accent. "Ha! Ha! Ha! Okay, we're gonna autograph this bitch and we're gonna shut this bitch down, you hear? All right, tell her, *Don't settle for the less when you can have the best. Without the headaches and the stress.* At the same time, I really mean that. I'm really, really tryin' to tell her, you know what I'm sayin' . . . *Look, all the complications, all the trials, we don't have to go through that. I'm gonna keep the one honey, you know? I'm gonna do my thing and you're gonna do your thing, but at the same time we gotta respect each other while we're doing our thing, you feel?"*

"Do you want me to write that down?"

"No!" he says. "Hell no! I'm just sayin' that's what I'm basically trying to say. You the fuckin' writer, here's where you come in, you hear? You can't be no motherfuckin' writer if you can't make her see what I'm tryin'a say, you hear?"

"You're probably right." I laugh.

"Now at the end put *a murble nigga like me.*"

"A what?" I say. "A dog nigga?"

Vincent turns quiet. "Now, hold on, hold on," he says sharply. "Now we're cool, right? I don't never wanna hear you say no shit like that again or we ain't never gonna be cool again, you hear?"

"I'm sorry," I say. "I thought that was what you said."

"I'm just sayin', I know what I said but you don't have to repeat what I said, you hear?"

"Okay, sure, sorry."

"A'right. Just put, like I said, *a thug nigga like me*."

"How do you want to spell the *N* word? *N-I-G-G-A?*"

"Yeah, like that. A'right, thanks, John. We're one hundred, man. But I don't really think about the *N* word and shit, man, real talk. It's just that I've had a lot of bad experience with a lot of white folks, you hear? I don't play by no kind of *nigger* word, no *monkey*, none of that shit," he says. "That shit gets to feel real bad, you hear?"

"Sure."

Vincent laughs. "At the same time, man, you're gonna go straight to her house and deliver her the card. I want her to have a card, teddy bear with some chocolate and some roses."

I scribble *Card, teddy bear, roses, chocolate*.

"Make sure you get a teddy bear that she can hug at night, you hear?"

"Sure." I laugh.

"Now don't be tellin' me you're gonna do shit if you don't mean it, man."

"I'm going to do it," I tell Vincent. "Why not?"

"That's what I'm sayin'—why not?"

"What's the address of the girl, though?" I ask.

Vincent says he doesn't have the address. He'll hit me back with it. She's not returning his calls right now.

"I was talking to her and we got emotional and shit and she started a little argument with me—'You ain't right for me.'"

I look up. The old man is waddling around the pool, still sulking because I scored the gazebo. A growl rolls up the corridor of East Mississippi prison.

"Hey, go to Facebook," Vincent says. "You can go to the computer right now and erase my Facebook, you hear?"

"Erase it?"

"You gonna get on there and erase that motherfucker. When you come in to penitentiary they ask you if you've got Facebook. I told them I ain't had no Facebook. 'Cause they'll be all up in your business and shit. They'd be asking, 'Do you disapprove of MDOC checking your Facebook account and shit?' I told them I ain't gotten it."

I pluck my silver laptop from my bag and creak it open on my belly. I tell him I've been on Facebook myself this morning.

"You been on *my* Facebook?" Vincent snaps.

"No, *my* Facebook!"

"If I find out you're the conspiracy, you're trying to trap me or something, I'm gonna knock your noodle."

"No, I'm writing a book, it's not a conspiracy to trap you. By the way, the police have already trapped you. They've already got you in jail. They don't need anything else."

"Man, I don't feel comfortable giving you my password," Vincent says.

Then he spits out the digits.

"Seventeen people want to be your friend," I tell Vincent.

"Don't answer that shit. Erase my Facebook account. Hey, go check my messages real quick."

I tell him a girl called Jasmine has written, *I've been texting but you won't text me back, what's up with that?*

"You tell her she mustn't be textin' the right thang," he says.

I type, *U musn't be textin' the right thang*, and hit send.

"Hey, but listen," he says, "go on ahead and delete my account, right quick."

"I'm trying to figure out how to do it. Just a sec," I say, fumbling through the toolbar. "Do you go to account privacy settings or account settings?"

"Say what?"

"I'll work out how to do it," I say. "When we hang up I'll talk to a friend who will know how to do it."

"A'right, listen. I'll hit you back soon, you hear?"

Vincent hangs up, and I stare at his Facebook message box.

I scroll down.

A white girl has messaged:

> Hey, what's up, you are beyond gorgeous. My name is Katie, I saw your face on TV.

I scroll down.

A person named Falona has messaged:

> SICK SICK HUMAN. ALL YALL DO IS TALK THAT HOOD SHIT AND FUCK UP. YALL MAKE ALL BLACK MALES LOOK BAD. I HOPE THEY MURDER YOUR ASS IN PRISON. NO ONE HAS D RIGHT TO TAKE ANOTHER'S LIFE. YOU WILL SOON BE BACK WHERE YOU BELONG IN A CAGE FOR LIFE LIKE THE ANIMAL YOU ARE. WILD BEAST NEED NOT BE IN CIVILIZED SOCIETY . . .

I scroll down.

There's a message to Vincent, and a reply from Vincent, on April 21. Why is that date itching me? Why is there a tickle running up my arms?

My brain pulls itself together.

That's the night Vincent wandered down to Richard's home and jumped on Facebook and began typing, then stood up from the keyboard and killed Richard Barrett.

I squint at the screen. Vincent's brother, Justin, has typed:

> Nigga where u at

And Vincent has typed back:

getting money

oh lets do it.

The Flower Drop: Justin and Sherrie McGee

The first time I drifted into the McGees' I could hardly see the McGees. This time the world blows its light into the living room.

Vincent's sister Sherrie has shorn her hair, and lanky Justin seems closer to the ceiling than last time. Tina is somewhere else.

"Vincent wanted me to give this to your mum," I say, floating in the doorway.

"God, they pretty," says Justin McGee.

"He dictated the card over the telephone," I say. "You can tell your mum I'm leaving Saturday so I won't be annoying your family anymore."

"Yeah," says Sherrie from the couch, "but, you know, you ain't no problem, you're okay."

I pull out the affidavit and run Justin and Sherrie through Daniel Earl Cox's story.

"It's really hard finding stuff in Mississippi," I say. "Lots of secrets."

"Mm-hmm," says Justin. "It's something else down here."

My fingers reach in my bag and pluck out the shirtless photo of Vincent.

"The lawyer Mike Scott showed me this picture," I say. "He was saying it was taken down at Richard's. And that the person in the reflection is Richard Barrett."

Justin blinks at the photograph.

"Oh, that picture," Justin says. "No, I took it."

Justin leads me through the living room to the hallway. The cream walls running down the McGees' hallway match the cream walls in the photo. The doors in the hallway match the doors in the photo, too. The mirror glimmering in the photograph glimmers in front of my eyes.

"It must have just been the flash," I say. "Because the flash makes the arm look white."

"Yeah, I took it right here," says Justin.

I deflate. One of the smoking guns is no smoking gun after all.

"Me and my little brother Eric," Justin says, "Richard wanted us to help him one time. And we said, 'How much money you going to pay us to help you?' He said, 'You shouldn't wanna get paid every time you do some work.' And I was scared 'cause he looked gay."

"So what do you reckon happened?" I ask him. "Do you reckon Vincent was angry 'cause he didn't get paid, or do you think Richard tried to attack him or something?"

"Oh no," Justin says knowingly, "he got paid."

"So you don't think it was because of that?"

"No," he says definitively.

"You think maybe . . ."

"I think there was something going on," Justin says.

Sherrie rustles on the couch.

"Some people do things," Sherrie says. "You need things and you'll do it, but it's not always the best thing, you know? Vincent would continue to do things for money. Big, large-lump sums of money, hundreds of dollars, you know? It's just, if he need it, he would do it, but you don't want the world to know it, so that's the situation."

I scrunch up my nose. I wasn't expecting this. Vincent's brother and sister are steering me to the story embroidered with homosexuality.

"Wow," I say. "Because it'd be a big taboo for everyone to know that?"

"Yeah, it would be embarrassing, right?" Sherrie says. "He couldn't enjoy his life after that. Especially since he didn't want to come out. I'm not judgmental. But anybody that prefers the same sex, they're embarrassed about it, they hide it."

I'm crumpling my brow trying to sort out exactly what Sherrie is getting at. *Anybody that prefers the same sex.* Is she talking about Richard or Vincent?

"Do you think Vincent . . ." I stop. I back up and rephrase. "It would have been just for money, though, wouldn't it have?"

"It would have just been for the money," Sherrie says. "But at the end he got a good feeling behind it. If you're getting whacked off, sucked off, you know, you're gonna enjoy that."

"What, Vincent?" I say.

"Yeah, he gets everything," Sherrie says. "I don't think he was doing the man. I don't think he was suckin' him. So he would be on his back and getting chopped off, as they say—his penis sucked. He was the one who was getting the service, but he was getting paid for his services—to be worked on, you know?"

My face tightens. I'm flustered by Sherrie's sharp turn into these vivid details. Is Sherrie speculating? Has Vincent talked to her?

"How do you know that?" I say.

"Because I don't think he could be the one lickin' anything, you know?"

I blurt an awkward laugh. Sherrie and Justin laugh at my laugh. Sherrie makes another sharp turn.

"If you notice the door on that house, they had bars on them," Sherrie says. "If you don't have the keys to those, you cannot get out of the house. So I think the only reason that Vincent would react that way is if everything was locked, you know, and the man had, you know, like, some kind of weapon and telling him, 'I'm going to do this and do that,' and Vincent had to do it in order to get out alive."

I think about Vincent telling me what happened and the feeling that there was something missing from the story of who did what first. What was the spark—did it originate in sex, or race, or money? They're the three questions I had in Melbourne. But after asking them for so long, I've come to wonder whether they're really three different questions at all. They *are* for the lawyers: When I asked Michael Guest whether there was a race factor to the crime, he said that would be a third explanation, after Vincent's other explanations involving sex and money. But I don't know that they are for Vincent, or were for Richard. For them, I think they're all the same question. Everything I've found out seems to show that for both Richard and Vincent, race, sex, and money were all intertwined. They were all about power.

Tina drifts in the doorway from outside. Her eyes meet the lilies in the vase and her face washes over with delight. The flowers overrule any apprehension she has about me. She pulls out the purple envelope tied to the vase with a white ribbon.

"I thought I'd give you one of these, too," I say. I hand her a copy of the affidavit and blabber out the Daniel Earl Cox adventure once again. "It kind of validates what you said happened. Who knows? It might come in handy one day."

"Okay." She smiles. "Thank you."

I leave Tina to read the card Vincent dictated to his secretary, John Safran, while clomping around his cell in Meridian at the East Mississippi prison for the criminally insane.

Dear Mom,

I'm glad that you've been down with me during the good times and the bad times.

You made me a better man by letting me learn the hard way.

And I'm thankful every day that you're still here with me.

With Undying Love,
Your son Vincent

The Black Man Who Cried

I found my way into one more house before I left Tina's street. I saw a man getting his mail, began chatting, and he invited me in.

The investigator Tim Lawless told me there was a black man who cried when he told him Richard Barrett had died. That black man is Moses. He's sitting on the couch with his wife, Michelle. Why was Moses fond of him? Moses says Richard helped him with a legal matter, a civil one. That he was a nice man. And—this I almost can't believe—Richard didn't charge him! But there was more than that.

"Summertime," Michelle says, "he would stop and visit with my mother."

"Is your mother still alive?" I ask.

"Uh-huh," Michelle says. "She's in the nursing home. He came and sat and talked with her. He wasn't a person in the neighborhood that you were scared of because he didn't bother nobody."

"Why do you think he chose your mother to speak to?"

"I don't know. He was a peculiar person, and I guess he just decided that she was all right and didn't hold no prejudice toward him for what people said and what he was portrayed to be."

Richard the white supremacist sitting with the old black lady at the nursing home. That image will stick in my mind as surely as Richard's body lying out on the lawn.

One More Secret

Giles Farm is up this way, and I'm not sure I'll be here again. I creep up Jim's dirt path one last time to say good-bye. I catch him carrying a Netflix envelope from his mailbox to his trailer. He seems happy to see me. We have a chuckle over the time Earnest accidentally endorsed him in the *Jackson Advocate*, confusing him with a black candidate called Giles.

"Yeah, that was funny," Jim says.

He wishes me luck with my book and tells me my next one should be about the Parkers, the white family murdered in 1990. I eye his Netflix envelope and ask him what DVD he's rented. He tells me he can't remember, but it's clear to me he can. He slinks off to his trailer. One more secret. Why not?

Erma McGee

Okay. Pulled into the dust outside the shack. Clothes hung on the barbed-wire fence stretched out front. A homemade wheelchair ramp ran up to the doorway. A brown dog yawned at me. There was a cat figure-eighting my legs as I knocked on the door. An old man opened. I said, "Hey, these are for Erma. Does Erma live here?" Behind him a young-looking woman in a black T-shirt was stretched out on a mattress without a sheet, watching a staticky TV.

"This is Erma," said the old man.

I felt like I'd walked into someone taking a shower. I say, "Vincent wanted me to pass these on to you," she says, "Thank you," and I say, "Cool. Okay. No worries. See ya."

I heard her fingers tearing the purple envelope as I pulled the door shut.

Dear Grandma,

I know I've made mistakes. But every day I've strived to be a better man.

I seek knowledge, wisdom, and understanding. And everything I do is for you.

I remember all the lessons you taught me and I love you to death.

Hopefully I'll get back to the streets and be the upstanding man you want me to be.

I'm praying for you every day.

Love your grandson,
Vincent

Chywanna Again

"Hey, Chywanna," I say into the phone—yes, Vincent's mysterious woman was her. "How are you?"

"Okay," she says.

"Hey, I just thought I'd ring you up because I dropped off something from Vincent, but you weren't there to tell you about it."

She says nothing.

"Hello?" I say.

"No, I got it," she says.

"Oh, yeah, sure. But I just wanted to . . . Because I was in a bit of . . . I didn't really . . . I was a bit uncomfortable about it because obviously Vincent's in jail and stuff. But he asked me to do it, and I thought I'd do it as a favor or whatever. But I just . . . yeah. I just wanted to make sure you weren't uncomfortable about it."

"No."

"Okay, cool. Sorry. Yeah, yeah. 'Cause I just . . . yeah, 'cause as I said on the phone last time, even though on the one hand, you know, I like Vincent and, you know, he's fun to talk to and everything, he is, like, obviously a murderer, so that's why I obviously . . . I felt a bit uncomfortable about just leaving the flowers there 'cause it might have seemed threatening to you or something."

"No. I'm fine."

"Okay, cool. I'm . . . Well, as long as you didn't feel threatened by getting flowers from a guy who's in prison for killing someone, then that's good. Yes. Okay."

"So . . . okay."

"Okay. No, that . . . I just . . . yeah, I just wanted to make sure that you weren't, like, scared or anything like that."

"Oh, no. It was fine."

"Okay, cool. Okay, excellent. Okay, see you later."

"All right."

Janet

What would Janet Malcolm think?

12.

THE RING

The Interrogation Room

Maybe because I'm leaving tomorrow, everyone in Mississippi has rolled on down the road and left me here. There are new dramas. New murders. I bumped into investigators Tim Lawless and Wayne Humphreys today at lunch. They told me they'd just driven interstate to retrieve a human head. Things have come a long way since the DA wouldn't let me peek in his manila folder the first time I stopped by. Now he's letting me watch Vincent's interrogation room footage, alone, on a computer in his boardroom.

Michael Dent's mother, Vicky, is boxed in a white cube. She sits in a chair in a pink-and-white-striped jumpsuit, a desk before her. The camera angle, high and pointing down, means only the investigator's fingers, resting on the desk, have made the shot. It is Trip Bayles.

Why Vincent Killed Richard, According to Vicky Dent

"My boy Michael never went down the house!" she pleads. "Vincent did!"

"Vincent did it all?" asks Trip.

"He did it all, baby!"

"Let me give you some history," Trip says. "Has anybody told you this? You saw it on the news, right?"

"Yeah."

"What did you learn about the dead man on the news?"

"That he was a good man and he tried to help people."

"Is that what you saw on the news?"

"Just saw a bit," Vicky concedes.

"He was a white supreme-ist."

Vicky leans in. "I don't know what that means," she says seriously.

"That means he didn't like black people very much."

"Well, I like everyone."

"Me too," says Trip. "They one of those people that perform with the skinheads," Trip says. "You ever heard of that?"

"No."

"They're really extreme racist white people."

"Oh, well," says Vicky, "that's his business. Long as he doesn't mess with me, I love him."

"Well, he was one of them. You think Vincent killed him because of that?"

"Maybe . . ." she says doubtfully, shaking her head. "I tell you the truth."

"Tell me the truth."

"I say Vincent killed that man and if he would have got away with it he would have killed another man."

"You think so?"

"Baby, look at his eyes. That tells you everything."

"I haven't talked to him," Trip says. "Why do you think he killed him? To rob him or something?"

Vicky shoos that away with her hand and leans in again.

"He did it just to kill a man," she says, then explains her reasoning. "They say when he was little he worked for the man and he gives a dollar. And they say on the news he's mad 'cause this time he gave him twenty-six dollars. If someone gives you a dollar in the first beginning, why you go work for them again?"

Now I've been given another explanation. Vincent needed to get a killing out of his system, and he knew Richard would rip him off, giving him the excuse.

Vincent Pulled into the White Cube

Vincent is slumped in the chair in his yellow jumpsuit in the white cube. This is ten hours after Vincent tried to light up the crummy little house. Trip Bayles's fingers tap on the desk.

"All right, man, tell me how it is," says Trip.

"This is the story, man," Vincent says.

"Let me hear it."

"Ah, I went down to his house—I'm telling the truth, can you give me a plea, man?"

"We'll see what we can do."

"A plea, you know what I'm sayin'? Something I try and come back out murble, you know what I'm sayin'?" Vincent looks up at the camera. "Is this being recorded?"

"Everything you're saying is recorded, audio."

"I need a lawyer here first."

The door of the interrogation room snaps open. Investigator Tim Lawless bursts in and sits behind the desk. This distracts Vincent from following up on his request for a lawyer. Was that on purpose?

"Me being in the situation I'm in, there ain't no way out, whether I'm right or wrong," he says, stressed. "Y'all know what happened, every-thing I'm gonna tell you is gonna be the truth. Y'all saying I killed the guy, you ain't got no evidence."

"Tell us what happened," Tim Lawless says.

"I didn't kill nobody, though."

"Tell me what happened," says Tim.

"When I left the house, he was still in good health."

"That's not according to your momma," says Trip.

Vincent knows his mother has made a statement to the investigators.

"The whole situation is, Vince, we know what happened. Okay? We know," says Tim.

"Is there a camera here?" says Vincent, looking up at the camera.

"It is," says Trip.

"You've gotta give me one more cigarette."

"Well, here's the deal," says Tim, "and I ain't trying to bribe you, 'cause I ain't doing it. I'll help you, but you gotta help me. Try to close this out. Take care of something. Sit down and talk. Look, what's weighing on your mind?"

"I can get another cigarette, though?"

"Oh yes," says Tim, "I'll get you another cigarette. I've been straight up with you. We tell you we're going to let you do something, we're gonna let you do it."

"Where you gonna put me when I leave outta here?" says Vincent. "I ain't violent, y'hear?"

"We're just gonna put you in a cell," says Tim.

"Like, in the back with the rest of everybody else?"

"Well, yeah," says Tim. "I mean, you know, I can arrange it if you want me to put you in isolation. I can do that for you. I can put you in the back, back there where it's just you back there, your own place."

"No, I wanna be around other people," says Vincent.

"You want to be around other people?" says Tim.

"I can't function all by myself," says Vincent.

"I'll put you in with three or four folks if that's what you want," says Tim.

It breaks my heart that not being left on his own is the best plea bargain he can negotiate.

"Listen, here, okay," says Vincent. "Okay, I went to the house, you know what I'm sayin', yesterday. Yesterday. I went to the house. And I was down and I asked him, you know what I'm sayin', 'cause I'm on Facebook. I asked him about getting on Facebook. And he said yeah. All been approved. And he was like, 'Vincent, come in here, in the kitchen.' So I go in the kitchen, where he asked. And he was like, 'Oh,' he started talking weird. He started talking about all types of different kind of things. And I was like—because I ain't feeling this, because you know what I'm sayin', he had, like, some type of cord, I don't know if it was an extension cord or something. He's trying, he was trying, you know what I'm sayin'—"

"Right," says Trip.

"He was trying to get me to do sexual favors for him. You know what I'm sayin'? And so I'm, like, I don't get down like that. I'm like, you know what I'm sayin', I snap. I ain't gonna lie to you. I snap. I'm like, 'You need to get out of my face, y'hear?' Murble. And so he kind of forced himself upon me. He was taking his pants off. So, he took his clothes off, and he still had his underwear on. And I was like, you know what I'm sayin', 'Wha' murble? Hey, man, get off murble.' All I'm sayin', you know what I'm sayin', he tried, he reached out and grabbed me. He grabbed me and I murble the nearest weapon."

"What kind of weapon was it?" says Trip.

"A knife."

"Where was the knife at?" says Trip.

"It was in the kitchen."

"Where is it now?" says Trip.

"Don't know."

"You don't know what you did with it?" asks Trip.

"Oh, it was so messed up in my mind. I don't even remember, I was so scared, terrified."

"I'd be scared, too, man," says Tim.

"I been so terrified, I didn't know how to control the situation. I want to go tell, you know what I'm sayin', the police. I couldn't, 'cause I know I'd been wrong. Even though in the circumstances I did it, I know I did wrong. I just couldn't come out and call the police."

"How many times did you stab him with the knife? Do you re-member?" says Trip.

"I just blanked out, it could have been numerous times, could have been one, I don't even know."

"Wha-wha-what happened after that?" says Trip.

In a tangle of murbles, Vincent tells Tim and Trip that he didn't want to get caught up in anything because he was just out of prison and he knew this would get him back in.

"Why did you burn the house down?" says Trip.

"Because I knew what I did was wrong. Even though I did . . . in my mind . . . in my mind I knew I was protecting myself, I knew I was doing wrong."

"Did this man ever try to do this before to you?" says Trip. "When you were a young boy, when you worked for him years ago when you were seventeen? Did he molest you then?"

"He used to touch on me."

"He ever make you perform sex on him?" says Trip. "Said he was going to kill you? Hurt you? What's the deal with that?"

"You know what I'm sayin', he used to tell me about some guy that died, he was the only black person he knew, he used to work for him, he used to help him out. And I used to think he was just talking about work. Until one day he just rubbed on my inner thigh, he tried to grab my manhood, you know what I'm sayin'?"

"When did he start doing this type of stuff to you?" says Trip. "How many years ago?"

"I was young. I was, ah, about, ah, when it first happened about seventeen, eighteen."

"How much money would he give you when he'd try to touch you, so you wouldn't go and tell folks? Did he ever pay you money to keep you quiet?"

"One time he give me two, three hundred."

"Who'd do that type of stuff?" Tim says, disgusted at Richard.

"He'd be asking me about neighbors and how they'd be acting," Vincent says. "And I'd tell him they seemed like nice people, but not the kind of people I hang out with, and then I told him I'd been to the penitentiary. He started asking about 'Is it rough in there?' He was like, 'Are there homosexuals?' And I was like, 'Yeah.' And he was like, 'Where do they keep them there?' And I was like, 'You know, most of them murble discreet, people don't like them in the population.' I knew then that he was trying to make sexual advances again. You know what I'm sayin', he used to always try to get me to do him."

"Man," says Tim. "Well, tried to make him do you from behind? That kind of crap?"

"I ain't like that, though," Vincent says, not really answering the question.

"I—I know, I'm with you," says Tim. "Something wrong with that man, I'm with you, brother. That man, doing those type of things, that ain't *right*. I want you to know, that that wasn't right, what that man was doing to you, what that man was trying to do to you, was *wrong*."

"I know I did wrong. I know, I know I did wrong, but I was trying to protect myself. He was trying to—I don't know how far he would have went. He grabbed me around my neck. I got scratches, he scratched me, he tried to force me, you know what I'm sayin', do sexual favors with him. I was provoked—I'm not a bad person, I was provoked. Minding my business, I got on Facebook. I'd shown him some of my pictures. He wanted to see my pictures on Facebook. And if you look on there, I got a lot of pictures with my shirt off. And I'm like, he was looking at my pictures and stuff, and I don't know if they could have turned him on or whatever, know what I'm sayin'? That's when he called me up to the kitchen. And he wanted to know . . . murble."

"That's messed up," says Trip.

"Sure is," says Tim. "Let's have a cigarette, let's smoke."

The tape cuts to four days later.

A shaky camera follows Tim, Trip, and shackled Vincent, stamping across Richard Barrett's lawn. There's something there that had been removed by the time I snooped months later. Thick Greek columns frame the front door and the back door. More of these columns are placed around the house to give the impression they are holding up the roof. Richard's apparent attempt to turn his crummy little house into a Southern mansion. They arrive at the back door.

"Did you knock on the door, Vincent?" asks Tim. "Or did . . . How did you get in? I mean, did you know or was it unlocked?"

"He let me in. Yeah."

"He know you were comin' or didya knock?"

"He knew I was comin'."

I'm inside the house for the first time. Sunlight cuts through the window shades, but it's dark overall. A flashlight beam rolls onto Vincent. He stands in a tiny kitchen area.

"This is where we got, right here, that's where I had . . ."

"Is this where you were sitting on top of his back?" Trip asks.

The camera pans down to a red blotch on the floor the size of a Richard Barrett.

"Murble," Vincent says. "Remember he had a knife," he adds, "he was tryin' to use a knife on me."

"Where'd he get his knife from?" Trip says.

"I guess it been here." He motions. "I think it was over on the counter at first. When he had the knife, I grab his arm and bend his arm, and the knife drop. And then, you know what I'm sayin', I tried to restrain him."

Vincent pokes his tongue when he says that.

"So I grabbed his belt. And he was on the ground, his pants were already off when he was on the ground. I grabbed his belt and I tried to tie his arm up. And know what I'm sayin', he kept struggling. All he kept sayin' was, 'Let me get to the room.' And I'm thinking, *If he gets to the room he gonna shoot me or kill me or somethin'.* Well, that's when, know what I'm sayin', I blanked out. Just started usin' the knife I had."

"Now, you brought a knife down here with you?"

"Yo." Vincent tries to pull the "yo" back into his mouth. "No. It was already there."

Trip turns and grins to the camera.

The three shuffle down the kitchen area, a corridor more than a kitchen. The flashlight rolls over this, then that, then that. Clay pot on top of the fridge. Cane stool on its side. Metal bin tipped over.

Vincent guides us through the dark to Richard Barrett's master bedroom. Vincent lifts his cuffed hands and flicks on the light. A four-poster bed appears. It's gorgeous and looks antique. The cloth canopy over it is frilled around the edges, with a golden tassel hanging at each corner. It doesn't belong in such a small room.

"I see this didn't burn so good," Vincent says.

"No, it didn't, did it?" Trip says. "What did you use, a lighter?"

"Mm-hmm. Pour the gas, run it out, light it up, whoosh."

Trip looks around at the chest of drawers and closet, a beautiful match to the bed.

"What was the reason for doing it in the bedroom? Any reason in particular?"

"Nah, I thought the whole house would burn. Burn the whole house down."

Vincent takes us to the other end of the house, the flashlight rolling over candelabras and antique table lamps on the way. The fire worked in the guest bedroom. The walls and floors are silver and black with ash.

The three men end up in what I'm guessing is the front room.

"Let's get out of here," says a voice in the dark. It's Tim Lawless.

"You scared?" says Vincent.

"No, it stinks," says Trip. "We just don't like the way it smells in here."

There's a rustle and a *click click click*.

"Put the light on us," says Trip to whoever is holding the flashlight.

The light rolls on. Trip is lighting a cigarette dangling from Vincent's lips. Behind them is a baby grand piano.

ater, the investigators and Vincent are striding up the road.

"Get me Jessie Jackson, Al Sharpton. Need those guys!" says Vincent with a half laugh.

"This is gonna be, like, kinda the Jena Six, hey?" says Tim. Five years ago, blacks united across America to protest the jailing of six black students in Jena, Louisiana.

"The Jena Six, y'hear!" shouts Vincent.

"They're gonna call you the Rankin One," says Tim.

Vincent laughs.

"And they gonna come down from everywhere," says Tim.

"Yeah. The white supreme-ist hollerin', 'Hear! Hear! Hear!'" says Vincent, imagining the white supremacist crowds furious he's killed Richard Barrett.

"You think about the name of your book?" says Tim.

"Yeah," Vincent says. "I think it gonna be *Consequence*."

"*Consequence*!" Tim and Trip laugh.

"It's a good title," Tim says. "I like that. You do me a favor? You write that book now, I'm gonna give you one of my cards, you make sure you spell my name right in your book. I want credit, too, now. I give you a card. Tim. They call me Tiny Tim."

Sherrie

Vincent's sister Sherrie has phoned me and I don't know why. The clock radio is glowing 10:07 p.m. Tiny moths block the glow from the lightbulb above my bed.

"You're leaving tomorrow, my momma said. I'm sitting here watching TV," Sherrie tells me. "I'm not doing anything. Do you have your stuff packed?"

"No, not yet," I say.

I'm trying to figure what to ask her on my last night in Mississippi.

"My momma and her boyfriend are not here," Sherrie says. "And I'm in her room. My uncle's asleep or he's drunk and, you know, he has a brother here. He's handicapped and he keeps calling my name. He's getting on my nerves. I don't know what I'm going to do. I have a headache. I don't feel well. I'm just stressed out."

"What are you stressed about?" I ask.

"Everything," she says. "Do you believe that the world is coming to an end?"

"Tonight? I don't think it's going to come to an end."

"This year?"

"No, I think it should be okay."

"Sherrie!" cries the tangled tongue of a man.

"That's my uncle's brother with the handicap," Sherrie says. "Have you read the Book of Revelations?"

My mind winds back. I remember when I first dropped by the McGees', Sherrie was shambling in the dark with her fat, floppy Bible.

"Yes," I say. "I've read the Book of Revelations."

"Did you read about the moon turning red?"

"I can't remember everything. I read it a few years ago."

"Did you see the moon turning red?"

"What, in real life? Like, up in the sky?"

"Yeah. Last week. It was red. It was so red. It was scary, but I was not scared because I knew that it was going to happen and I've been good forever."

I drift over to my window and poke my head out, but I can't find the moon.

"I'm concerned with this," Sherrie says, "because I know this girl named Crystal and I hear things and I think that she is the devil, and every time I talk, she talks."

"The Bible devil?" I squeak.

"Yes," she says. "The other night, I was lying in bed. I was on the floor, actually, I don't have a bed. So I was there on the floor wrapped up in the blanket and I started hearing her. She put her soul into a dog and she told me to 'Come out here. Come out here.' You know, trying to scare me to death."

"She put her soul in a dog? And it was a dog that was outside your house?"

"Please don't think I'm stupid."

"I don't think you're stupid. I'm just trying to follow the story."

I now know what I'm going to ask her on my last night.

"Do you reckon Vincent has got the devil in him?"

"I think he has," says Sherrie. "Well, I know he's there now because he killed a man. You know, murder, that sends you straight to hell. So he's probably one of his people. One of the devil's people."

"Do you reckon the devil made him kill Richard?"

"I think so. Probably. I have no idea. I don't know. He was just a violent person and it led him to death and now he's marked with sixes."

I think of the devil's beard that sprouted from Vincent in the courtroom, and the last three digits of his social security number—666.

"Sherrie!" cries the tangled tongue.

"Vincent told me when he was really young one of his relatives made him round up dogs to hit," I say. "And that's why he thinks he might have started to get violent."

"That's possible. You know, you hang with the guys in the streets, these kind of guys are rough and like fighting dogs. When we moved to Jackson in '95, '96, he met a lot of guys. They were doing things, hopping in cars, hopping over car fences, stealing cars, doing different things. People he hung out with got him into things. Those were the people that accepted him, and he stayed in there with them, you know? And he's always seen violent things. So when he grew up and thought he was a man, he thought, *Okay, I've seen men hit their women.*"

"Did you know China, his old girlfriend? I heard he beat her up."

"He did. They just used to fight all the time. She was Korean and black. She was a very pretty girl. I believe the first woman he ever hit was China."

Vincent, Sherrie says, wasn't like this when he was small.

"I think he mostly got violent when he was in prison," she says. "Because he had been stabbed and, you know, you can die in the prison. In prison the guards are never always there. And the prisoners all clique up into cliques. Being in there for so long and having to see what was going on, he knew either he was going to fight or die, so he had to defend himself. And, you know, when he got out of prison, his mind was still in there. Once you've been somewhere and once you've been used to something, your mind is set on that. When you're sixteen, seventeen, in and out of a detention center, from detention center to prison, back and forth, every three or four years, not being used to the world because you're always in jail, you feel more comfortable in jail than you do home. And it's just a lifestyle. It becomes your life, because when you get out here in the world, you're lost because you're used to having a schedule: You wake up, you shower, you clean, you go out, you get back to your room, you eat, and you do those things."

Vincent, Sherrie says, didn't handle Richard like a free man would have.

"He's been in jail and has almost faced death because four or five guys jumped on him, and he knew either he was going to fight or die. And so, you know what I'm sayin'? So he comes out and he did what he did when he was in jail."

"I wanted to know, when Vincent was in court, how come none of the family came?"

"Nobody was keeping in touch with me, telling me too much of anything. And I wanted to be there for him and help him out, but no one told me. So that's the only reason I wasn't there. Every time I see him on TV and the papers, I want to cry, because I know he's going through so much and to have no family there for him, it hurts bad, man. I was locked up in a detention center. Nobody ever came to see me, you know? And I wonder, everybody else locked up had a visitation every other week. My momma never came and when she did come, it was on the wrong day."

"Sherrie!" cries the tangled tongue.

"I don't know if he's better out or in," Sherrie says. "Nobody likes to be locked up against their will, but, see, he's so used to it. It's really just his life. He's never had a chance to get out here and work, get a decent job, have a decent home, a decent family. He's never experienced that. And I know how he feels, but I just handle my things differently from him. So I understand what he went through, but I know that wasn't the best alternative."

Sherrie breathes out.

"But we're at the end of time," she says, "so none of us will be dealing with this much longer. I don't know if I'm going to die or get killed or what, but I haven't done anything to anybody."

"I don't think anyone's trying to kill you," I say. "I think you'll be fine."

"Well, you know, reading the Bible has taught me that two people . . . two people are going to get killed and that they'll be put in the holy city. What is the holy city? Do you think it's Pearl?"

"Why would the holy city in the Bible be Pearl?" I ask.

"What is the holy city? Jerusalem? They're going to take me away to Jerusalem?"

Sherrie tells me she thinks "the rose of Sharon" in the Bible's Song of Solomon is referring to her, because Tina wanted to name her Sharon but her daddy said no.

"I can read some to you," Sherrie says. "The Song of Solomon. I want to read the part where it states about Sharon."

"I've got a Bible with all my books," I tell Sherrie. "I'll just go and get my Bible, too."

And Sherrie takes me through the Song of Solomon. It must be talking about her, she says, because Verse 1:5 reads: *I am black but lovely.*

Pull the Trigger

There's this true crime book about an Aboriginal death in custody. The author paints precisely what happens the morning of the man's arrest. He was wandering down the street like so. A woman was lounging over by that house. He was whistling this specific tune. The sun shone like this. The police van pulled over like that.

It bugged me, the precision with which the author knew about the morning, while I was still floundering over whether Richard pulled up outside the McGees' in a black SUV (like Vallena told me) or a bicycle (like Tina said). I spoke to the author, and as it happens, she didn't really know any more than me. She just committed herself to a fair-enough version of events. None of the true crime writers know any more than me, they just commit. They just pull the trigger. Safran, pull the trigger.

S o here's what I think happened. Richard had come to Mississippi because it's a place to hide if you're a little queer. People will overlook it, act ignorant. From Vincent's side, his community is decimated by poverty, partly the legacy of racism. Pain has been cascading toward Vincent's house since before the Civil War. A black guy at my apartment complex told me, "You know why they're called McGee? Why these Africans have a Scottish name? Vincent's ancestors, their slave master would have been McGee."

I once interviewed this ex–Christian minister, excommunicated after being caught having gay sex. He told me about his first gay encounter. He was in his midteens, in the 1960s. He knew no one gay in his rural Australian town. No one spoke of it one way or the other. He hadn't really processed he was gay himself. One night he went walking. He ended up ambling along the side of the road just out of town. A car slowed down, pulled up twenty meters ahead of him. He headed to the car and climbed in. He had sex with the man in the car and left. Nothing was said before, during, or after about what they were doing. I asked the ex-minister, "How did you know to go to the car? How did the car know to pull over?" He said he didn't really know, everything just drifted together that night on automatic.

I'm going to guess something like this went down with Richard and Vincent. Nothing said about what they were doing before, during, or after. Vincent with his prison rules that you're not gay if you give and don't take it. Richard the Grand Dragon of Cognitive Dissonance. That night in the crummy little house, Vincent and Richard danced their unspoken dance of sex for money. A tinderbox of self-loathing over sex and bitterness and exploitation and small lives caught fire that night. That's what happened.

And Richard pulled up on a bicycle.

God and/or Fate

Not ten minutes have ticked past since finishing the Song of Solomon with Sherrie and my cell buzzes again. It's Vincent McGee. He sounds different.

"I need a wedding ring," Vincent announces.

"You need a what?" I ask.

"I need a wedding ring. Think you can get me one?"

God and/or Fate gave me the perfect entry point to this murder. Because He wanted me to be here and document all this. And now, the night before I'm scheduled to leave, He gifts the story again, with a winding up of sorts, where otherwise there would be no winding up.

"You need a wedding ring?"

"Riiiight," he says. "So I can propose."

"No way!" I say. "You need a wedding ring for who?"

"You already know who it's for," Vincent says bashfully.

"For Chywanna?"

"Riiiight."

A moth flutters in the window and lands on the arm of the couch. I toss up lying that it's a butterfly for the book.

"No way," I say. "Have you spoken to her since the flowers?"

"Yeah," he says. "We been talking since she got the flowers, you know? Murbleandstatic."

"I can't believe . . . You've spoken to her since and you think . . . What did she say to you?"

"You know, so we did chat it up a bit and murbleandstatic . . ."

"I'm leaving tomorrow, so I won't have time to get a ring."

"You can go to murbleandstatic."

"Where can I go?"

"You can go to Walmart, they sell rings, you know? It ain't got to be no ten-million-dollar ring, you know what I'm sayin'?"

"Yeah, but then what happens? I go to her house and I give her the ring?"

"Sorry, wha'?"

"How do I get the ring to her?"

"Just go to the house! I ain't told nobody but you. You go over there."

"But how do you know she wants to . . ." I trail off.

"Murbleandstatic."

"It just seems a bit weird to me."

"It *seems* weird, but I'm like staticandmurble."

"Yeah, sure. But my flight. If I did it I'd have to do it at nine a.m., or even earlier, like seven a.m."

"Like I said, I ain't got nothing else on. I wake up easily about four in the morning."

"Yeah, sure, but what about *her*? Will she be happy if I ring on the door at seven in the morning?"

"Murbleandstatic."

"Just say she says no, though?"

"If she says no then I've still got it for another one . . ." Vincent interrupts himself. "Nah! She ain't gonna say no."

"What about her? You're not going to get out for about thirty years or something. What is she meant to do?"

"That's not even in the . . . We ain't worried about that right now. We just need a ring. That's the only thing we're focused on. I'm dead serious, dude."

"Yeah, I know you're dead serious."

"Hey, listen. Don't you call her up and tell her, 'cause I know you got her number."

"Yeah, sure. I won't call her up. I did call her today 'cause I felt . . . 'cause I didn't see her yesterday when I dropped off the flowers."

"What did you say when you talked to her?"

"Yeah, I just said to her that I hope it's okay that I dropped off the flowers. That's all I said to her."

"What did she say?"

"She said it was fine."

"Oh, yeah?"

"You know, I've got to be on both your sides. I'm on her side and I'm on your side."

"You're on both our sides?"

"I was slightly worried, to be honest, today, after I thought about it. I was slightly worried she might think it's a bit unsettling—that suddenly flowers were just left there, you know, so that's why I rang her up. But she said she was fine."

"A'right," says Vincent McGee. "This is some serious-ass shit. Asking a female to marry you, yeah, that's a lifetime commitment. You don't know how this shit turns out."

"Yeah, sure." Out the bedroom door my eyes catch the Leaning Tower of Pisa of dishes in the sink. When will I wash those?

"You're like a motherfucker!" he snaps. "You put shit together just to see how it turns out."

He's right of course. This wasn't only God and/or Fate. I delivered the flowers. There was and/or me in the mix.

"You wanna see the outcome!" Vincent continues.

"Yeah, why not?" I say. "The wedding ring was your idea, though."

"Yeah, it was my idea," he says proudly. "I'm just sayin', though, you still wanna see if I'm gonna get the girl, or shit."

"Definitely!" I laugh.

"You know, I'm tellin' you, failure ain't an option."

My thumb hangs up. Before snapping the cell shut, I spot a flashing envelope. Vincent sent me a text half an hour ago when I was in Bible study with Sherrie.

**I NEED A WEDDING RING A.S.A.P. I WANNA MARRY MY
SHORTY. IF YOU CAN MAKE THAT HAPPEN I OWE YOU MY
UNDYING LOYALTY. TRUTH. AND RESPECT. CAN YOU DO IT?**

His new signature is:

"PRESIDENTIAL"

Walmart, with the Dictaphone

Oh my Lord. It's 10:52 at night. That's that. I'm in the little Ford Focus bullet now. I'm exiting Ashland Apartments. It's chilly on my legs because my only pair of long pants have chocolate stains on them and are wearing away at the hem. So I look like a hobo unless I wear my shorts. I've put on weight—I'm going to have to lose weight for the book tour. The radio is saying, "Would you kill Hitler if you knew he was going to kill all those people?" It's about abortion.

Okay, I'm at Walmart. Nearly had a car crash on the way. I have to get back home and start catching the trams. I seem to be nearly driving into traffic every day now.

I'm walking into Walmart, past big cardboard boxes of pumpkins for Halloween. There are huge ones stacked on the outside. Walking past the in-Walmart Subway. A military man walks past on the other side. Halloween cards. Fruit. Mickey Mouse balloons. Bibles. Magazines. Post-it notes. Underpants—no doubt not many mediums or smalls. Oreos. Paper plates. Girls' clothing. Shoes. Babywear. There's the in-Walmart TV network playing. Past the Green Dot cards. There must be jewelry here somewhere. Tire & Lube Express. Toys, where I bought my Scrabble set. Oh, I see. Yep, over there.

Cool, thank you very much.

A black man pulling cardboard boxes has just pointed me toward the jewelry.

Oh, Lord. Lots of jewelry, watches . . . I guess I can be a cheapskate on the ring, can't I? What's anyone going to know? There's lots of . . . I don't want to be a real cheapskate. Oh no, they're just earrings. Digital clip watches. Girl Power key rings. Hmm, rings, rings, rings. Thankfully no one's at the counter, which means I can look without being awkward. It looks like the most expensive one is $198, but it looks a bit garish. Oh, here are some more expensive ones. How high do I really want to go, though? Do I just go for a crappy one? Here we go. I don't know. I wish there were a girl here to tell me. What's simple but nice? I just don't know. I guess I've got to be grateful that there are wedding rings here at all, that there's a place that's open at eleven at night in Mississippi. Aren't wedding rings meant to be plain rather than have big things on them? I don't really know. Since I can't really get an expensive one, shall I just go for a seventy-buck one? There's a couple . . . they're looking at jewelry themselves. Maybe I'll ask them. Wedding bands.

Okay, I think I found the one. It's not 'cause I'm trying to be cheap, but it's just because it's got the least garish stuff on it. It's ninety-eight dollars and it's called "Bridal Collection," so you know, that should be good. It just occurred to me—this is meant to be, like, an engagement ring, though, isn't it? It's not a wedding ring. So maybe it *can* be a bit garish. It doesn't have to be all thin. Oh, God. Wish there were someone that I could talk to about this. It's all too embarrassing. I'm going to go up to someone to ask them how I can buy something from the jewelry department.

Okay, I bought a ninety-eight-dollar ring. I'm in the Ford Focus driving out. I promise I was willing to go up to five hundred, but it just seemed . . . they seemed garish. It's like, the simplest ones seemed . . . It's got, like, one little diamond in it and it just seemed, to my eyes, the least risky, 'cause it looked the least garish. But I could be wrong. 'Cause maybe this is meant to murble . . . Oh, I don't know. It's too late now, and it's a ring.

Lord, I'm on the wrong side of the street with my headlights off.

The Morning

My silver Ford Focus is tucked under a tree on the corner of Highway 469 and Chywanna's dirt road. Vincent McGee's file sits next to me on the passenger seat.

"My girl ain't around," Vincent says from my cell phone on the dashboard.

Vincent had called Chywanna's home. He wanted to smooth my arrival.

"I don't know where she's at," he says. "She might be asleep, she might be out at somebody's—I don't know, she ain't around."

"So what should I do?" I ask. "Should I ring on her bell?"

"Hell!" sheepish Vincent says.

Screams, from a prisoner or a guard, bounce off the walls at the East Mississippi prison for the criminally insane.

"I don't want her people to be in on this, you hear?" he says. "I don't know what her people might do. When you went there last time, were her people there?"

"Yeah, yeah, there was her brother-in-law, I think . . . Not her brother-in-law, I think maybe her stepbrother or something, and then there was also a little boy."

"I'm not talking about them!" Vincent says. "I'm talking about moms and dads—those all motherfuckers."

"No, no, they weren't there," I tell him.

"You know what I'm sayin'? There are a lot of people that stay over there. But look, if that's what you wanna do, man, she didn't answer the phone, so I ain't told her what happened. If you want to go over there and knock on the door and give her the bag—that's what you do."

Knock on the door and give her the bag. Vincent must think she is there. If so, she didn't pick up his call, or someone else in the house pretended she wasn't home.

"Okay, cool," I say.

Each boot step down the dirt road, toward the house, raises a puff of dust.

"Here we go," I say. "Stay on the phone."

The woods shadow me on both sides of the road.

"You're there at the house?" he says.

"No, no. I'm still . . . I'll be about one minute, I'll be half a minute."

I clomp on, a big aqua bag with the ring swinging by my side.

"Murblestaticmurblestatic."

"What's that?" I say. "I didn't understand that."

"I'm saying you gotta hit Walmart up before you leave, too, man. You gotta go get the Green Dot card, you know what I'm sayin', you hear?"

"Let's just get rid of this first. Deal with this."

"Okay, we're going to deal with the main problem here."

I clomp on.

"How much did the motherfucking ring cost, though?" he says.

"Maybe a hundred dollars."

"You bought a ring for that?" he squeaks.

"What?"

"Man, you're bullshitting."

"What, is that too cheap?"

"Hell yeah!"

"Well, you can buy her another one later. It wasn't my fault—it was the best-looking one. There weren't that many at Walmart."

"What color is it?" he asks. "Gold or platinum?"

"No, it's silver."

"It's got a little diamond in it?"

"Yeah, it's got a little diamond in it."

"A real one?"

"Oh, who knows? Who knows? I knew I should have got . . . I would've . . . Can I tell you the truth? I would have been happy to . . . The ones that looked a bit more . . . The ones that cost more, I didn't think looked as good. They looked like . . . you know. The ones that weren't as simple didn't look as good. But I didn't really know what I was doing. I didn't really know what I was doing."

"Man," Vincent says. "You've got me on some strangest Australian adventure–type shit."

I clomp on. The white house rolls closer.

"I'm outside the house now. Okay, just a sec. I'll go . . . so I'll go ring on the bell."

My finger presses the silver buzzer.

An elephant starts thumping from somewhere deep in the house. The elephant thumps closer and closer, louder and louder, until it arrives at the other side of the door.

The door creaks open. I look down. It's a small boy.

"Are you the delivery man?" he says, hypnotized by my aqua bag.

"Yes," I say. "I have something for Chywanna."

The boy creaks shut the door. The elephant thumps up the stairs. The elephant thumps down the stairs. The boy reopens the door.

"She'll come down in a moment," he says. "She's just goin' to change and piss."

Four tiny children and a yelping dog spin out from the home. The kids are giddy and want me to tell them what's in the aqua bag. They're stomping up puffs of dust. The dog won't shut up.

Beneath it all I can hear a tiny shouting murble. I press the phone to my ear.

"Who you talkin' to?" Vincent says anxiously. "Who you talkin' to?"

I head away from the house toward the trees.

"Just kids, I don't know," I say. "Chywanna's upstairs, but she's coming."

"I don't even know why I did this shit!" he says. "Why am I doing this shit?" The dog at my feet is howling like an inmate in the East Mississippi prison. "This ain't how it's supposed to be, you hear?"

Through the murble and static, Vincent screams that I've messed it all up. I was meant to text a photo of the ring from Walmart. Vincent says he can't propose with a dog barking. I can hear his feet thumping about the cell.

A basketball patters to my feet. I kick it back to the kids, dusting up most of my pants.

"Yeah, but you've got to look at it this way," I say. "It's, like, after I go, there's not going to be anyone else to go and buy the ring and then kind of drop it off. You've got to take advantage of the situation."

"I need to take advantage of the situation, right?"

"Right."

"Where you waiting at?"

"I'm waiting by the trees and they're . . . It's a bit farther back from the house. Hang on, here she comes . . . I think."

A woman in a pink quilted dressing gown and blue towel wrapped like a turban walks through the cloud of dust.

"Do you want me to pass the phone to her?" I say.

"WARDEN!" screams an inmate.

"Hi. Chywanna?" I ask.

The woman nods.

I hand over the aqua bag.

"This is what he wants me to pass you, and he wants . . . He's in prison or whatever," I say.

I hand over the phone. I've sticky-taped a lapel mic to the phone. I'll be able to hear Vincent's end of the conversation later.

She slides the phone to one of her ears poking from her turban.

"Hello?" says Chywanna.

"I swear to God, that white dude is crazy, you hear? I don't know what he's got going on, you hear?"

"Yeah," she says flatly.

"You know what I'm sayin', I said, 'Go get me a ring.'"

"Oh my God!" she exclaims.

"Yeah," Vincent says. "Listen, I'm trying to be down with y'all. I'm sayin' I'm not gonna mistreat you or nothing like that, you hear?"

"Yeah," she says flatly again.

"But listen, get the bag from him, tell him to give you the bag."

"I got it."

"Oh, I've got a question and I wanna know the answer. You know what I'm sayin'? Do you wanna be Mrs. McGee?"

Chywanna's face twists to shock.

"This is how I feel, you hear?"

"Mmm, I don't know," says Chywanna dryly.

"Yo, the white dude got you a ring."

"But . . . but . . ."

"But look, at the same time . . ."

"Hmm-mm."

"Are you gonna wear my ring or what?"

Chywanna winces.

"Yeah, I will," she says, not exuberantly.

"So, that's all I wanna say, but look, shit, the white dude, that's my nigga—we're cool, you hear? At the same time, I ain't just trying to shit on him, but he got a cheap ring."

"Yeah."

"You were sleeping?"

"Yeah, I was asleep."

"Look, you know what I'm sayin', you ain't gotta get all mad and shit at me, right?" he spits a little angrily.

"Okay."

"Put him back on the phone."

I take the phone and my fingers motion to Chywanna that I will return. I walk through the dust to the trees.

"Man!" Vincent laughs.

Vincent and I giggle uncontrollably.

"But look, I appreciate you doing that, man, you know what I'm sayin'. She says she's gonna wear my ring."

I congratulate him.

"Well, listen, man," he continues. "You need to be heading for the closest Walmart, you hear? For a Green Dot, you hear?"

"Yeah, yeah, sure, sure, sure. Okay, see you."

I hang up and walk back to Chywanna. I run my hand through my hair and dust dances off into the sky.

She has plucked the ring from the box and is holding it between her thumb and forefinger.

"That's it—so he asked me to do it," I say. "He asked me to come, if that's okay."

"That's okay," Chywanna says.

"Sorry. Just be . . . you know, so just be careful with him."

"Okay."

"If you know what I mean. Like, he did sort of . . ."

I fumble out a photo from my bag and hold it up to Chywanna. Vincent's knife glistens in the dead grass.

She returns her gaze to me.

"I'm gonna call him anyway," she says.

"Okay, cool."

"Okay," she says.

"Okay, see you later."

The little children buzz around Chywanna as she slides the ring on her finger and holds it to the sun.

D'Lo Water Park

I want to tell you about a detour on the way to the airport. I would have made it a daylong adventure, but my plane leaves in a few hours.

Two nights ago I knocked on the door of a fifteen-year-old boy. Well, he was a fifteen-year-old boy in the 1967 FBI file. He dragged a Viet Cong flag around the State Capitol with Richard Barrett and then lit the flag on fire. He's now an old man. He lives in a cedarwood house that he built over the course of a year from trees he chopped down. His name was blacked out in the FBI files, but I eventually found out his name. L. E. Matthews. His father was a big deal in the Klan, said the files.

At the door of the cedarwood house he became immediately suspicious I was secretly taping him. I told him I had a Dictaphone in my bag but I hadn't pressed record. He told me to remove the Dictaphone from my bag and made me remove the batteries. We sat in rocking chairs in his study and drank bourbon. He had a DON'T TREAD ON ME flag on the wall, like John Moore had in his pencil holder.

He told me Southerners were their own racial group.

He goes, "Oh, the thing about Richard, he wasn't a Celt. He wasn't a Celt, and that's why everyone was suspicious of him." And L.E. talked about how his own family came here in the 1600s. He said, "I'm not American. I'm Southern."

He asked, "How would you describe an American, John?" And I said, "Oh, I don't know. There's lots of different types." And he said, "Exactly. That's the problem." He said, "As soon as you have too much diversity, you don't have one thing, and it's . . . You don't have history pushing forward in the same direction."

He and I drank and drank.

"A cat with a chicken, does that make sense to you?" he said. "A black man and a white woman make as little sense as that."

He told me that in a couple of days' time (so today) there would be one hundred and fifty to two hundred people gathering for a white nationalist event.

"The Klan!" I squeaked with a slur because of the bourbon.

"Not the Klan!" he hissed with a slur.

He told me it would be a meeting of the Council of Conservative Citizens (CCC), some of whose directors had long ago been on the White Citizens' Council. The group is holding a political meet-and-greet at a water park. Mississippi is entering election season. Everyone from county sheriffs to school supervisors is running for office. The Council of Conservative Citizens ran notices in the newspapers inviting candidates to come down and address its members. This is a tradition going back to the 1950s.

We stumbled out of his cedar house and pissed against the trees together. I told him I'd be there.

Anyway, that's the background. So I drive from Chywanna's for an hour, to a town called Mendenhall, and pull into a forest. I thought *water park* would mean fun slides and dolphins leaping through hoops. But in this case it's simply a forest with a river cutting through it. Perhaps a hundred white Mississippians are here at D'Lo Water Park. They are heating up barbecues and huddling around their pickup trucks. The sky's mainly blocked out by the tall trees. There are a lot of mustaches. There are many fishing hooks pinned to trucker caps. Women are straightening tablecloths on picnic tables and pulling cakes out of the backseats of cars.

I've built up a little trust with L. E. Matthews after the bourbon and piss. He asks me to keep my Dictaphone in my bag, but doesn't demand I pluck out the batteries before his eyes. He tells me not to tell people I'm a writer.

There's an area with rows of chairs. Out in the front of this area is a podium with the state flag on either side.

Hang on. Not everyone here is white. Slouching in a chair near one barbecue is a swarthy woman. And a black woman is chatting to a white woman under a tree in the distance. And there's a teenage boy who would be white in Melbourne, but not here. There's the slightest slant to his eyes. What is going on here?

John Safran, Race Detective, swings into action. I drift to the teenage boy, my brain snapping together patterns.

The boy tells me he's come with his parents. He points out his dad. He's a bald man with a belly and a Confederate flag vest. He's a Christian minister with the League of the South, a group that wants to secede from the rest of America. The boy points to his mum. She's the swarthy woman slouching in the chair, one-quarter Cherokee, the boy tells me, making him one-eighth. When the whites first conquered America, they found most Native Americans to be savages, but, he says proudly, they found the Cherokees to be one of the "Five Civilized Tribes."

So that explains the swarthy woman at the white nationalist rally.

The boy's dad, in the Confederate vest, walks to the podium and recites a prayer. Then L. E. Matthews strolls to the microphone and tells the crowd how the day will run. He has a list of candidates who have asked to talk to the CCC. They will go first. If anyone else wants to make a political statement on the microphone, they should wait till afterward.

L.E. reads out the first name with a hint of pain: Audarshia Lee Flagg. She's running for superintendent of education, Simpson County. The black woman I saw in the distance bounces to the podium to polite claps. She's young and cheery. What is she doing here?

She tells the people about her teaching degree and how she loves children. Lord, she loves children! she tells us, and loves to see them happy!

The white crowd is awkward. There's quite a bit of scratching arms and looking at the dirt.

"And I share your conservative values!" she chirps. "I want prayer in school! I will not be told I cannot teach the children to pray!"

Oh, Lord. Audarshia hasn't Googled. She thinks the Council of Conservative Citizens is just a bunch of conservative voters. She's young and has grown up in a new Mississippi. She doesn't know she's in a forest with a hundred white nationalists.

It is beautiful.

She continues chirping away. I look over at L. E. Matthews. He is miserable. He mopes to the microphone and reads out the next name.

Samm Tittle. She's running against Barack Obama and Mitt Romney to be president of the United States! A white Southern belle makes her way to the front. A beautiful woman in her sixties.

"I don't need a microphone!" she shouts as she paces back and forth in front of the podium. "I'm here for you, and it is an honor and it is a privilege to be in front of all you great Americans. Why don't you all step in just a little bit more? Just a little tighter. I wanna make sure you all hear this 'cause this one's for you, if you please. I'm proud, I'm proud and honored, to be standing here with all of you, my brothers and sisters, in this Council of Conservative Citizens. If Barack Obama can speak to the Congressional Black Caucus, I can speak to you, my brothers and sisters, conservative, God-fearing Americans who love our Confederate flag and honor it the same way we honor our American flag—because that is a beautiful history!"

A roar floods through the forest. Every person I can see leaps up and cheers. This is what they came for! L.E. is thrusting his fist above his head.

"That's our history! That's our history!" Samm says, pointing at the Confederate cross on the state flag.

Samm looks down at Audarshia, sitting near the front. Audarshia is beaming, still unaware she's at a white nationalist rally.

"And," Samm says with much energy, "it doesn't have anything to do with a race, color, creed, white, black. Let me say to you that you are all fine people. You are God-fearing patriots, just like me!"

L. E. Matthews looks miserable again.

"I'm a Southern-born and -bred girl. From a poor family, may I say. I struggled . . . I struggled . . ."

Samm seems briefly distracted. She turns her attention back to Audarshia and points a finger.

"That lady right there. You take a look at her, because she's done a lot of hard work and education and she's just my kind of lady. And I don't care whether she's Democrat, black, white, Muslim, Jew—I don't care!"

Only three other political candidates have come to D'Lo Water Park to pitch themselves to the CCC. Incredibly, *another* of them is black.

L.E. sits on a stump with his beer, deflated. How has it come to this? Decades ago the most powerful men in Mississippi—governors and senators and mayors—would line up to curry favor with the group. Now only four candidates have turned up. No big names. And two of them are black! I feel I'm watching the birth pang of a new era.

The beaming black woman unaware she's at a white nationalist rally. The white nationalists too Southern and polite to cause a scene and tell Audarshia what's really going on. There is no one in the world—not one of the seven billion—who would appreciate this bizarre scene more than me. I've been on a piece of elastic my whole life, being drawn closer and closer to this meeting in this forest today.

Jackson–Medgar Wiley Evers International Airport

"I'm saying, though, I'm trying to club with you, man."

I think Vincent's saying *club*, but I don't know what it means. I'm scratching around my pocket. I can't find my boarding pass.

"You know what I'm sayin', I'm trying to get clubbed to Australia, see what you all got going on over there, you hear?"

"Oh yeah?" I say. "You want to come to Australia?"

"Yeah, I might escape from penitentiary, man, I might need somewhere to go. I might need you to put me up in a house for a couple of days, you hear?"

"You can't be serious," I say. "That's a joke. Tell me that's a joke."

"No . . . yeah . . ." Vincent half laughs. "I wish that I could do that, you hear?"

"Yeah."

"But shit, I'm saying, though, man to man, real shit, you hear? If I was to break out the penitentiary and me and you would be in conversation, we'd be chilling, we'd be kicking, and I ran to Australia, you wouldn't let me come kick it with you?"

"Yeah . . ." I say, not sure how to answer.

"Man, you lying, man."

"Well, I don't know," I say. "I'm a bit confused 'cause you sound very funny on the phone—like, I like you, except then when I look at the police file and then I'm like, *Oh my God!* Just say you have another spell and you suddenly start stabbing me or something . . ."

"I can see that, too, I can see you worrying about something like that, but shit . . . You know, man, fuck this. I was just thinking I'd come over there, man. Like I say, okay, if I was to break out, how would I get to Australia? What I gotta go through? Besides getting a passport."

"No, you need a passport and a plane ticket. But I think that sometimes they know if you've got a criminal file—they know that you've got it so they stop you at the airport."

"I'm saying, do you know where I can get there on a boat?"

"Oh! Maybe you can," I say, suddenly lost in Vincent's train of thought. "That's a good idea. No, there's people who come—that's true. They don't usually come from America, they usually come from the Middle East and they come from Asia. But yeah, people are always coming over on boats to Australia. So yeah, you can get there that way."

"There's some black people over there?"

"Yeah, we've got black people. Well, we've got Aboriginals—they're like the black Australians, but we've also got some black Americans, and then also some people from Africa."

"Oh yeah?" he says. "Hey, we're gonna kick it, though, man, real talk. If I get out of this here . . . Have you ever been to the ocean?"

"Yeah, I've been to the ocean."

"Yeah, I want to go to the ocean, you hear? I ain't talking about no Mississippi Gulf Coast shit, you hear? I'm talking about the real blue ocean where you can see the bottom of that thing."

"And you've never been to the ocean before?"

"I ain't . . . I been to the bullshit, the little water, man, but I ain't been nowhere, you know what I'm sayin', the nice ocean, you know what I'm sayin', you see on TV, you hear?"

"Yeah, sure. And what, to go fishing or something, or just to swim?"

"I wanted to swim. I don't really like the fishing, you know what I'm sayin'? Take a couple of females down there and just, you know what I'm sayin', have fun, you hear?"

"Well, you've kind of screwed it up a bit by being in prison, haven't you?"

"Man, I told you, I ain't gonna be locked up long, you know what I'm sayin'? I'm talking about I got a plan to get up out of here, man."

"Which ocean do you want to go to?"

"I'm gonna go to the Atlantic Ocean," Vincent says. "Where that located at?"

"I don't know. I'm sure you can get there. There's lots of good oceans in Australia if you manage to smuggle your way to Australia."

"I can smuggle myself to Australia?" he says hopefully.

"Yeah," I say, in the moment, half believing he can.

From my window seat I can see Jackson shrinking below me. I crack my neck.

I pull *The Commission* from my backpack, turn on my reading light, and continue where I left off.

So many wild stories. Richard is fighting with his father. Richard tells him he killed a wildcat and his dad doesn't believe him. He's angry at Richard for lying. Richard returns to the woods and drags the wildcat back home. His father still doesn't believe him. *"How do I know, Richard, someone else didn't kill the cat? Things are not always what they appear to be."*

Then on page 282, Richard writes—although he didn't know it at the time—an obituary to himself and his half-made-up-in-his-head white nationalist way of life:

> *Swallows return to Capistrano, elephants to their burial ground, and salmon to their birthplace. Englishmen go down to the sea in ships. Without the flock, the herd, the community, or the nation, the species withers, falls prey to its enemy, and dies out.*

EPILOGUE #1

Vincent's Profile · John Safran Official Page's Profile · Vincent's Wall

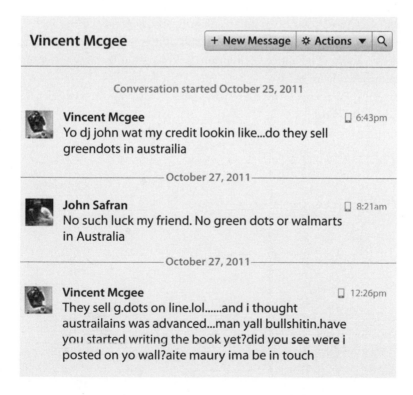

Vincent McgeeJohn Safran Official Page
Good lookin out on that bizness me and chy workin thingz
out...john safran saved my marriage..lol

EPILOGUE #2

Vincent Mcgee

[+ New Message] [⚙ Actions ▼] [Q]

Conversation started October 25, 2011

Vincent Mcgee   📱 6:43pm
Yo dj john wat my credit lookin like...do they sell
greendots in austrailia

———————— October 27, 2011 ————————

John Safran   📱 8:21am
No such luck my friend. No green dots or walmarts
in Australia

———————— October 27, 2011 ————————

Vincent Mcgee   📱 12:26pm
They sell g.dots on line.lol......and i thought
austrailains was advanced...man yall bullshitin.have
you started writing the book yet?did you see were i
posted on yo wall?aite maury ima be in touch

EPILOGUE #3

April Fools' Day 2014, an e-mail pops into my inbox that I assume is a joke. It says that Vincent, not three years into his sentence, has been released from prison. *This offender will not be under constant correctional supervision. If you have any concerns about your immediate safety, contact your local law enforcement agency.* I soon learn it is not a joke. That day, Vincent, like Richard, had found himself facing a man with a knife. The man, a fellow prisoner, stabbed him through the eye. One month later I'm on the phone to Vincent's stepfather, Alfred Lewis. He tells me the last time he saw Vincent he was breathing through a machine, not moving, his head wrapped like a mummy. Doctors had removed the eye. Alfred tells me authorities won't keep the family updated on his condition. At time of publication Vincent has been moved back into prison, into the hospital unit of Mississippi State Penitentiary.

May 2013, Chokwe Lumumba is elected mayor of Jackson. February 2014, Chokwe is found dead. A Mississippi councilman says he was assassinated: *So many of us feel, throughout the city of Jackson, that the mayor was murdered.* National black leader Louis Farrakhan eulogizes: *You who know Mississippi . . . a black man being mayor and trying to do right by all the people is not a mayor that those people want.* The more conventional explanation is sixty-six-year-old Chokwe suffered heart failure.

May 2014, Precious Martin dies in an accident when his four-wheeler ATV hits a curve and flips.

ACKNOWLEDGMENTS

Thank you to Madeleine Parry for research assistance, photography, and general Harper Lee–ing in Mississippi; Earnest McBride for helping far more than reflected in the book; staff at Mississippi Department of Archives and History; all Mississippians in the book, and others who graciously gave their time and expertise; Lally Katz for Melbourne-based Harper Lee–ing; Team *Race Relations* from Princess Pictures and the Australian Broadcasting Corporation; Kevin Whyte, Georgie Ogilvy, and Token for care and haggling; Ben Ball and Penguin; and Laura Perciascpc and Riverhead.

I have changed the names of Richard's sister and Vincent's "white" girlfriend and her mother. Jim Giles's address has also been changed so you can't easily take him up on his offer to fight. I have also made minor edits to documents for grammar and clarity. A version of this book was published as *Murder in Mississippi* in Australia.

Check out the six-part *John Safran's True Crime* podcast via johnsafran.com.

Got a lead for my next true crime story? Hit me up at john@johnsafran.com.